The 'Unremarkable' Man

My encounter with cancer

Thanks to the NHS and my will

to live, I am able to tell my story

by Terry Barry

First published 2018

Copyright © 2018 by Terry Barry

All rights reserved

This book is dedicated to the memory of

Debbie Binfield

30th April 1969 - 10th March 1980

Contents

Contents		5
Preface		7
Finding Mr Diary		9
1	I had a pain	13
2	Life in hospital	33
3	A welcome break	77
4	Second session of chemotherapy	83
5	Another rest	113
6	The good news and the bad news	129
7	Home at last	173
8	Recovery	183
9	Returning to normal	215
10	My vitals	231
11	Pete	249
12	Fully engaging with life again	265
13	Looking to the future	315
Goodbye, Mr Diary		343
Acknowledgments		345
List of characters		348
List of Medical Terms		354

Preface

This book is about some experiences of mine over the five years from 2011 to 2016 and is based on my personal diary entries. I was born on the 17th August 1947, the same day as Davy Crockett, Robert De Niro, Richard Duke of York and Terry Barry. Maybe there is someone on that list that you have never heard of. That is probably me; the person that you pass by every day without a second glance. I have always been relatively unseen and unremarkable in almost every way. But that is ok with me.

I do not have any special skills to speak of but I get by. I have not climbed mountains, explored unknown territories, or been shipwrecked and survived raging seas. I am not a courageous soldier who has won medals for gallantry. I am completely unknown.

So why did I write this book? And why would anyone want to read it?

It began as a form of therapy during long periods of isolation in 2011 when I was confined to a hospital room because my immune system was at a critically low point. I wrote in my diary almost every day and eventually gave it a name, Mr Diary. During that time, Mr Diary became my constant companion but it was not until four years later in April 2015 that my diary entries would spur me on to write this book. As I started writing, I realised that my story was not just about me but about us, the world we live in, and how we all get by if something, suddenly and without warning, goes horribly wrong.

I suppose when I think about it and look back, I could say that, in a way, I have climbed mountains, I have been adrift alone in heavy seas, I have explored unknown territories and I do have courage. I just did not realise this before I began writing. Nor did I realise just how special the natural world is because I took it for granted. For the first time in nearly 70 years, I even discovered as I came towards the end of my story, who I really am.

This is a story that I believe will strike a chord with many people, regardless of title, wealth, position or fame. It is about receiving and accepting personal and unexpected bad news, coping with it, recovering from it, and living a full and happy life beyond it. It is about stirring fond memories from long ago to recent times. There are many ups and downs as well as twists and turns along the way. I hopefully show just how resilient we can be when we need to be.

I have avoided pulling any punches. My unfolding story covers fear, hope, courage, despair, love, devotion, grief and empathy as well as the odd bit of humour here and there. I didn't plan it that way, it just evolved as I put pen to paper. My story is not meant to depress or impress anyone. It is about the power and positivity of the human spirit that we all possess when faced with adversity. They say that it doesn't pay to wear your heart on your sleeve as it leaves you open and vulnerable but I wouldn't have it any other way because that is who I am.

Finding Mr Diary

My wife Chris and stepdaughter Hayley were on their way to London to see the stage show *Wicked* in the West End. The date was Saturday 18th April 2015. My plan for the day was to be completely self-indulgent and as inactive as possible. I stayed in bed until about 9.30 am.

Still in my pyjamas and dressing gown, I got up, went downstairs and cooked myself eggs and bacon. At the last minute, I popped a slice of bread into the sizzling bacon fat. It smelled and tasted delicious. I wouldn't have got away with eating bread this way if Chris had been around, as I was supposed to be keeping to a healthy diet. After breakfast, I reluctantly got dressed, drove to the local shop and bought the daily paper.

When I returned, I went out into the garden. It was a warmish, spring day. I stretched, yawned and looked about me. That was my exercise for the day. I sat on our garden swing seat with my paper in one hand and a mug of freshly brewed filtered Italian coffee in the other. I watched the blue tits timidly helping themselves to the nuts and seeds that we had left out for them in the feeder hanging from a nail on the garden shed. Our resident robin flew down onto the garden table to join us. I enjoy days such as these, I always have. I don't mean the bacon and fried bread. I mean these spring days. They make me feel good to be alive.

The sky was clear and bright blue. The air was crisp. There was a slight chill in the air. Spring was here and summer was on its way. I sat there gently swinging back and forth thinking how lucky I was and how happy I am. I have ten wonderful grandchildren. Five of my own and five inherited through my marriage to Christine. Christine's five grandchildren have known me since they were born. They all call me grandad quite naturally, which is lovely. I have four children of my own and three step children, who have more than accepted me into their world as a fully-fledged family member. I have a good job and I work for a great company. Chris and I like to have two holidays a year if we can afford it: one in May, usually to Majorca where we became engaged in 2005; and one in November in Tenerife for a bit of winter sun. So, as you can imagine, I have a full and active life. It is a normal life just like most people, with the usual ups and downs. I was previously married for twenty-eight years with a ten-year break before contemplating marriage again.

It was beginning to get chilly outside, so I went back into the house and made myself a cup of tea while I contemplated what to do next. Obviously, I was going to indulge myself further with chocolate and watch all the DVDs that I enjoyed and Chris didn't. That was the plan anyway. But after a while at about 3.30 pm, I felt that I was being perhaps too indulgent, too much of a slob. So, I decided to make myself useful by tidying up some of our cluttered cupboards and drawers. I eventually came across a drawer in the office that housed some of my old photos, birthday cards and two theatre programmes of *The Phantom of the Opera*.

At the bottom of the drawer, I found my old 2011 A4 day to a page diary. I opened it and skipped through until I came across the date of Tuesday 14th June. The first entry was a nurse's appointment at my local doctors at Forest End, Bracknell, for 3.20 pm. I sat down in a chair and read the open page. Suddenly my heart began to race. I shuddered and felt a chill go down my spine as I began to relive that day. I did not want to continue as I knew very well what I was going to read from that date on and what was about to unfold before my eyes as the next pages grew in content and horror. Did I want to remind myself of the hell Chris and I went through from that moment on? I hesitated, but temptation got the better of me and I did turn the page. My day of indulgence immediately disappeared into insignificance as I sat there and began to be engulfed in a story that I knew I had to tell.

1 I had a pain

Appointment with the nurse

Tuesday 14th June 2011
I had a pain in my kidney area that had been hanging around for a while and was now causing me some concern. I had previously heard some stories of people passing kidney stones and it was the worse pain that they had ever experienced. Being a bit of a hypochondriac, I thought I should get myself checked out as soon as possible. I made an appointment with the nurse at my local GP practice for 3.20 pm that day. I arrived at the surgery on time and eventually, the nurse called me in.

After a brief chat about my symptoms, she examined me and said, *"You seem to be a bit tender around the right side of your kidneys so I think you should see the doctor."*

She then made an appointment for me to see Doctor Marshall at 5.50 pm that evening.

After the brief but thorough consultation with the nurse, I went home, still not unduly worried. I spent the rest of the afternoon making some work-related phone calls. I also looked online to see where and how I could spend a Red-Letter gift voucher given to me by my employers. The Red-Letter Day is a company that offers various experiences, like ballooning, gourmet evenings and short breaks.

When I arrived at the surgery that evening, I was promptly seen by Doctor Marshal, a shy studious-looking man probably in his late thirties. He asked me to get up on the couch and proceeded to press down gently on various parts of my stomach, which I found to be quite tender in places.

As he was examining me he looked at me somewhat puzzled and said, *"I think I will send you to Frimley Park hospital as a precaution. I will give you a letter to give to a Doctor Black at the Surgical Investigation Ward. Just hand the letter over when you arrive. I will phone them and arrange this now. Just get yourself there."*

He then handed me the letter. I asked him what he thought the problem was that required me to visit the hospital immediately. He said that he thought that there might be some sort of problem with my stomach but he was not sure exactly what it was. But to be on the safe side it should be checked out by the investigation team as soon as possible.

This news shook me up a bit, but I thought okay let's do what the doctor orders and worry about it later. I left the surgery and went home feeling quite apprehensive. The news took Chris by surprise. She was in the middle of preparing dinner. We decided to stop the cooking just in case I did have a stomach problem that required urgent attention. I think we both felt that the visit to the hospital at our busiest time of day was a bit inconvenient, but agreed that it was better to be safe than sorry, in case I was about to pass a kidney stone, which I was still convinced was the problem. So off I went to Frimley Park hospital with my letter in hand, accompanied by Chris who was just as apprehensive as I was. I remember thinking at the time how hungry I felt. I was looking forward to eating Christine's homemade shepherd's pie, but hopefully I would still be able to enjoy it once we got home from the hospital.

When we arrived at Frimley Hospital, I handed over the letter to a young nurse who showed me to a bed in the right-hand corner of the 8-bed ward. All the other beds were filled with gentlemen of all ages, in varying degrees of discomfort.

I leant against the windowsill next to my bed and looked out of the window. I had my back to Christine, patients and nursing staff. Then, without any warning, a searing pain that I had never experienced before erupted in and around my kidney area and back on my right side. It felt like I was being stabbed by hot needles in rapid succession. The pain was so intense that I could neither breathe in or out. I gripped the radiator below the windowsill and began to panic.

I turned my head towards Chris and said, *"Get a nurse quick I can't breathe."*

She didn't waste any time. I turned back and faced the window again as I didn't want anyone to see the obvious distress that I was now experiencing. Before I knew it, there was a nurse or doctor behind me asking me to turn around and lay down on the bed. But I was rooted to the spot.

I felt that I was about to pass out when someone from behind said, *"You will feel the injection working. Can you feel it now?"*

It was one of the nurses. Her voice sounded reassuring and calm.

"It will help the pain," she said.

I had been given a morphine injection and, although I was still suffering, I could feel the effects of the drug working. Almost immediately, it began to reduce the severity of my pain and my breathing slowly began to improve. Another nurse gave me an oxygen mask, which I gladly accepted.

Assisted by two nurses, I turned still bolt upright, rigid like a manikin and laid down on the bed with the nurses' help. I was somewhat relieved that the agonising pain had subsided enough for me to cope with it. I also felt somewhat embarrassed that I had been the centre of attention in such a distressing way. I was sure it must have been entertaining enough for the other patients to forget their own discomfort for a minute or two.

I stretched out on the bed. Christine's face looked ashen, as if she had just gone through the same agony as me. I was not going home that evening. She stayed for a while, then left to get my pyjamas from home. In the meantime, a young nurse took some blood from me, then an older nurse who had the kindest of faces asked me if I would like some more pain killers, the best of which she said was to be inserted rather than swallowed. I opted for the one that would help the pain the most. I still felt embarrassed when she administered it, but it didn't seem to bother her.

She smiled and said, *"Get some rest. I will look in to see how you are later."*

I felt reassured. I was in safe hands.

Chris returned some time later with various food goodies, which I would not usually eat at that time of day. But my appetite had increased over the last four/five hours. She stayed until 9.30 pm. After she left it didn't take me long to fall asleep as I was completely exhausted. But before I did, I thought to myself, *"What is going through Christine's mind now walking into our empty house?"*. I can't imagine.

Meeting Chloe

Wednesday 15th June
I was woken up at 6.00 am with a cup of tea. I had some breakfast at about 8.00 am. I still had a slight pain in the kidney area. The nurse came in with her drugs trolley and gave me some

more anti-inflammatory medicine. Soon after, I was sent for an ultrasound scan. When I returned, a nurse arrived and took some more blood.

Later that morning, at about 11.30 am, three doctors in their typical white coats appeared at my bedside. One was a Registrar, a young smart dark-haired lady, who introduced herself as Chloe. The other two were male junior doctors whose names escape me. They pulled the curtains around my bed.

Then Chloe said, *"We have discovered a couple of abnormal cells in your blood that we think should not be there, but to be sure we are going to send the blood results to the laboratory for a more accurate analysis."*

She seemed to be waiting for a reply from me, so I did.

"What were these abnormal cells?"

"We are not sure. We will know more by tomorrow," she replied.

I still didn't feel too concerned, as I thought that my main problem was kidney stones or something similar.

After the doctors left, not much else happened. The nurses were in and out during the day. Chris came to visit as usual that evening, both of us still unaware at that point of anything being seriously wrong with me.

Thursday 16th June

I was gradually getting used to the ward routine. That morning I had tea, medicine and breakfast.

Chris phoned to see how I was, asking, *"Have the doctors been yet?"*, which they hadn't.

I replied, *"I will let you know later what they come up with."*

Both of us thought that the worst my condition could be was gall or kidney stones and having them removed would be a relief. Chris went to work not duly concerned and I was also in a good frame of mind.

The three doctors that came to see me yesterday arrived about 10.30 am. A nurse pulled the curtains around my bed to give us more privacy. The doctors stood at the head of my bed, looking quite solemn. An announcement of any seriously bad news had still not entered my head.

Then after the normal greetings of good morning and how are you today, Chloe said, *"We have had the results back from the laboratory and they have confirmed that there are definitely a few abnormal blood cells present in your blood."*

She hesitated then continued by saying, *"We have to do more tests to see how many abnormal cells there are."*

I became slightly more anxious at that point. There was an uneasy silence. They were waiting for me to say something. I didn't want to ask the obvious question, but knew I had to.

So, I came out and said it, *"Well what do you think the abnormal cells are then?"*

Chloe replied in a sympathetic voice, *"We think you have leukaemia."*

"Leukaemia?" I answered somewhat sheepishly.

"Yes, it's called acute myeloid leukaemia. As soon as possible, Professor Smith, our senior doctor, will administer a bone marrow test to see exactly how many of these abnormal cells are present in your bone marrow, after which you will be transferred to the G1 isolation ward."

It is difficult to explain my reaction to this news. But there was a time a few years ago when my son Damien was on a school skiing trip in the French Alps. I received a call from my father-in-law telling me to turn on the news. Four or five students on a school trip from our town had wandered off-piste at the same resort. They had fallen off a cliff face, possibly to their deaths although nothing had been confirmed. You can imagine, my blood ran cold, my body became numb from head to toe. I felt helpless, anxious and afraid. I rang the school but there was no answer; I rang the police but there was no news, except that it was true that children from our area on a school trip were involved in an accident. It was not until sometime later that we heard that our son was safe and the sad accident had involved pupils from a school just down the road.

> That is how I feel now, today, this minute. Cold, numb, helpless, anxious and uncertain, not in control of my feelings.
>
> After the doctors leave, I am obviously still in a state of shock and unable to fully take in my unwelcome news. I get off my bed. I feel invisible and completely *alone*, alienated from all my surroundings, trapped in a dark unknown place.
>
> I begin to walk out of the ward. An elderly man who is sitting on the bottom edge of his bed close to the entrance looks up at me and says knowingly, *"Bad news mate?"* His voice is almost an echo as I pass him by.
>
> I turn to him and say, *"Yes."*
>
> I continue to walk out of the ward. I don't know where I am going. I feel like a robot unable to think. Just

programmed to move. I just know I must get away from everyone and everything. I eventually find myself at the entrance to the hospital. I walk outside and start pacing up and down still unable to think straight or to comprehend what has just happened. I am still unable to take anything in. I feel like I am falling but have no idea if I am going to eventually land. I sit on a wall and phone Chris. I don't know what I am going to say.

She answers, *"Have you seen the doctors yet?"*

"Yes," I reply.

"Well, what did they say?"

I pause, trying to hold back the tears that seem to be emerging uncontrollably from the depths of my stomach. I manage to regain control of myself and say, *"They have told me I have some blood cells that should not be there."*

Chris replied after a short pause, *"What does that mean then?"*

"They think I may have leukaemia. It's called AML or something."

"Stop messing about".

She thinks that I am joking. But she soon realises that I'm not.

I continue by saying, *"They need to be sure, so I have got to have more tests. Don't worry too much, let's wait for the results."*

Chris came to the hospital almost immediately. We found our own way to the isolation room. It was early evening. Chloe, the Registrar, came to see me and said, *"You can go home rather than spend the night in hospital, but you must return to the hospital by 7.00 am tomorrow."*

We accepted her kind offer and left for home. As you can imagine I did not get much sleep that night. Neither did Chris, but we were both more than happy to be home.

Professor Smith's shocking conclusion

Friday 17th June
We were up early and made our way back to the hospital and the isolation room, which is a large, sparse, newly painted and very clinical room. Not the ideal place to wait for the final verdict that was due to be delivered sometime that morning. After a four-and-a-half-hour wait, Professor Smith arrived with his team to give us the latest lab results. The Professor looked every inch a Professor. He had a reassuring air about him that commanded respect without demanding it. His demeanour gave us both the confidence we needed in a doctor that was going to do his best for me. But I didn't think he would pull any punches and he didn't.

"You do indeed have leukaemia," he said.

His dulcet tone had a quiet authority. It was gentle but measured. It reminded me of Sir David Attenborough's voice and seemed to make everyone present listen intently.

"It is called acute myeloid leukaemia. I will need to perform a

biopsy to see what we are dealing with. Then we can start treatment, but it is not good", he said shaking his head from side to side.

I responded by saying, *"What can be done then, Professor?"*

The other doctors looked at the Professor in unison for some inspiration it seemed. Then he said, *"Well, we can cure it."*

I immediately grasped his reply with both hands and thought to myself, that's good enough for me.

I then said, *"Well what do you want me to do?"*

"You will be transferred to Onslow Ward at the Royal Surrey Hospital in Guildford where they will begin and continue your treatment until it has been successfully completed," "If it is left untreated you would become very ill very quickly so it is better for you that we begin treatment as soon as possible."

Unbelievably, for a moment I felt a real sense of relief. It was like my recent morphine injection working all over again. Now I knew what I was up against, so let's get on with it.

I asked the Professor, *"How long will the treatment take."*

"About five, possibly six months."

"How many times must I visit the hospital to have the treatment?"

"You will be an inpatient for five to six months."

At that point, I could not even begin to comprehend that length of stay in hospital. That obstacle was yet to be overcome. What the Professor didn't tell me and what I found out years later was that if my condition had been undetected and untreated I would have been dead within weeks. I am glad he didn't as it would not have helped me or Chris to know that at the time.

Before we left the hospital for the weekend, the doctors gave me some medicine to take. Allopurinol 300mg a treatment for gout and kidney stones I think, but also to stop the build-up of uric acid and ensures that you don't get tumour lysis syndrome, which can be fatal.

That evening, Chris and I went to the *Stag and Hounds* in Binfield. It is an old traditional pub, in a nice setting backing onto woodland. Chris thought it would take my mind off things for a while. We both ordered a steak, but I couldn't eat any of mine.

I looked at Chris from across the table and said to her, *"I don't feel too good."*

What a waste of good food I thought. But I was just not up to eating anything, my mind was elsewhere. Chris didn't attempt to scold me for leaving my food like she normally would, especially if it contained green vegetables.

Instead, she said, *"Don't worry, it doesn't matter let's just go home and have a nice cup of tea."*

We paid the bill and left. We did indeed have that cup of tea before going to bed early for some well-earned and needed rest.

Before I attempted to go to sleep I thought to myself, I wish that today had never happened. I woke up in the night soaked in sweat. Chris had to get up and change the bedclothes as they were wet through.

I said to Chris, *"I feel kind of weird. Is it me just getting stressed? Or is it the pills? Or am I still in shock after being told that I have leukaemia? Or is it the leukaemia itself?"*

Chris just shook her head slowly from side to side and said, *"I don't know, it's the shock I think, I don't know."*

> ### The diagnosis of acute myeloid leukaemia
>
> Acute myeloid leukaemia (AML) is usually diagnosed when a patient develops symptoms related to low blood counts: usually anaemia symptoms, easy bruising, bleeding or infection. A blood test is done that picks up abnormalities and leads to the diagnosis on blood and bone marrow tests. It develops over weeks and the longer it is left the more severe the symptoms are. Eventually, patients develop high white cell counts that cause 'hyper viscosity' (poor blood flow due to the number of cells in the blood stream), with headaches, visual disturbances and drowsiness. Without treatment, patients will deteriorate and die usually from uncontrolled infection or from the high white cell count problems over weeks.

Saturday 18th June

We went to visit Hayley, her husband Joe, their little three-year-old boy Oliver and new baby Daisy today. Hayley is the youngest of Christine's three children. She is a bright, bubbly, brown-eyed girl with the kindest of hearts. Christine's eldest son Darren was also there with his wife Angela. Darren is the strong, thoughtful, silent type. Joe is also warm and friendly and a West Ham supporter like me (but more about those two later). Angela is a smart career type of girl. We had a lovely day as we always do when we visit Christine's family. We enjoyed a nice supper of sausage and mash. Everyone did their best to make the day as normal as possible for me. This was just the medicine I needed. But it must have been difficult for them, knowing how ill I was. During the night, my sweats returned and my breathing was quite shallow. I got up and took some deep breaths and eventually went back to bed and slept.

Sunday 19th June

It is Father's Day today. Hayley made breakfast and I received cards from her and Joe, and Darren and Angela. I thought this was a very kind gesture as I am only their stepfather.

After breakfast, we went to a car boot sale where Hayley bought some toy dinosaurs for Oliver. I am sure she bought Oliver the toys because she knew that I liked anything to do with fossils and palaeontology in general. I have always passed on this interest of mine to little Oliver. In the afternoon, Joe and I went to buy some DIY items. We were all just trying to keep the day as normal as possible.

Later, at about 4.30 pm, Chris and I left the family and drove to Guildford to see where I would be staying for the near future, the Royal Surrey Hospital. We didn't know exactly where it was, so a trial run was required.

When we finally arrived home, my daughter Sacha came to visit with her partner Wayne and my grandchildren Immy and Lola. They stayed for a couple of hours. The children were oblivious to my situation and played happily at my feet. I joined them and made them both a paper aeroplane, something I always find myself doing every time any of the grandchildren visit.

When they left, I sat back and tried to relax. But as I did, those dark thoughts returned, just for an instant. Is this my mind's Gateway to Hell? Opening just wide enough to let in negative thoughts? Is this how it is going to be from now on? I hope not. It's just the unknown affecting me as I attempt to come to terms with the reality of my illness. I must think more positively and meet this impending health struggle head on.

Monday 20th June
It's Christine's birthday today. It's not much of a birthday for her. She opened her cards and presents at breakfast. We both tried our best to be as happy as we could on her special day. Chris is a quiet person but when she does speak it is usually worth listening to. However, today you could hear a pin drop as we went through the motions of what should have been such an enjoyable occasion.

Eventually, and reluctantly, we made our way back to Frimley Park hospital. At 3.00 pm, Professor Smith performed a bone marrow test on me. I was sedated so I don't know exactly what happened as far as the procedure was concerned. A bone marrow biopsy detects the amount of the immature cells (blasts) within the bone marrow. The procedure draws out the marrow through the hip. I have read in layman's terms it's a bit like twisting a corkscrew into your hip and sucking out your bone marrow. It sounds gross, but it is a necessary procedure that shows the extent of the immature cells in the bone marrow. This will help the Consultant Haematologist decide what treatment is required going forward. Chris left about 6.30 pm. I ate some hospital food and managed to sleep until 5.15 am the next morning.

Tuesday 21st June
5.15 am. I was wide awake. I felt okay, although the flush button in the toilet was not working. I decided to leave my room after a while and have a cup of tea with two of the nurses before returning to my room for breakfast, which arrived at 8.15 am. Cornflakes, followed by bacon, beans and a roll and marmalade. A nurse came into my room about 9.30 am with my pill allocation. Philip, a special nurse, arrived just after 10.00 am and took some of my blood. We chatted about his background which was in residential care. He had also been an army medic.

At 10.30 am another nurse came in and said, *"Professor Smith will be looking at your bone marrow test results at lunchtime, then he will come to see you."*

That awful feeling of uncertainty returned once again. I didn't want to think about anything until Professor Smith had revealed the results of my bone marrow test. By 2.30 pm, the Professor had still not arrived although a nurse put her head round the door to tell me that Doctor Tim, my heart doctor, had phoned the Hospital to say he was sending Professor Smith my notes. I have what's called left bundle block of the heart and Doctor Tim is the consultant who looks after me regarding that condition, but that's another story.

At 4.30 pm, I saw Chloe at the nurse's station. I asked, *"Where is the Professor?"*

"He is not coming today," she replied. *"The laboratory has put the wrong stain on the slide"*. Whatever that means.

"So, he could not see the cells. They are redoing it."

She went on to say, *"He will let you know the outcome sometime tomorrow."*

That's great, another 24 hours of hell. I was not amused. Chloe noticed that I was less than pleased and decided to let me out of hospital for an hour so that Chris and I could have a bite to eat at the pub just around the corner.

When we returned, we went into the relatives' room and watched some TV. Chris left about 8.30 pm. I went back into my room. I was feeling depressed. More worrying thoughts were beginning to work their way into my head. Not about my diagnosis but other things; I must let work know where I am. What if I do not get paid while I am off work? I have only been working for this company for ten months. How was I going to pay the bills? And so on. But I soon expelled those thoughts and drifted off to sleep, helped I am sure by a sedative given to me by the nurse on her evening rounds.

Wednesday 22nd June

I was awake at 5.30 am and Chris rang at 6 am. A few minutes later, the nurse arrived and took my blood pressure (139-72), which is a bit on the high side I think but expected given my circumstances. I went outside and joined the staff for a cup of tea in the staff room at 7.45 am.

I wandered into the relatives' room, which is very small, about 2.5 metres square. It has an armchair (two seater), a small television and a coffee table. This is the only place outside my room where I can sit and watch television for free. The room is for patients and staff. The alternative for watching TV was in my room but it was too expensive for me, especially as I was going to be a long-term patient.

I was beginning to get on my high horse a bit. If people didn't take our NHS so much for granted, maybe the car park and television viewing fees, amongst other things, would be less expensive. Maybe there would be enough beds go around for people who really needed them. It was just a thought that had come into my head. I was just taking in my new environment and situation and was beginning to think in a negative way about stuff that I didn't have the answers to. So I decided to park those sorts of thoughts, for now anyway. I needed to be clear minded and positive to be able to tackle what might be in store for me next, which is still unknown to me. I hate not being in control of my life.

At 8.40 am I ate some breakfast, took my medication and had yet another blood test.

Chloe and another doctor came into my room at about 10.00 am. Chloe said, *"There are indeed many alien cells (blasts) present in your bone marrow, about 60%, and you will now be transferred to Onslow cancer ward at The Royal Surrey Hospital in Guildford, probably tomorrow, where you will be under a new consultant haematologist."*

She continued, *"Also, tomorrow we are going to insert a tube into a deep vein near to the top quadrant of your heart. A trained technician/nurse will perform it."*

She hesitated for a second. She must have noticed by the look on my face that I didn't like the sound of anything so invasive, especially as it was going to be threaded through a vein so close to my heart.

She continued by saying, *"The technician who will be carrying out the procedure is really good at his job. You will be fine. It is very important that you have this done because of the nature of your upcoming and ongoing chemo treatment."*

I then said to her, *"What is this procedure called?"*

"It is called a PICC Line. A Peripherally Inserted Central Catheter."

I didn't like the idea of having this procedure, but if it had to be done, so be it. I phoned Chris with this latest news. She became very upset.

I tried to pacify her by saying, *"Hopefully they will let me out for the weekend before they start chemo on Monday."*

Chris arrived at 5.15 pm and went to speak to the ward sister in her office. I don't know what was said as Chris didn't say anything about it after she came out. At visiting time, my brother Paul and his wife Christine came all the way from Tonbridge in

Kent. It was great to see them. I am beginning to see just how important family and friends are when you are in this sort of situation, or indeed any crisis or trauma that you may have to go through in your life. The jungle drums were also beating, as I received messages of comfort and sympathy from colleagues, friends and family throughout the rest of the day.

Thursday 23rd June

I woke early this morning at 4.30 am. I dozed for a while and had some sips of water. The nurse arrived at 6.10 am and took my blood pressure, pulse, temperature etc. I thought, my God, once the NHS have hold of you, they don't let go do they? What busy bees these nurses and doctors are. After the observations, I fancied a cuppa, so I got out of bed and went and made one in the ward kitchen where I met and started speaking to a young Nepalese nursing assistant who had been in the country for seven months because her family wanted her to come to England. But now she wants to go back home as she is homesick. After our brief but pleasant chat, I returned to my room. At 7.45 am the tea lady arrived followed by two other nurses who came in just to see how I was getting on. That's nice of them, I thought.

I began to read a Macmillan diet book, thinking I must improve my eating habits. I didn't realise just how much water, fruit and veg you needed to keep healthy. I now realise just what a rubbish diet I had had up to now, although I didn't drink much or smoke at all so that must be something. But it's a bit too late to worry about that now. At 10.15 am, I was still waiting for this PICC line procedure that doesn't sound very pleasant. I was also waiting for news about my impending transfer to Guildford.

At 11.30 am the nurse came in and said, *"Has the PICC line specialist been in touch?"*

I replied somewhat indignantly, *"No one has been in touch!"*

"We are still trying to arrange your transfer," she added.

At midday Professor Smith, Chloe and two other doctors came in to wish me luck. Nice touch, I thought and thanked them for what they had done for me so far. The PICC line procedure finally took place at 2.50 pm by a chap called Graham, who talked me through it in layman's terms before he began.

He then injected a small amount of local anaesthetic underneath the surface of my skin at top of my left arm close to my shoulder. Then, using an ultrasound machine to help identify the best vein for the PICC, he inserted a needle into the suitable deep vein. Next, he threaded the PICC tube through the needle into the correct place. As the PICC was being gently threaded up the vein, he asked me to turn my head towards him and angle my chin downwards towards my shoulder. This helped him guide it into the correct position. He secured the PICC and covered it with a dressing. He then sent me for a chest X-ray to check that the PICC was correctly inserted. This sounds gross but it is no worse than having a blood test. Well, only a bit worse. Chris arrived just after the procedure was completed. I was transferred to Guildford Onslow Ward almost straight away.

2   Life in hospital

My new home for a while

Thursday 23rd June 2011 (continued)   7 days since diagnosis

We made our own way to The Royal Surrey Hospital. When we arrived at the ward I remember thinking what a dismal looking place it was compared to Frimley Park. We checked in with the nursing staff and we were shown to room ten, which was a small eight-bed ward. There were several other patients in there, all looked very old and extremely ill. A few of them seemed to be away with the fairies. The nurse came in and performed various tests including a blood test, the results of which were:

HB 129 WCC 6.00 PLATELETS 191 NEUTROPHILS 1.6

Fascinating, but what do these tests mean? As far as I understand it, my blood stats are very important regarding my condition. So, I want to present these results that were taken throughout my illness in an accessible way.

HB or **H**aemoglo**B**in is the protein found in your red blood cells that carry oxygen throughout your body. The normal count in an adult male is 136 to 177. I'm going to call this Oxygen carrying.

WCC is your total **W**hite blood **C**ell **C**ount, that helps fight infection by attacking viruses, bacteria and germs that invade the body. White blood cells originate in the bone marrow but circulate throughout the bloodstream. A normal count is between 4-10. I'll call this Infection fighting.

NEUT is your **NEUT**rophil count, which is related to the defence of your immune system against infection and is part of the WCC. The normal range is 1.5 to 8. I'll call this Bacteria fighting.

PLT is your **P**late**L**e**T** level. Platelets are the smallest cells in our body that circulate within our blood and bind to the site of any damaged vessels. Basically, they stop us from bleeding to death by causing the blood to clot. Example: when you cut yourself a crust forms around the bleed. A normal count in an adult is 150-450. In my case, if the platelet count was too low I might have to have platelets in the form of a blood transfusion to stop potential bleeds. And I'll call this Clot forming.

So, using my own nomenclature, my blood results look like this:

129	6.00	1.91	1.6
Oxygen carrying	**Infection fighting**	**Bacteria fighting**	**Clot forming**

Now, those numbers don't mean much to you, do they?

So, to try to help explain their relevance, I'm going to use smileys to indicate if the result is good, okay, bad, or terrible!

 Good. This measurement is in the normal range for a healthy adult male.

 Okay. This measurement is near the bottom of the normal range.

 Bad. This measurement is outside of the normal range.

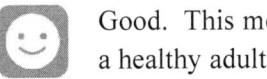 Terrible. Oh, dear - this is not good!

So, combining the smileys with the different blood results, we get:

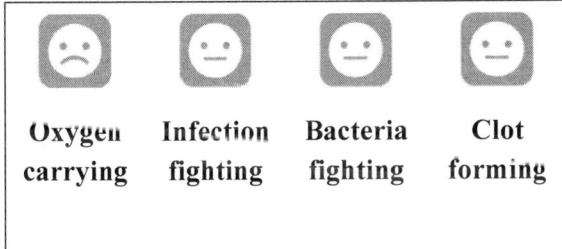

> In addition to these basic results, the doctors have confirmed that the blasts or abnormal immature white cells in my bone marrow are in fact 65%. It should be no more than 3 to 5 % maximum in a normal human being.
>
> Blast cells are not typically found in the circulating blood of healthy individuals. These abnormal blasts begin very quickly to take over the bone marrow and prevent the production of adequate numbers of other types of blood cells, such as platelets, red blood cells and healthy white cells. In fact, production of leukaemia blasts may get so out of control, that the immature cells spill out into the circulation causing anaemia, bleeding problems and infections. The presence of blast cells on a complete blood count is therefore very indicative of leukaemia.

At about 6.00 pm, I met a junior doctor called Andre, and the consultant who was going to look after me, Doctor Louise. Doctor Louise informed me that my chemo would start on Monday and that my blood count (WCC - infection fighting) had dropped a bit. She also told me that I was to have another bone marrow test with no sedation this time. If I opted for the chemo AML Trial 17 treatments, there would be a bone marrow test for every session of chemo. My first impression of my new consultant and future guardian angel was that I had better behave or she would wrap my knuckles. Chris left about 8.00 pm. I walked with her to the ward entrance and as I was about to go back to my bed, I saw two groups of people who were obviously visitors walking towards me. Two or three were crying. I didn't want to think about why they were upset. You can only imagine how I felt as they walked past me as if I wasn't there.

I spent a very uncomfortable night on the ward. The chap opposite me fell out of bed and cut his head badly. He was so drugged up I don't think he felt a thing. I called the nurse and they took care of him. All through the night the rest of my inmates were having conversations with themselves. Sometimes I thought they were talking to me. Sometimes I thought they were talking to a sergeant major on parade. Occasionally there was a cry for help. The chap to my left, who had to be at least 90, was shouting for his mum. So, you can imagine, Mr Diary, I did not get much sleep. I felt sorry for them all but I wished that I was somewhere else.

I've been adopted

Friday 24th June
I woke up at 5.30 am. As mentioned, I couldn't sleep due to all of the goings on from the very confused collection of people around me. The smell of vomit, the constant cries for help and the mutterings from my fellow inmates in their sleep were making me consider getting up and discharging myself. The ward environment was making me feel uneasy and out of my depth. Just before breakfast, a lady appeared and asked the guy who had cut his head if she could take a photo of his wounds. He agreed and she took two photos with her phone; very odd. Later that morning, I wandered out onto the main ward area and met a chap called Pete. He was a bit older than me - I would say in his late 60s – and looked quite frail and underweight. I asked him how long he had been in hospital and what was his specific condition. He said that he had been here since January 2011 and he has AML (the same as me). He would be going home as soon as his blood count was at a level to be discharged, hopefully tomorrow. I was to find out more about the science of blood

count levels and other treatments as time went on.

Pete seemed to have taken me under his wing.

He kept saying to me, *"You will be all right. They are great here. You are in safe hands."*

Obviously, Pete had already been through what I was about to go through. It was quite reassuring to have someone to talk to who was going through the same illness as me. He decided to show me the ropes from then on, including the best place to walk or sit and what he did to keep busy, like getting up and dressed and going for a walk, instead of lying in bed every day. He even gave me the lowdown on who was who in the ward. Everyone from the tea trolley man to the consultants was fantastic as far as Pete was concerned.

When I asked him about the dreaded bone marrow test he said, *"Sue the specialist nurse is the best one to get to do it, she is gentler than the registrar, but you will be all right it is not that bad."*

This was the thing about Pete, everything was or would be okay, even if you thought it wouldn't be. His positive, calm attitude gave me some peace of mind and some reassurance. This was something to cling onto, although when I think back on it, it's a bit like the priest saying to the condemned man just before he is to be executed:

"Don't worry it will be over in no time."

We popped down to the hospital entrance where we sat and chatted over a coffee. I also managed to get Chris a three-month parking ticket for a reduced rate of £1.50 per day, which would be yet another thing off my mind. The expense of Chris travelling from Bracknell to Guildford every other day and the parking costs were beginning to concern me now that I had got over the initial shock of my diagnosis. So were other practical things like will my employers be contributing financially while I am off sick and the mortgage and day to day bills. How would Chris cope? It was all right for me in a way as I was in hospital being looked after. But Chris was at home alone.

I returned to the ward where I met Doctor Andre who had a great bedside manner. He told me that he was going to start some medication for a fungal infection on my foot that I had had for some while. I also filled in a consent form for the AML17 chemo trial. It was full of technical information that I did not understand but in the name of hope, trust and research, I signed the form. Well if you can't trust your doctor who can you trust?

I did ask my consultant if this trial treatment was different from any other treatment. I was told that there was no evidence that it was and the way I look at things, I didn't have the time or inclination to do much research. I just wanted the professionals to get on with the job in hand. We are all different though. Some people may want to know everything about their treatment, their illness, or their life expectancy in detail. That's up to them, I am not that kind of person. I would rather put my trust in the system and the professionals. I preferred in this instance to accept my current situation and deal with everything else as and when I needed to, as far as my health was concerned anyway. The way we handle trauma of any kind is down to the individual. Doctor Andre came in to tell me that I could go home for the weekend. I immediately phoned Chris with the welcome news and she came to get me as soon as she finished work.

Chris and I had decided that I needed another distraction while I was in hospital. So, we visited Sacha and Wayne at their home in Ascot. Wayne is a computer expert and he was going to see if he could adapt my laptop, as there was no Wi-Fi connection at the hospital. Thankfully he managed to find a solution. So now I don't have any reason to get bored. When we returned home, I put my feet up and watched some tennis. Chris made me omelette, chips and beans. You would be surprised what you dream about eating when you are a long-term inpatient. It was not long before I became tired and went to bed as I hadn't slept much the night before. This is what I have missed. My own bed, my wife and family, and some good, honest, comfort food. Even lying on the settee listening to the birds singing outside in the garden seems to be all I need.

My perspective on life was beginning to change. Almost everything that I have taken for granted in the past is becoming more important to me as my future seems to have been put on hold and I live for the day. My world has been turned upside down. It's changed, maybe forever. I am beginning to absorb every morsel of my existence. My senses are on a different level since I accepted the reality that my life may be shorter than I expected. Let's hope not. I believe they call my new perception of my surroundings mindfulness.

Saturday 25th June

I had a great night's sleep, I woke up at 5.30 am and I took some horrible medicine that the hospital gave me called Itraconazole, an anti-fungal treatment for my toe. At 6.00 am, Chris went downstairs to make us both some early morning tea. I got up about 8.00 am and showered. I had a bad tummy ache that I couldn't seem to shift. At 11.00 am, although I still felt a bit uncomfortable, we made our way to Maidenhead, where I had my haircut. We met up and had a cup of tea with my old workmate Chris and his partner Yvonne. It was nice to see them and they were very sympathetic towards me and to Chris for obvious reasons.

We arrived home about 1.15 pm. I still had a bad stomach ache.

I phoned the nurse at the hospital.

She said, *"See how it goes and if it persists phone me again."*

Chris attended a wedding reception that afternoon. I was just going to chill out on the settee and relax while she was gone. She returned home at about 7.00 pm, I don't think she enjoyed herself much and she was very quiet. Sacha and Wayne came around for a brief visit with the children just after 7.00 pm and Wayne set up my laptop. For the rest of the evening, we just chilled and didn't speak much, mainly because I kept falling asleep whilst lying on the settee.

Back to hospital

Sunday 26th June   A hot Summer's day

Still at home. I took my medicine at 5.30 am and after breakfast at about 9.00 am, we went to the supermarket to get some grapes and other bits and bobs for me to take to hospital. We then took a trip to Windsor for a couple of hours until I found myself getting too tired to continue, so we returned home. Christine's youngest son Matt came to see us with his children Harrison and baby Louis. Chris was busy ironing and getting all my bits together. We left home at about 7.00 pm. The front tyre on Chris's car was a bit flat so we hunted for a garage with a working airline. We then continued our journey to check me back into the hospital.

When we arrived, we were both somewhat sombre. I was not looking forward to returning to the ward. The reality was beginning to sink in again as I entered Ward 10. We looked at each other at the same time with tears in our eyes. We had a bit of a hug and said our goodbyes. I was back with the sick people again in the eight-man ward - same smell, different day. Hopefully, I would get a room to myself soon. I have been told that once treatment begins I would need to be isolated because the treatment would reduce my immune system to zero and I would be more prone to infection.

Monday 27th June

Chris texted me at 6.00 am and then phoned, *"Are you awake?" (!)*

We spoke for a few minutes and after our brief conversation, I debated with myself whether I should take a shower.

> I love showers but the preparation required for such a simple task is extensive. I have to water-proof myself by cling-filming the PICC area on my arm. Then get a supermarket plastic bag, cut a hole in it for my arm to pass through and cover my arm and shoulder to ensure that the water from the shower doesn't get through to the attached PICC line. Luckily, I have an endless supply of plastic bags which Chris has brought in just for that purpose.

After my shower, I didn't know whether to get dressed or get back into my pyjamas. Decision made: I got dressed. At about 11.00 am, Sue, the specialist nurse came in and asked me to make my way to the anteroom on the ward where she was going to give me the dreaded bone marrow test.

Sue, who looks like a cross between Natalie Wood and a young Linda Bellingham, told me that she was a 'key worker' (someone to guide you through your treatment to make your journey as easy as possible). They are a point of contact for you. Sue carried out the procedure by giving me a local anaesthetic first. Then when all necessary parts were numb she began to carry out the job in hand as gently as she could, reassuring me all the way with general chit-chat about this and that, just to put my mind at rest. She did talk me through the procedure without it sounding too bad, which I found reassuring. She knew exactly when to stop, push and pull; she was obviously very good at her job.

When it was time to perform the pull part of the test and extract the bone marrow Sue said, *"Your leg will jump up in the air when I pull the needle out."*

And sure enough, up went my leg; it must have looked like I was getting off a bike.

"All done", Sue said. *"Just stay there while I put the dressing on."*

I obliged. I dreaded having this done. I was sweating profusely and I was glad when it was all over but it wasn't that bad at all. It had to be done so that was my incentive to endure the treatment without being knocked out completely. All I did was grip onto my mobile phone tightly and chat to Sue nervously until it was all over.

Later I took a stroll around the hospital and met up with Sue again. She took me to the Fountain Centre which is a place where in/out patients can go for a read and a cup of tea as well as get all sorts of information, like travel insurance for cancer patients and many more things besides. It's a bit like a citizen's advice centre but more informal. You can chat to patients and staff alike while sitting in a comfortable armchair.

We then made our way to the St Luke's garden and the St Luke's coffee shop where you can sit and watch television. I left Sue and returned to the ward. At about 2.30 pm, while a male nurse was extracting copious amounts of blood from me, a screen was put around James in the bed next to mine. I overheard the doctors telling him that he would be better off in a hospice. I didn't really want to hear this, so I got up and walked out of the ward. I really wanted to escape. I wanted to go home. My confidence in my ability to struggle on with my illness had just taken a knock. James' reality was temporarily becoming my own. With nowhere to go, I returned to the ward and sat on the chair beside my bed. I felt cornered, trapped. At 4.00 pm, Doctor Robbins came in to see me and told me that the preparation for my chemo treatment was due to start at 5.20 pm.

Sister Carol arrived and sat down beside me and started treating me with an anti-itching solution. She said that the chemo would begin at 8.00 pm and could go on to midnight. Carol also looked the part. I could imagine her being the matron on the TV programme *The Royal*, or a resident army sister: very disciplined, straightforward and doing things strictly by the book with a clinical kindness that you could warm to as you got to know her. She seemed to be a dedicated professional just like all the Angels working in the Onslow Ward. Carol's trademark was a thick red banded belt. Whenever she entered the room I felt that I should stand to attention at the end of my bed and step forward when ordered. Carol left after a short while but came back soon after. She told me that she could not go on with the treatment as my consent form, which I had signed, was in the possession of the Registrar and he had left for the day; my chemo treatment would have to be delayed for another twelve hours. As you can imagine I was not very pleased to hear this news, but Carol reassured me that the delay would not affect my current condition. Today's blood results were:

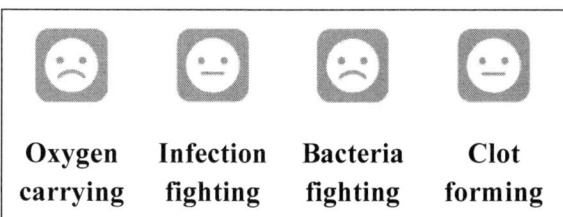

And my weight today was 93.1 kg. I am aware that I am losing weight but unsure whether it is due to my chemo treatment or the cancer itself. I find myself trying to weigh more on the scales by standing very flat on my feet, whereas before my illness, I always stood on tip-toe to try to weigh less!

So you see, Mr Diary, my weight recordings, just like my blood tests, are significant to me.

First session of chemotherapy

My Chemo course

Course 1 **10 days**

a. Cytarabine (Ara-C) — Twice a day for 10 days
b. Doxorubicin (Red Devil) — Once a day on day 1, 3 and 5
c. Etoposide — Once a day for 5 days
d. Mylotarg 6 — Twice during course day 1 and 3

Course 2 **8 days**

a. Cytarabine — Twice a day for 8 days
b. Doxorubicin — Once a day on day 1, 3 and 5
c. Etoposide — Once a day for 5 days
d. Mylotarg 6 — Twice during course day 1 and 3

Course 3 **5 days**

a. High-dose Cytarabine — Twice a day on day 1, 3 and 5 with eyedrops

Each item is applied intravenously via my PICC line and takes from 1 to 4 hours.

Tuesday 28th June **Chemotherapy starts**

The first course would take 10 days. Courses two and three would happen after my body had recovered from the first course.

The first infusion of Cytarabine began at 6.30am. I remember thinking after the nurse had made sure the contents of the bag began to flow down the tube into my arm, "Here we go. There is no turning back now. I hope this works."

I was not feeling that great at the time. I was still suffering from an upset stomach. The chemo continued in the early afternoon with Doxorubicin (with the wonderfully familiar name of 'Red Devil') which was administered by Jincy, the sister who sat with me for an hour chatting to me as she slowly pumped the syrupy, toxic drug into my veins. I felt dizzier as the day passed by and I had a severe headache. At around 4.00 pm the second bag of Cytarabine was put on flow. I had no appetite. Chris arrived about 5.00 pm and stayed with me until 8.00 pm which made me feel a bit better, although during her stay the nurse came in to administer more drugs. This time it was one called Etoposide. One bag of this dripped into my PICC line for an hour or so. The last of the chemo arrived just after Chris left. This time it was a drug called Mylotarg. This was a new drug that was going to be used as part of my clinical trial. The sister sat beside me once again because she needed to monitor me very closely due to the possibility of side effects which some people experience. Luckily my body showed no early signs of any serious reaction. It was about 10.30 pm before everything around me seemed to quieten down, although I had visits from the night sister just for monitoring purposes and the usual OBS. How did I feel after such a long day of treatment? In a word, knackered! I felt weird and somewhat apprehensive even though all of the day's excitement was over. I didn't spend too much time thinking about it, it was time for a well earnt sleep.

Today's Chemotherapy

6.30 am	Cytarabine	for 1 hour
2.00 pm	Doxorubicin (Red Devil)	for 1 hour (supervised due to toxicity)
4.00 pm	Cytarabine	for 1 hour
6.00 pm	Etoposide	for 2 hours
8:30 pm	Mylotarg 6	for 1 hour (supervised due to toxicity and possible serious reaction)

Wednesday 29th June

The second day of chemo. I felt slightly better today but I still had no appetite. I've been moved to room 1, which is a great room. I have it all to myself. It is an isolation room, which is a prerequisite as far as my condition is concerned as my immune system is about to drop to zero. I have also requested a sick note for work, yet another thing for me to think about. What if I am off work for six months or even longer? How will we survive financially? I should have taken out some medical insurance. I should have done a lot of things but it's a bit late now. I decided to park those 'wish I had' thoughts as they were not doing me any good and I needed to stay in a positive state of mind. In the meantime, my chemo continued, although it was not as intensive as yesterday. Chris is not coming in today so me and Mr Diary got together again for a while. My last session of chemo started a bit later than usual. The bag of Etoposide was empty by about 9.15pm. Another day of chemo over. It didn't take me long to close my eyes and drift off to sleep, although I knew that the coming day was going to be as intense as the first.

Today's Chemotherapy

6.00 am	Cytarabine	for 1 hour
4.00 pm	Cytarabine	for 1 hour
6.30 pm	Etoposide	for 2 hours

Thursday 30th June

I woke up at 4.00 am. I dozed for a while until the nurses arrived and woke me up again at about 6.30 am to administer the Cytarabine. I was feeling sick yet again. The chemo continued throughout the day. The doctor came to see me on his morning round and told me that I was neutropenic, meaning that my immune system was at zero. I was now well and truly cocooned in my new room.

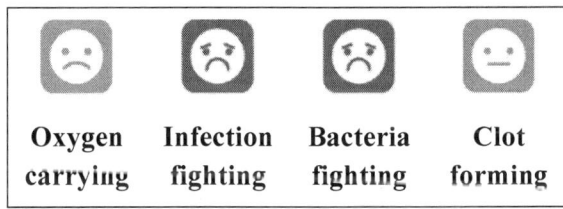

| Oxygen carrying | Infection fighting | Bacteria fighting | Clot forming |

Now that my immune system is at its lowest, I am at the mercy of any bug that might be around. Any minor ailment could turn into something major. So, I need to be very careful from now on. I can't leave my room until my immune system gets back to an acceptable level, which could take three or four weeks.

The nurses have been in and out of my room like busy angel bees. They weighed me. 92.4 kg, that's about (14s 5lb), they have also taken some blood and have given me my daily medicine. Anyone would think that I was ill! My temperature hovered around 36.4 which was normal. My Blood Pressure (BP) was 109/70. Occasionally, I intend to show my blood pressure and body temperature in the same way as the other blood results:

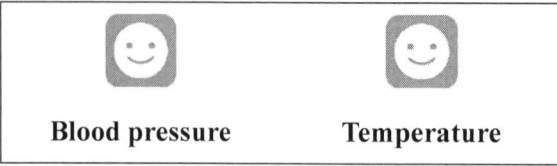

| **Blood pressure** | **Temperature** |

> Just of a matter of interest. The top BP number is called *the systolic blood pressure number*. When your heart beats, it contracts and pushes blood through the arteries to the rest of your body. This force creates pressure on the arteries. It is the highest level your blood pressure reaches when your heart beats. The bottom number is called *the diastolic blood pressure number*. It is the lowest level your blood pressure reaches as your heart relaxes between beats. The ideal reading should be *120/80 or below*. So, my reading of 109/70 was just fine.

My blood oxygen level (SAT) was 94%, just below the normal range of 95 to 100%. My respiratory rate (RR) was 17. The normal range for a healthy adult is 12-20 breaths per minute, so that was okay.

Carol returned to administer the big red toxic dose of Red Devil at about 3.30 pm. I wondered what was going through her mind as she sat there beside me. Her big blue eyes looking up at me and smiling as she pumped the potent drug into my veins. I sensed that she already knew what was going to happen to me. What a responsibility! I am glad that she is looking after me. I didn't realize just how time consuming administering some types of chemo can be. Doxorubicin, for example, is a syrupy, gloopy drug that has to be infused a bit at a time due to its consistency. It takes a senior trained nurse to give patients drugs such as Mylotarg and The Red Devil. That's why my daily chemo infusion time schedule changes occasionally when they are so busy out on the ward. At 5.00 pm, Chris arrived but I was not very talkative due to my ongoing nausea. I hadn't been out of bed all day apart from visiting the little boy's room. Another sister, Sarah, came in to tell me that she would try to get me into a double room tomorrow. Sarah is a young blonde haired angelic looking nurse. She reminded me of how, as a child, I imagined Florence Nightingale should look like. This young lady is another Onslow angel.

My consultant haematologist Doctor Louise arrived with her posse in white coats at about 6.00 pm. She told me that she was happy with everything so far, which was good to hear. My last session of chemo (Mylotarg) was supervised by the night sister and started at about 9.00 pm and it finished just after 10.00 pm. That was enough excitement for the day, it was late and I was completely worn out. I remember thinking to myself I hope these drugs are doing their job. Maybe it's too early to tell. What if my body rejects the chemo? What happens then? I didn't know what to think so I didn't. I just closed my eyes and drifted off to sleep.

Today's Chemotherapy

6.30 am	Cytarabine	for 1 hour
2.00 pm	Doxorubicin (Red Devil)	for 1 hour (supervised due to toxicity)
4.00 pm	Cytarabine	for 1 hour
6.00 pm	Etoposide	for 2 hours
8:30 pm	Mylotarg	for 1 hour (supervised due to toxicity and possible serious reaction)

Friday 1st July

I was awake early again, 4.00 am. I still felt ill but not quite as bad as yesterday. Nothing much to report much today. Not being able to go outside of my room is now a reality. I hate the restriction but the confinement is for my own good so I will just have to put up with it. Any visit would have indeed been welcome but most of the time I was on my own, unable to even peek outside into the busy ward. I had a few visits from doctors and nurses who continued to monitor me throughout the day. The last bag of Etoposide emptied at about 10.00pm. As I drifted off to sleep, I wondered yet again how my body was going to cope with all these toxic drugs. I will have to wait and see. Oh, I forgot I. I had my OBS taken at 3.30 pm and my daily blood results were:

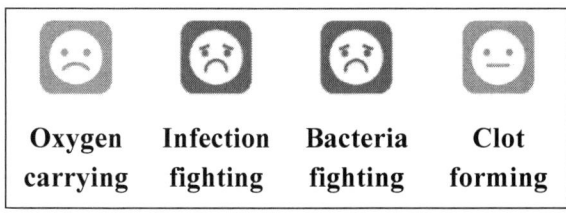

| Cytarabine | 1 hour x2 |
| Etoposide | 2 hours |

Saturday 2nd July

Chemo began at 6.15am. The highlight of my day was a visit from Chris, Hayley and Joe at about 2.00 pm. Hayley is what any step father could wish for in a step daughter. She is kind, supportive, considerate, warm and always welcoming when you meet her. Just like Joe. I defy anyone not to like them both within the first moments of meeting them. Joe was carrying a portable television to help stem my boredom, while I was in isolation. It was great seeing them and it lifted my spirits immensely.

After they left, Carol came in to give me another infusion of the Red Devil. She sat with me for just over an hour.

Doctor Robbins came in to see me at 6.00 pm. He is a consultant haematologist, a keen cyclist and all-round nice bloke; I find him easy to relate to. I made a few entries in the diary until about 9.00 pm when I felt too sick to continue. I had the mother of all headaches so I decided to stop writing as all I wanted to do was sleep.

My bloods for the day were:

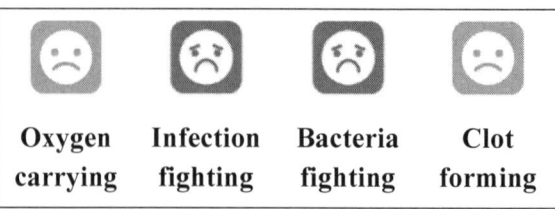

Cytarabine	1 hour x2
Doxorubicin (Red Devil)	1 hour
Etoposide	2 hours

Sunday 3rd July

Sacha, Wayne, Immy and Lola came to visit me today. Sacha phoned me from the car park. I had previously told them that it would be best if the children just waved to me from a suitable viewing point below. My reasoning for this was that my immune system was now zero and I was at risk of infection. I knew the children were just getting over some sort of bug, so it was better to be safe than sorry.

I looked out of the window. Sure enough, they were looking up and trying to get a glimpse of me amongst the multitude of windows above them. Eventually, they saw me waving. They waved back and jumped up and down enthusiastically. It was a great feeling, but sad at the same time. I would have loved to have given them a hug. But I also didn't want them to see me in my current condition. Nor did I want to catch anything from them.

In hindsight, I wished they had come up. Sacha came up to see me while Wayne took the children into the hospital coffee shop for some refreshments. It was great to see her. I think she was a bit upset, but she tried not to show it.

One of the first things she said was, *"We didn't see that one coming,"* referring to my diagnosis.

We chatted for a while. When she left, she made sure the children gave me another wave from the car park below.

Chris arrived in the evening with her sister Elaine and her husband Dave. Again, it was nice to have visitors and we chatted for some time before they left an hour or so later.

> It is 9.30 pm and I am now in room 15, a self-contained isolation room. I am also on some new medication which is giving me stomach cramps. I feel depressed and I don't know why. Maybe it was seeing the children today, so near to me and yet so far away. I must snap out of this dark mood and begin to think of the day I am cured and get back to having a normal life again. Just before I closed my eyes a thought came to me, *"I wish I had spent more quality time with my own children when they were young".*

Cytarabine	1 hour x2

Going downhill

Monday 4th July   7th day of chemotherapy

I received a visit from the whole medical team today. Doctor Louise seemed to be happy with me. I was still neutropenic. Chris arrived at 3.30 pm and stayed till about 7.00 pm. I was not good company for her or anyone else. I constantly felt sick and tired and I still had stomach cramps. It must be so boring for her but she never complains.

Cytarabine	1 hour x2

Tuesday 5th July

I was woken up by a nurse at 2.00 am and again at 4.00 am so that the nurses could take some observations. Did they know something I didn't? At 6.00 am the first bag of chemo was put on flow After breakfast, Susan the dietitian was here at around 10.45 am. She is attempting to put me on an appropriate diet. Best of luck with that one. I was not being very helpful because I have no appetite. Chris is not visiting today. My stomach cramps are still hanging around. Evidently Pete has been taken into intensive care, I don't know the details. Poor Pete, he thought he was going home soon too. Nothing else to report, apart from feeling like a prisoner. I couldn't concentrate on anything much and I felt rubbish. I must try to snap out of it. Last infusion of chemo on flow around 7.00pm. Watched television for a while and then slept.

Cytarabine	1 hour x2

Wednesday 6th July

I was awake at 4.00 am with stomach cramps again. At about 6.00 am the nurse came in an attached another bag of chemo on line. Chris phoned at 8.00 am to say that she couldn't visit due to being unwell herself. I didn't feel like eating breakfast. At 10.45 am, Doctor Andre came in to see me. He wanted me to produce a urine sample for some reason. Another bag of chemo was attached to my PICC line at about 6.30pm. Not much more to report today Mr Diary. I was not in the mood to write or talk to anyone. I was just going to watch television and catch up on some sleep. I felt quite miserable for some reason.

| Cytarabine | 1 hour x2 |

Thursday 7th July   10th day of chemotherapy

I woke up this morning feeling very ill. Chemo began at 6.00 am.

The doctor came to see me at 8.30 am and I said to him, *"I don't feel good. I have a sore throat and I feel hot. There is also a nasty rash all over my arms and legs."*

He noted my discomfort, examined me and left without much comment. Chris phoned and because she was still ill herself, she would not be coming to see me today.

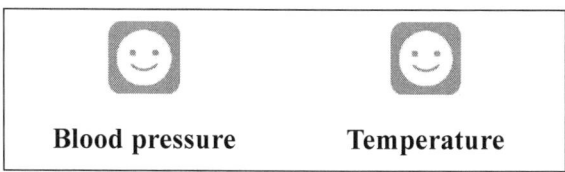

I felt dizzy again and I was shivering. Susan the dietitian came in at 10.00 am. She is very persistent in trying to get me to eat. But I have only managed two crackers and a Scandishake (a high-energy drink supplement for people who are suffering from involuntary weight loss). Even though it comes in various flavours, it tastes disgusting!

It seems that the nurses were quite concerned about me and have noted that I looked unwell. My temperature was normal though, 36.8. But I still had severe stomach ache and upset stomach. I needed to have close observation because of an evolving sepsis.

> **Sepsis**
>
> Sepsis is a potentially life-threatening complication of an infection. Sepsis occurs when chemicals released into the bloodstream to fight the infection trigger inflammatory responses throughout the body.

I have been sick. I also had to provide a stool sample this afternoon. Yuk. More chemo arrived at 6.30 pm. A nurse came to see me again at 8.30 pm and gave me a strong anti-sickness drug intravenously. Overall, a rubbish day again but the nurses certainly have been keeping a watchful eye over me all the time. They also weighed me: 89.4 kg. Good old NHS, it will not let me down I thought, especially with a team like the Onslow Angels looking after me. Today was the last day of the first chemo course. Thank God for that! My neutrophil blood count is now at zero so it could be 3 or 4 weeks before they rise and my immune system is at an acceptable level to go outside this room. Now the long wait in isolation has begun.

Cytarabine	1 hour x2

Friday 8th July

Bloody awful day again and it began very early in the morning. A nurse came in at 1.00 am to take my temperature. It had risen to 38.2 which is quite high and, as I said previously, may be an indication of sepsis. She gave me some antibiotics intravenously. She also informed me that my platelets were quite low. At 6.00 am another nurse visited me and took blood cultures. The rash that I have developed recently was now all over my body. I still felt sick and I had persistent diarrhoea. I was so very tired and I was sweating profusely. At 9.00 am my blood pressure was taken, it was 95/60. which was also quite low.

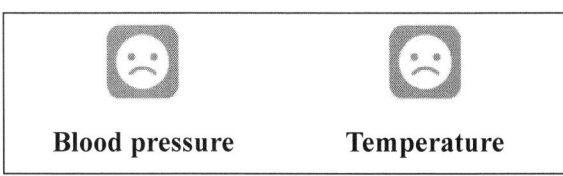

My throat was still sore. 10.30 am Sister Carol came in to see me and attached a pool of platelets to my drip, followed by another soon after. 11.40 am another nurse came in to see me and asked me to provide a urine sample. 5.00 pm I was sick again. I was getting really fed up with being ill. The diarrhoea had worsened and I was now on oxygen. Chris arrived at 5.30 pm and she managed to get me to eat some yoghurt and a small piece of orange. At 10.00 pm my temperature had risen to 38.4. Blood pressure was 116/67. I can't remember what time Chris left. I wished that I was going home with her. Not much fun today was I Mr Diary?

Saturday 9th July.

I felt very ill again today. How much longer was I going to feel like this? I have had a rubbish night's sleep and I have dozed on and off all day. Chris came to visit me late afternoon and helped me wash, as I just couldn't be bothered. The nurses came in and extracted more of my blood. At one point during the day, my temperature had gone down to 37.2. I felt slightly better than I did this morning.

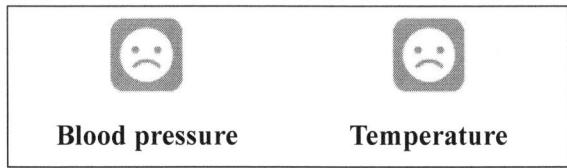

Sunday 10th July

Sorry to write this again, but today was a bad day due to my constant stomach problems, let's call it D from now on as it sounds horrible and I have trouble spelling it anyway and its more information than you want to know, Mr Diary.

For the record, Chris witnessed me trying to stop the dreaded D with my hand when I couldn't make it to the toilet in time. I had to get out of bed with a PICC sticking out of my arm attached to a bag hanging from a pole on wheels and travel six feet at speed to the toilet door when I felt as weak as a kitten, dizzy, sick and disoriented. It was so embarrassing trying to clench my cheeks and knees together, as I tried hopelessly to shuffle across the room to the toilet, and when I didn't manage to get there in time, I collapsed onto the floor. I was on my knees, too weak to get up, unable to stand, my head was spinning and I was still clenching the pole with one hand and my embarrassment in the other. I began to weep in frustration.

Chris and Atish, who is the ward's health care assistant, came to my aid without any hesitation and began to clean up the mess that had soiled my pyjamas and was now all over the floor in front of me and behind. That's my dignity gone out of the window, I thought. The experience had made me feel helpless, ashamed and insecure. But Chris and Atish took the situation in their stride and showed me a side of humanity that I had not witnessed before today and I was eternally grateful.

My son Damian and his wife Nicola came to visit soon after with my granddaughter Scarlett. They brought me some nice goodies including a Nike baseball cap to cover up my now slightly balding head. Thanks, Dame and Nicky, you are most thoughtful. You have made me feel much better. Especially after my earlier accident. Now I can keep my head warm.

Damian is my middle son and he is a quiet lad; thoughtful, generous and has a kind heart. Well I would say that, wouldn't I? But it's true. He was a skilful footballer in his time, as were his two brothers, and he has a dry sense of humour. He has his own business in Bournemouth and adores his children. I really appreciated his visit.

There is a sore or tear on my backside which is most uncomfortable, probably due to my too frequent visits to the bathroom. Poor Chris, this isn't fair to her. The nurses were busy with me today. They were taking various stats and bloods. My temperature was back to normal 36.7 which was good. My BP is 94/52 which is a little low. Maybe I was a bit dehydrated.

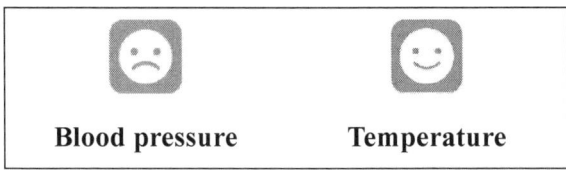

My bloods were:

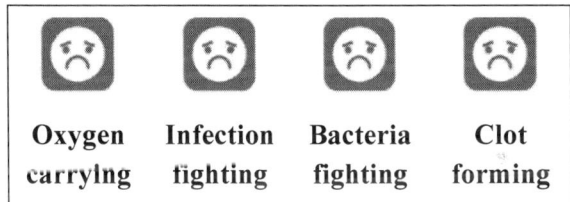

Four very unhappy faces equals one very sick person! My C-reactive protein (CRP) reading was 147, which is a bit on the high side. This means that I am not on top of the infection. Another stool sample has been taken and I received yet another transfusion of blood, this time very late at 11.30 pm. I can't get rid of this rotten headache and the sick feeling remains constant as well as the D. What a day, I was glad it was nearly over. Unfortunately, D, headache, nausea and fever are all side effects of chemo treatment. I have been told that we all react differently to the treatment. That's no consolation though. I am doing my best to be positive but I couldn't concentrate for long enough to have any positivity at all. But I know I will snap out of it eventually. If only I could get rid of this headache first.

Pete is back

Monday 11th July
Good Morning Mr Diary. It is a better morning. Doctor Andre popped in to see me. He gave me some medicine for the D. We chatted for a while. He hopes to go to Australia and work in the Accident and Emergency department of a hospital out there. Good luck to him. Also, Toni, another great and caring nurse, came in and dressed the sore on my rear end. Hopefully, if the wound heals and the D subsides, I can concentrate on food. The doctors have also changed some of my medicines today. They have introduced different antibiotics and at some point it seems that I am to have an X-ray. They think that there might be an infection on my lung. Whatever next? My old mate Pete the patient, Peter Small, is back on the ward. This is good news, as he had taken a turn for the worse recently and got an infection which was so bad that he had to go to a critical care unit. No Chris today, but overall it was a better day, more sleep, no D. I was drinking more but still not eating much and I was still neutropenic. My temperature was up a bit again to 37.2. Today was also day 14 of the AML Trial and for the record, my rash is still present.

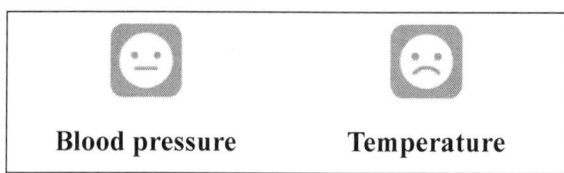

Tuesday 12th July

I woke up early this morning at 4.30 am. I have been having trouble sleeping on my current mattress. But I have been told that it would be changed today, to one which is far more comfortable for patients that must spend more time in their bed and of course I am spending more time in it than I want to. The last thing I want now are bed sores.

My appetite has also improved. That will please Susan the dietitian. I had Rice Krispies, orange juice, a yoghurt and three cups of water at breakfast time; but I was still not drinking enough liquid.

Susan arrived to see me at 2.30 pm, followed by Chris. Susan told me that there is to be a diet change. No hot food from now on, just protein shakes and I must drink much more water. So, that's me told but she isn't the one who feels constantly sick.

The new air bed arrived and Chris has brought in a mini fridge which Atish has kindly brought up to my room. I also had a CT scan of my chest. So quite a busy time of it. My temperature is still hovering on the high side at 37.4.

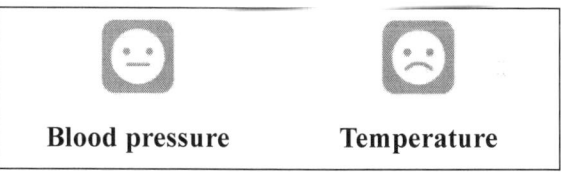

All of this was completed by 3.30 pm. I was also given the results of the CT Scan from earlier today. They have found multiple pulmonary embolisms. Basically, that means that I have multiple blockages in the blood vessels that carry blood from the heart to the lungs, in short, blood clots. Oh, and some scarring. Scary stuff. With that bit of news, I felt I needed to go up a gear regarding my own positivity, if only I could find the mental and physical strength required to do it. There seems to be no consistency regarding how I feel. It is just as well that I am here in the right place so that the medical team can act quickly. I know how lucky I am. But I have been struggling with my current mental condition. I have been finding it all a bit tough to cope with. I feel as if I am losing some ground.

I needed to escape from my situation for a while but how was I going to do it? I cannot leave the room or the hospital. I was even finding it difficult to get out of bed.

There have been times when I have used my imagination as an outlet to break free from the real world and there was no better time than today. One memory that comes to mind was when I was a child of about nine or ten years old.

> There was a farmer's field opposite Grandma Oakley's house in Romford called Fowlers Field. There were two ponds in the field. The smaller one was a bomb crater from the Second World War that was filled with water. I used to go there and collect frog spawn and look for newts and frogs with friends. The other was larger and deeper. About three or four feet from the water's edge there was a large, fallen oak tree trunk that was partly submerged. It was about eight feet in length and about two to three feet wide. It was a challenge to jump onto it and stop myself from falling beyond it. But once I was safely aboard I was in another world. I was the master of a fine ship. Sometimes my vessel was no more than a raft made from coconuts and timber found on an undiscovered desert island that I had been shipwrecked on. I even gave myself an imaginary name, Jim, after Jim Hawkins the cabin boy from Robert Louis Stevenson's Treasure Island, my favourite childhood book. Occasionally an imaginary shipmate joined me

because I felt lonely out there on the high seas with no one to talk to. We would sail the ocean together and had many adventures for hours on end without interruption, or until I became hungry, or cold. Or sometimes my grandma used to send grandad over to get me because supper was ready.

There was not much room on my ship for anyone else although it would have been nice to have real company and occasionally some real friends did jump aboard. But they either became sea sick or bored and wanted to go home before I did. Anyway, there was always more exciting places to visit and I wasn't lonely for long after they left as I could still conjure up an imaginary shipmate if I wanted to. Just like today with Mr Diary.

Wednesday 13th July

Today my rash began to really itch. It's all over my body and legs. I felt irritable. The doctor came in to see me at 10.40 am. He prescribed Piriton to ease the itching. He also said that I was to have two units of blood around 7.30 pm this evening, plus one pool of platelets. My OBS were stable and as always, the staff have been checking me over regularly. My PICC line was nice and clean.

I also had a surprise visit from my uncle Les and his son, cousin Chris. They came all the way from Winchester and their visit was most appreciated. Chris who is a paramedic, helped me into the shower as I was very unsteady on my legs. To top that my hair had begun to fall out in chunks when I tried to dry what is left of it on my head. They both noticed the clumps of hair on the towel and the bald patches that were now visible but they tried their best to ignore it.

This latest development didn't over worry me but it well and truly cemented the realisation that I was having treatment for cancer. I must admit I have been struggling to come to terms with some of the ongoing side effects of nausea, headache and D amongst other annoying symptoms. But I know that these symptoms will subside once the treatment finishes. On a lighter note, the fridge is working. A Health and Safety check has been completed, so cold drinks are now on offer, which is most welcome. Christine has also brought me in a CD player, oh and I forgot I ate some Rice Krispies and two mini Jammy Dodgers and a shake for lunch. I didn't feel too sick today either and I was relieved that there was no D present. Given the circumstances, I have had a very enjoyable day.

Thursday 14th July

I had a good night's sleep and managed to eat some breakfast of cornflakes/water and juice. The doctors arrived at 11.00 am. They were talking about my blood clots. Excuse me I am in the room! They chatted amongst themselves, about the possibility of inserting a stent to stop clots returning.

I decided to speak up at one point and said, *"I don't like the idea of having a stent."*

Doctor Robbins seemed to agree. He said, *"It may not be necessary."*

They agreed that as an alternative, they would consider giving me Clexane injections instead. They also said I must have a blood transfusion today. This began at 4.30 pm and included two pools of platelets. My daily blood results were:

THE UNREMARKABLE MAN

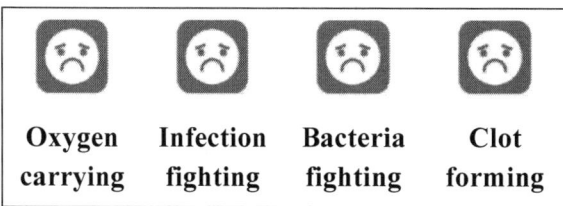

| Oxygen carrying | Infection fighting | Bacteria fighting | Clot forming |

As they left, the doctors told me that I was improving even though I didn't feel particularly well. But the doctors' encouraging words made me feel slightly better. I settled down for the night at about 11.30 pm.

> **Clexane**
>
> I had a pulmonary embolism which caused a blood clot to form. Clexane was used to disperse the clot and I later transferred to warfarin. Clexane also has the effect of thinning the blood and because the blood was already thin due to the low blood count, the risk of bleeding was high. So a transfusion was required to give me more platelets to minimise this risk.

Friday 15th July

Again, I had a good night's sleep. Early this morning, at about 7.30 am, I tried to eat a biscuit. Colin the tea man arrived and gave me a cup of tea, which I couldn't finish as everything still tasted horrible. I felt sick again. I know it's the combination of the chemo, antibiotics and just being sick. But you know what they say: *If you find a path without any obstacles, it probably doesn't lead to anywhere.* So, I must go with the flow I think and get on with it.

I have been told that I am to have a scan on my lower limbs early next week and it will take two hours. Today's bloods were still very poor:

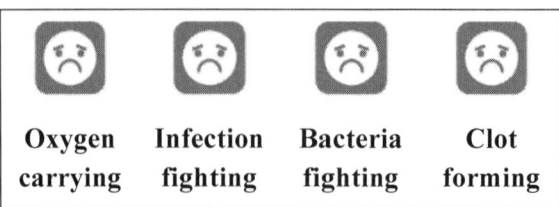

I have had a Clexane injection and there is to be ongoing platelet support if the medical team decide that I need it. I slept for most of the day. At 7.00 pm the door to my room opened and to my surprise, in walked a mate of mine, Barrie Gould. This was a nice surprise and he cheered me up no end. This is typical of Barrie. He has always been a thoughtful person and always manages to do the right thing at the right time. Thanks mate, I will not forget it.

Saturday 16th July

I was awake at 3.20 am this morning and I felt nauseous again. The duty nurse came in and gave me an injection for the sick feeling. I managed to get some sleep until breakfast time when I woke up feeling slightly better. I had the usual water, biscuit and cereal. I even managed some soup at lunchtime. Doctor Robbins came in at 3.00 pm and again at 5.00 pm. My bloods today were:

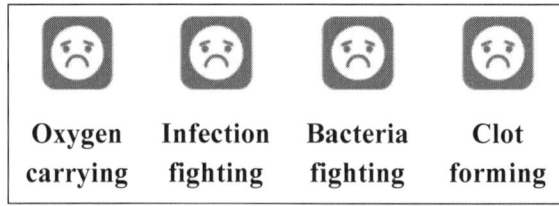

Sunday 17th July

I slept well. Breakfast included a banana, that's a first. I had a shake at lunch time and some water. Chris isn't coming in today. The doctor arrived at 3.00 pm. He seemed to think that I was okay. Everything is going in the right direction it seems. Toni the staff nurse came in and has removed the dressing from my rear end which is healing nicely. PICC line okay, bloods were:

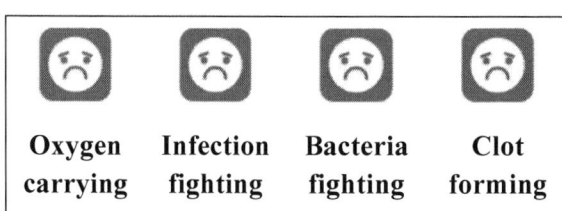

My youngest son Jamie came to see me for a brief visit at 7.00 pm. It was the first time that he had seen me in this condition and I think it shocked him somewhat but he did not say anything.

Sometime after Jamie left he sent me a text which said, *'Night dad I was sad seeing you today I just wanted to say I love you loads.*

I slept well that night. It is not like Jamie to show such emotion even though it was only a text. Thank you, son.

A visit from Barbara

Monday 18th July   12th day of isolation
Doctor Andre was here to see me at 10.00 am. I had a nasty cough so he examined my chest. He seemed to think that it was nothing too serious. I also had to go for the 2-hour scan on my lower limbs this morning. Maybe I must have the stent inserted that the doctors were on about, I hope not. The ultrasound was eventually completed. It covered my arms and legs and

stomach, no clots found, only overlying bowel gas. Well, I have always had plenty of that. Whoopy! That means no stent then. Great result.

Then it was back to the ward and my room. Barbara Binfield, a friend of mine for over 40 years, was due to visit me this afternoon with her daughter Kerry. One of Barbara's daughters Debbie, died of leukaemia many years ago, when she was about 10 years old. Her death had a profound effect on me then and is even more relevant now. So, without reservation, I dedicate this book to her everlasting memory.

I managed to eat some ice cream and some cake today. At 5.15 pm I had to ask the nurse for a sickness pill. I also seemed to be coughing more. I was very tired and the dreaded D had returned. I was slowly beginning to get really fed up again. I had to snap out of it as I was due visitors. It was 6.30 pm and Barb and Kerry arrived as expected. It was lovely to see them both, although a bit embarrassing. I had to visit the toilet at least three times while they were here, which as I mentioned previously is difficult when you are attached to a PICC line, which is attached to a bag of medicine dangling from a drip stand. I hope they didn't mind. I tried to act as normal as possible so that they would not feel too awkward. I think they knew I was struggling because of the way my knees and bum cheeks were clenched together as I sprinted to the toilet door. They did their best not to show that they had noticed my obvious predicament. When I think back, it must have looked like a funny scene from a Carry On film, in a macabre sort of way.

It's strange but while I was waiting for them to visit, I felt apprehensive. When they finally arrived, I felt an overwhelming sense of guilt as well as embarrassment but they both did their best to make me feel at ease. I just didn't want to remind them of seeing someone as old as me with leukaemia and still alive.

It's ridiculous I know, but that is how I felt. Debbie was so young when she died and here was me, sixty-four years old and still here. After Barb and Kerry left, the nurse took some more blood. There cannot be any left surely? My blood results today were:

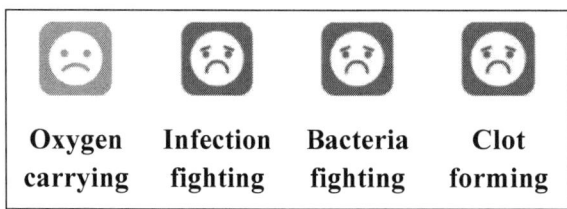

Tuesday 19th July

I slept well last night. My breakfast consisted of cornflakes and some water. I still couldn't eat much food as it tasted tinny, which was awful. At 9.35 am, Susan the dietitian visited me again. My weight today was 84.6 kg which is a 10% weight loss in three weeks. By all accounts, this is clinically significant. I explained to Susan that I was not eating because of the taste of the food, probably caused by my chemo treatment, but she still seemed concerned.

The doctor arrived about 10.00 am, OBS were taken.

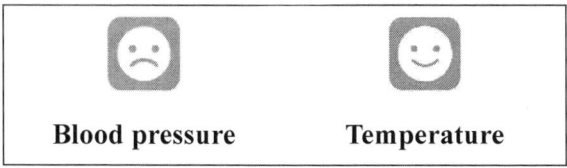

The doctor came back just after midday. He checked my rash and said that the area around my PICC needed a bit of a clean-up. At 7.00 pm the doctors were here again. They are going to start me on Levomepromazine. This is for my nausea and I hope it does not affect any of my other conditions. This evening I had a Clexane injection plus one pool of platelets. Blood results today were:

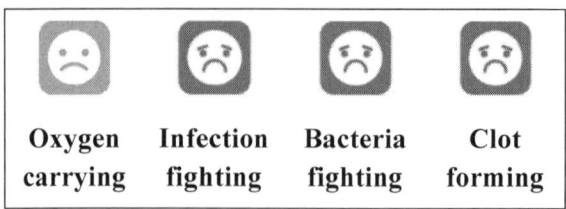

Wednesday 20th July

I was awake at 8.00 am. Shortly after, a nurse came in and told me that I had to have a CT scan today. She inserted a needle into the back of my hand. It was a painful experience as it took her 2/3 attempts to do it as she couldn't find a suitable vein. I did say to her that I was not aware of any CT scan. At 10.35 am Doctor Andre arrived and just checked me over with the usual observations. I waited all day for this scan but no one came to get me.

I eventually called the staff nurse, Shay, and asked her, *"Why have I not gone down for the CT scan?"*

Shay looked bemused and said, *"I thought you had gone down."*

There seems to be a lack of communication somewhere along the line. My daily blood results:

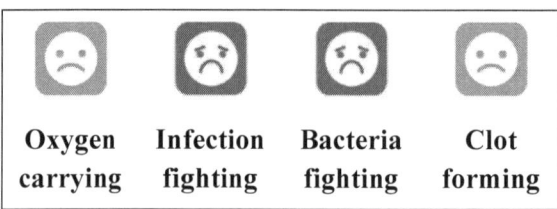

My leg was swollen but not painful. This was due to an

abnormal accumulation of fluid in the tissues surrounding my knee and is called a *Pitting Oedema*. My temperature was 36.8 this morning and 37.6. later that afternoon. It now transpires that my CT scan is to be done tomorrow. So, that means another needle in the back of the hand. Ouch!

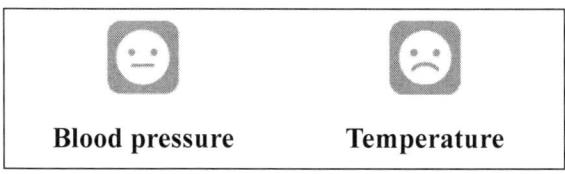

At 7.00 pm I was given one pool of platelets plus a Clexane injection. Why was I still feeling sick? I have been given a bit of good news though. I might be going home at the end of the week for a short break if my blood counts are at a suitable level. Then I will be re-admitted again for my second session of chemotherapy.

Thursday 21st July

It has been 35 days since I was first diagnosed with Leukaemia and 23 days since my first session of Chemo treatment began. I tried to eat some breakfast consisting of a bowl of cornflakes and half a cup of tea provided by Colin the tea man but I was still struggling. At 10.00 am in came Susan the dietician. I told her that I had a muzzy head. She was not too happy with my fluid intake. She also told me that she was going to prepare an eating plan for when I get home. This young lady is so thorough. At 10.30 am, Doctor Robbins arrived. He checked my PICC line and said that it was okay. He said that they would show me how to inject myself with Clexane while I was out of hospital. The nurse came in early afternoon and took some bloods.

Today's results were:

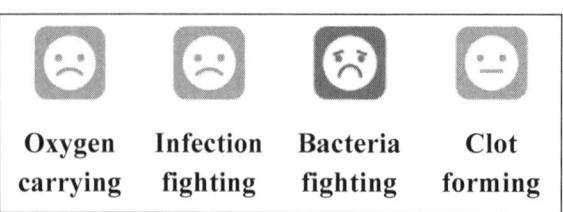

At 11.00 am I went down for the CT scan that I was supposed to have yesterday. Lunch today consisted of a Scandishake and a mandarin orange. The rest of the day was routine: read, write, sleep, look out of the window and drink more water.

I heard a commotion outside my room and so I ventured out onto the ward at about 2.30 pm (although I wasn't supposed to). I saw a young lady aged about eighteen or so supported by a young man walking past me and out of the ward. She was crying, which was a most distressing sight. She was obviously in a state of shock and oblivious to me and my situation or the rest of the patients. In her eyes the only the sick person was the patient that she had just visited. I felt sorry for her. Poor girl. Poor family. Poor patient. Who was the patient? Lucky me.

I made my way back to where I should have been all along, cocooned in my room. I sat on the bed and felt somewhat shaken by what I had just witnessed. The young visitor brought back the memory of when I was first admitted to Onslow, when I walked out of room 10 only to witness a similar scene. This time I thought I could handle the situation in a more positive way. But I can't imagine myself getting used to it. I wonder if the nurses and doctors do? I doubt it somehow.

The rest of the day and evening was uneventful apart from the odd text and phone call and of course Chris was here beside me as usual. How do people cope if they are in hospital long term without family support? One thing is for sure, if you're in hospital for the long haul, emotional support must be a vital part of recovery, both for the patient and close family. I was beginning to realise this, as the long days passed slowly by and I was feeling low. One day, you can feel uplifted and full of hope. The next you can feel alone, vulnerable and in a deep hole full of darkness and despair. You must sometimes force yourself to be positive and think about getting well again.

The long days reminded me of when I was young and the summer evenings seemed endless. I remember lying in bed thinking: *"I know it's bedtime but I should be outside enjoying myself with my friends because it's still light"*. And of course, I couldn't sleep no matter how many sheep I counted.

TERRY BARRY

Bed in Summer

by
Robert Louis Stevenson

In winter I get up at night
And dress by yellow candle-light.
In summer, quite the other way,
I have to go to bed by day.

I have to go to bed and see
The birds still hopping on the tree,
Or hear the grown-up people's feet
Still going past me in the street.

And does it not seem hard to you,
When all the sky is clear and blue,
And I should like so much to play,
To have to go to bed by day?

3 A welcome break

Home for a while

Friday 22nd July 2011 **Isolation ends - 27th day in hospital**

Thank God, it's Friday. I was awake early and I could hear the busy angel bees of Onslow buzzing about outside my isolation room. The tea man, who rarely speaks (apart from uttering the words tea or coffee), came in. I have nicknamed him Costa Colin. He was followed soon after by a nurse with my breakfast. I got out of bed at about 9.30 am. I was still very tired but I had to make the effort and have a shower, which I did.

As I was no longer neutropenic and was now able to leave my room, I got dressed and wandered out of the ward and down to the Fountain Centre. It's a support centre in the hospital for cancer patients and their families. They offer advice and leaflets as well as a cup of tea and a comfortable chair where you can relax, read a book, or chat. I wanted advice on car parking for my wife who obviously was a frequent visitor and her current discount card was running out. A member of staff gave me a form to fill in that enabled me to get a discounted parking card extension for Christine, which was fantastic. They also gave me a form for disability parking should I need it. I will tell you more about the Fountain Centre another time.

I was still having this Clexane injection into my stomach which I was now doing myself. The injection doesn't hurt if you do it right and if you have enough tummy flesh to squeeze into a fold, which is affectionately known as a muffin top. It enables the needle to go in without hurting. I just stab it once and it works. Well sometimes.

This afternoon I was given the results of yesterday's scan of my abdomen and pelvis. It showed that there was a tiny amount of linear atelectasis at both lung bases (collapse of lung tissue at both lung bases). Everything else was normal. Well, that's all right then. Or is it? Blood counts were.

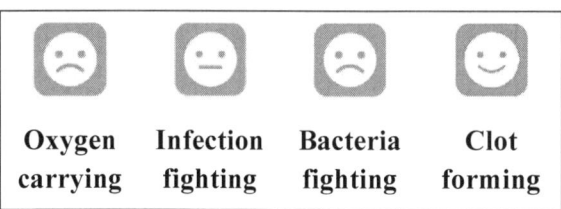

| Oxygen carrying | Infection fighting | Bacteria fighting | Clot forming |

Now for some great news. The doctors have finally given me leave to go home for a while as my immune system, although still low, has improved enough for me to be let out. Chris came to pick me up at about 6.00 pm. We left the ward and collected my medicine from the pharmacy. Then, together with my discharge letter and medication, we left the hospital for a most welcome break.

When we arrived home, I got out of the car and slowly made my way to our house. Although only a 10-metre walk, it made me realise that I was still very ill, as I was very unsteady on my legs and short of breath. But what a great feeling to walk through my own front door once again. A thought crossed my mind as I took those few steps. I didn't think I would be able to do this simple thing again, not really, not recently anyway. But here I was at last, at home. Within a few minutes, I was sat on our sofa watching television. I could smell bacon cooking in the kitchen. Chris was making me a sandwich, which I had been dreaming about for a while. This was odd, as I couldn't eat anything in hospital without feeling sick. But now I was sitting in my own armchair, about to eat a crispy bacon and soft yoked egg sandwich in my PJs, slippers and dressing gown, and chatting with the wife. Happy days' best medicine ever. After about two hours I must say I was exhausted. So up the stairs I went, to my own comfortable bed. This was bliss. Goodnight Diary.

Saturday 23rd July
This morning I felt somewhat different when I woke up. I felt more alive. This was an overwhelmingly happy feeling. I had already experienced what I called being close to the Gateway to Hell. Today I felt something new. Maybe it was the Gateway to Heaven, who knows. I got up and leant out of the bedroom window, the sun was shining on my face. The birds were singing their morning songs and sounded far more distinctive and beautiful to me than ever before. Was I getting soft? Why was I having these emotions? I gulped some more of the fresh warm air. It was a fantastic feeling and only I knew what that felt like. I know I sound a bit over the top, but so is having leukaemia; my perspective on life and the world that I live in has changed, maybe forever, who knows.

Chris got up first, she went downstairs made a cup of tea. We both sat up in bed drinking our tea and chatted until Chris finally decided to get up again at 9.30 am to make breakfast. The remainder of the day for me was just relaxing and getting used to being back home, even though it was only temporary. I just wanted to be like anyone else who are living normal, healthy, low profile lives. So, don't expect too much from me Mr Diary.

Sunday 24th July
Same as yesterday, doing nothing much, sleeping quite a lot, but felt very happy.

Monday 25th July
I woke up at 6.15 am. It was a lovely sunny day again. We had

a nice breakfast and sat out in the garden. At about 11.00 am Chris and I went out for a ride to Windsor just to get out of the house. We parked the car and took a slow walk up the hill past the castle and sat down on a bench watching the world go by. I was out of breath and exhausted but it was good to get out and about even if only for a short while. We arrived back home at about 2.00 pm. I mentioned to Chris that I had quite an appetite, which was great for her to hear. She made me poached eggs on toast and I also had a doughnut to follow and some orange juice and ice cream. At 6.00 pm we had dinner, two lamb chops with potatoes. Sorry, Mr Diary, for keeping on about food but I am just making up for lost eating time.

Sue the specialist Worker Bee

Tuesday 26th July
Today was a reminder that I was still under hospital care. I was awake at 6.00 am and at 7.30 am I had breakfast - three rashers of bacon, poached egg on toast, juice and a cup of tea. Today was bone marrow test day. So off we went back to the hospital. We arrived for my 3.00 pm appointment with Sue, the specialist nurse. She really looks after me. She greeted me with her usual smile and together we went into the procedure room.

The procedure took about 25 to 30 minutes. I got on the couch in the required position and Sue began with the local anaesthetic. I will not go into the gory details but I just gripped my mobile phone tight in one hand and all through the procedure Sue talked to me about anything that she thought would take my mind off what was happening and to put me at ease. Great skill. I was also trying to talk to her as if nothing was happening but I don't think I was kidding her. The whole process was not that bad, thanks to her. When the bone marrow test was over we went home and did nothing much so it was goodnight Mr Diary, see you tomorrow.

Wednesday 27th July
Nothing to report today, just taking it easy.

Thursday 28th July
Today I used the Red-Letter Day gift voucher that my employer gave me. We are going to stay at the famous Lilly Langtry Hotel in Bournemouth. While there, we will also visit Damian, Nicola and Scarlett. This will do nicely, as Chris and I need this short break away from it all.

We arrived at the hotel at about 10.00 am. We dropped our bags off into our room, then took a stroll in the beautiful gardens before driving down to the seafront at about 11.30 am. We sat on a bench just people watching and enjoying listening to the sea lapping on the sand. I was exhausted and before too long fell asleep. After half an hour, Chris woke me up and we walked slowly back to the car. We then drove to another of our favourite places, Haskins, a popular garden centre with a very good restaurant. We treated ourselves to a bowl of roast potatoes, a slice of apple pie and a cup of coffee. After lunch, we walked back to the car and just sat there. Chris noticed that I was tired again and suggested that I took yet another nap which I gladly did for fifteen minutes or so.

We returned to our hotel and relaxed for a couple of hours before having a delightful dinner in the hotel's restaurant. We then returned to our room where we relaxed for the rest of the evening as we were both exhausted.

Friday 29th July
We checked out of the hotel after breakfast and drove to Damian's where we were going to stay the night. We received a great welcome. Scarlett was very attentive, which made me feel

great. After a while, Damian sent out for a takeaway meal. We all just chatted for the rest of the evening without too much conversation about my current illness. I was enjoying the freedom and family time, but again I was very tired.

Saturday 30th July
We said our goodbyes after breakfast and made our way home to Bracknell. My eldest son Nick and his Polish girlfriend Beata arrived late afternoon all the way from Stockport where they live. Nick, who is my eldest son and is in his early forties, suggested that we went out for an early evening meal at the Yorkshire Rose in Warfield, which we did. Afterwards, we returned home and settled down and chatted until it was time for bed. Yet again it was great to have a father-son catch-up. Nick works for the government in Customs and Excise.

Sunday 31st July   9th day of freedom
A lovely day again. Chris had put herself out once again to make our guests welcome. We all sat out in the garden around our garden table. We even had to put up the umbrella to shade us from the emerging sun. Chris produced a fantastic breakfast spread, including bucks fizz. I am so proud of her; she is my anchor and I couldn't live a happy life without her.

After Nick and Beata left, Chris and I just relaxed in the lounge with our feet up. I noticed that we were both a bit quiet as we separately, but in unison, contemplated my return to hospital the following day for my second course of chemo; neither of us were looking forward to this.

Yet again, I must endure weeks of treatment and isolation and Chris must endure the waiting game and loneliness of being on her own after coming to see me in hospital every other day. I do not know what's worse; we are both isolated and alone most of the time.

4 Second session of chemotherapy

Bald and back for round two

Monday 1st August 2011   **25 days since the last chemotherapy**

The quiet around the house continued today. After breakfast and with Christine's help, I collected my things together to take back to hospital. You could hear a pin drop. I don't think either of us knew what to say to each other without facing the realisation of me going back into hospital and her being at home alone again. As the hair on my head was now no more than a few scattered clumps, I suggested to Chris that we visit the barber's and get him to shave off the remainder of my locks so that my head would look a bit neater. Not so good if you are a female, methinks. So off we went to the local barber, where he did the job in no time at all.

I did not know it at the time, but while I was sitting in the barber's chair chatting away to the barber as you do, Chris was sitting behind me in tears. This was due to her own realisation that I had cancer. As an afterthought, four years later, I asked her to record her thoughts about the whole experience and her account is near the beginning of chapter 7, under the heading *Christine's Letter.* I found her account very touching and amusing at the same time. My wife does not share her innermost feelings openly, especially amongst strangers and for her to share her thoughts and feelings in writing is unusual.

We arrived at the hospital at 8.00 pm. We stood outside the ward entrance, looked at each other and simultaneously wept. It was a very emotional and spontaneous moment for us both. We said our goodbyes and I went into the ward to face the job in hand and Chris went home. We were separated again and alone and it hurts.

After I had settled in, the doctor on duty informed me that my 2nd cycle of chemo would begin tomorrow. She also noted that I had mouth ulcers and my rash seemed to be getting worse. The rest of the arrival checks have been done and I was back in a bed and in a place I didn't want to be in but we cannot always get what we want when we want it, can we? Sometimes we must be patient and wait and go with the flow. Goodnight, Mr Diary.

Tuesday 2nd August
3.15 am. Interrupted sleep. The night nurse came into my room and took some blood. The results were pretty good apart from my haemoglobin count.

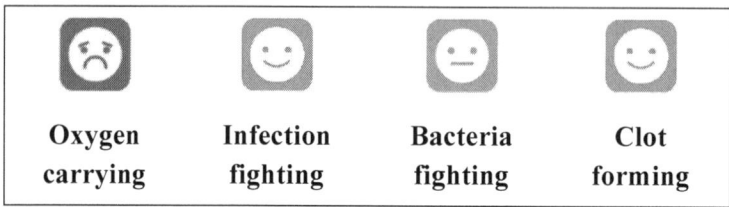

I managed to eat some breakfast at 8.00 am and at 9.30 am, the doctors came in to see me. Everything seemed to be fine and in order apart from my itchy skin and mouth ulcers. The latest bone marrow test results were also back. 3.3 blasts (I think these are the immature cells detected when you have a bone marrow test, so it was okay to proceed with the chemo which started just after midday). Chris arrived about 5.00 pm while Carol was still feeding the Red Devil into my veins and stayed here until about

7.30 pm. A nurse came in soon after Chris left with more chemo. The night sister arrived at about 9.45 pm with the last of the day's treatment. There was nothing more to talk or write about. It was late and I was tired. I am still trying to get used to being back on the ward after having a week in the comfort of my own home. It was a bittersweet experience going home and then coming back to hospital knowing what to expect next, but on balance I was so glad I had the break. I needed it if only to get through today's events.

Today's Chemotherapy

12.30 pm	Cytarabine	for 1 hour
2.30 pm	Mylotarg 6	for 1 hour (supervised due to toxicity and possible serious reaction)
4.30 pm	Doxorubicin (Red Devil)	for 1 hour (supervised due to toxicity)
7.30 pm	Cytarabine	for 1 hour
9.30 pm	Etoposide	for 2 hours

Wednesday 3rd August

Day 2 of chemo started at 6.00 am. My nausea was still present and I had a bit of a chesty cough.

At 9.45 am Doctor Louise arrived and examined the rash on my body and legs as the itchy red blob had migrated downwards and said, *"I think I will get a second opinion regarding your rash."*

What could be more irritating than itching all over on top of everything else? Susan the dietitian arrived at midday and informed me that I should be on a high-protein diet. Two full-fat yoghurts, Forceval multivitamin tablet and a Scandishake.

She also said that I could speak to the hospital canteen about the food I could eat if I was not neutropenic, providing the medical team agree. The last of the chemo infusion began at about 7.00 pm. It was Etoposide, which lasted for two hours. While I was waiting for the bag to empty, I began thinking about my diet and health and I wondered whether my dietitian would approve the following memory of an old NHS diet:

> When I was a young boy, I was sent to convalesce in the country because of my severe asthma. We were all fed very well. Breakfast started with either shredded wheat or porridge with plenty of sugar on top followed by streaky bacon and eggs. I can't remember much about lunch but at dinner time, we quite often ate savoury and sweet suet puddings or breast of lamb. Then, just before lights out, which was at about 8.00 pm, we had a plateful of bread and dripping for supper with a glass of milk to wash it down.
>
> We did however get some things right as far as diet was concerned in those days. 60% of the adult population had allotments, so fresh vegetables were in plentiful supply, so our parents thought that we did have a reasonably healthy diet.

Cytarabine	1 hour x2
Etoposide	2 hours

Thursday 4th August

I had some cereal this morning, a Scandishake, two or three quavers and a nibble on a croissant and jam. At midday, Susan came back to see me again about my diet. She told me that I had excellent weight gain while I was at home. 85 kg to 89 kg on re-admission, but now my nausea was back and worse than ever. Carol came in mid-afternoon and gave me some anti sickness pills after she had finished giving me more of the Red Devil. I had more chemo that evening from 7.00 pm onwards. I settled for the night at about 11.15 pm.

Cytarabine	1 hour x2
Etoposide	2 hours
Doxorubicin (Red Devil)	1 hour
Mylotarg 6	1 hour

Friday 5th August

I felt ill today. Chemo started at about 6.30am. OBS were taken by the nursing staff and were satisfactory. Bloods for the day were

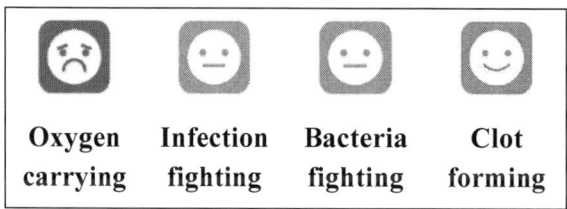

CRP was 10, which could be the start of an infection. Doctor Louise came in at 10.10 am. She examined my rash again, it was now all over my body. She is in contact with the dermatology department and is still waiting for a second opinion from a Doctor Wong. A nurse came in, Toni, a very caring individual. She changed my dressing to the PICC line. After she left, I wandered downstairs to the Fountain Centre and sat there for a while. Chemo continued again this evening, ending at about 10.30 pm.

Cytarabine	1 hour x2
Etoposide	2 hours

Saturday 6th August

Nothing much to report today, Mr Diary. Doctor Louise came to see me just after midday. She said that my OBS were stable, but she was concerned about my mouth and throat ulcers. I was not particularly concerned about these myself, but medication was on the agenda. Chris arrived with some books for me to read and sat with me. We decided after a while to get out of the ward and take a slow stroll down to the reception area by the hospital entrance where she had a coffee. We said our goodbyes at the hospital entrance and she left for home.

I made my way back to the ward and waited for sister Carol to prepare and administer that evening's chemo, Red Devil. OBS were taken at 6.25 pm. I watched some television and read for a while. It was about 9.45 pm when I began to get very tired. It was time to turn in for the night and get as much sleep as possible. As I drifted off to sleep, I wondered what tomorrow might have in store. I hated being alone, especially at bedtime.

Cytarabine	1 hour x2
Etoposide	2 hours
Doxorubicin (Red Devil)	1 hour

Sunday 7th August

I am now in room 17. This was my worse day so far of this second period of treatment. I am fed up with having D, feeling sick and itching all over, and now I have a sore ulcerated throat and mouth. I am thoroughly cheesed off and let the nursing staff know it. I just didn't know what to do with myself. I couldn't concentrate on anything for long and I was fed up with trying to be positive. There was one good thing about today. It was my brother Paul's birthday. Happy Birthday Fred (that's his nickname). The ward sister came back at 7.00 pm and continued with another session of chemo. She also wanted a stool sample (nice).

| Cytarabine | 1 hour x2 |

Monday 8th August

I felt a bit better today. A bit more positive after feeling sorry for myself yesterday. I even had a bit of an appetite. I ate some cornflakes and enjoyed a biscuit with a cup of Colin's tea.

You may have wondered, Mr Diary, why I keep writing and talking about food and my weight. It is most important that I record what I am eating and drinking. If I get a tummy bug, the medical team need to be able to get to the source of the bug as quickly as possible, especially as my immune system is so low. My weight recording is also most important. If I was to gain or lose too much weight in a short space of time, it could be medically significant. So, it might be a bit boring to read, but it is essential to record.

It was 10.45 am when the doctor arrived and looked at my rash without much comment. At 12.15 pm, Susan came in and gave me the third degree about my lack of food/fluid intake. She weighed me: 84.6 kg, a decrease of 2 kg over five days. I told her about the itching, the metallic taste in my mouth, and my nausea, which seemed to get worse when I ate hot food. I also mentioned that I had some difficulty in swallowing and I had a constant headache and three episodes of D, and it was still only just after midday. No wonder I was losing weight. Apart from that, I felt much better. She has now decided to put a diet plan together. More fluids required, Forceval and Scandishake (as a meal replacement). I declined her option of puréed food and external tube feeding. Wouldn't you, Mr Diary?

I stayed in bed until 3.30 pm. An hour later, I had a visit from Doctor Louise, one of my senior guardian angels. She checked my PICC line and asked about my sore throat, which I said was slightly better, but I was still very itchy all over the front of my body and arms. It was then that she confirmed that she has made me an appointment to see Doctor Wong the dermatology consultant tomorrow at 4.10 pm. Thank the Lord for that.

Cytarabine	1 hour x2

Tuesday 9th August
The doctor arrived at 10.00 am. My neutrophil count was 2.8.

Bacteria fighting

Now for the long wait until the neutrophil count goes down to zero. My rash became worse overnight. It's now all around my lower back and the top of my legs. I was waiting for new drugs to help with the irritation. My sore throat was better and I had managed some breakfast.

I visited Doctor Wong the dermatologist consultant that afternoon. Her verdict was that it was drug related.

"Probably chemo," she said. *"The more chemo you have, the worse it will get."*

That's great. She had prescribed a strong steroid cream and tablets which I must take four times per day - Atarax and Betnovate cream. Let's see what happens from now on. I am sure it will work. I also had stomach cramps, but still managed some banter with the nursing staff throughout the evening.

Cytarabine	1 hour x2

Wednesday 10th August

It's my youngest son Jamie's birthday today, so I texted him "Happy Birthday" and shortly after that, I phoned him and we chatted for a while.

It was not a bad sort of day, although the routine remained boring. The doctor came in at 9.45 am. My mouth ulcers were improving but I still had stomach cramps, which get worse when I eat. Hooray, I have started applying my rash cream. Chris arrived at 2.00 pm with a boiled egg and bacon sandwich. I also had a call from my sister Linda. She is coming to visit me with her husband Geoff. Just as a point of interest, they are both teachers from Kent; Linda a PE teacher, Geoff a deputy head. They should be here this Friday afternoon. They intend taking me out to a pub for a bite to eat. The doctors are stopping the Clexane injections today and the second cycle of chemo has ended. Chris left at about 7.00 pm.

Cytarabine	1 hour x2

Thursday 11th August

Good Morning, Mr Diary. I had a good night's sleep. After breakfast, the nurse helped me put on the itchy skin cream. She did a much better job than I did yesterday. At 10.00 am my OBS were taken. PICC site clean.

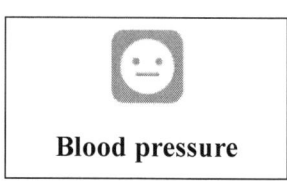

Blood pressure

She is back. Susan the dietitian with many more questions. She weighed me: 85.1 kg, a decrease of 1.5 kg in 7 days. She asked me about my fluid intake which I was unable to recall. She told me of the consequences of eating perishable food from home or anywhere outside of the hospital, i.e. contact with food that can cause infection. Well, that's told me yet again. Good old Susan, she means well. At 4.00 pm, Doctor Louise arrived. She noticed an improvement in me and said that I could go home for the weekend, although I needed to come back to the hospital on Saturday for a blood test. I told her that my wife was away for the weekend so I declined her kind offer and decided to stay in hospital. Chris visited as usual. She is going to stay at our good friends Maureen and Paul down in Somerset. It will do her good to get away and I know that they will cheer her up.

Friday 12th August

I had a good night's sleep and, when I finally managed to get out of bed, I treated myself to a nice shower.

I had some breakfast and then phoned Chris, *"Have a nice weekend and be careful on the roads. Can you bring some more Waitrose bags next time you visit, please?"* and of course I asked her to give my love to our friends.

At 9.30 am, Doctor Andre arrived to ask how I was feeling and confirmed yet again that my second cycle of chemo was indeed completed on the 10th August. He examined me while a nurse took some routine observations of temperature, blood pressure and pulse reading.

Blood pressure

I mentioned to Doctor Andre that I was constipated. I only

mentioned this to him because it was the opposite of what I have been used to since my treatment began. Sorry to share this with you, Mr Diary. I don't know what's worse: the dam being blocked or the dam bursting.

Linda and Geoff visited this afternoon. We went to a Beefeater pub a few miles outside of Guildford, which of course was a welcome break for me. It made me feel great seeing them again, especially as they had travelled so far to see me. As we walked to their car, which was only 100yds or so from the hospital entrance, I felt sick and dizzy. I found it difficult to keep up with them (it's usually the other way around). I didn't even have the breath to call out and ask them to wait until I caught up with them. A reminder, yet again, of just how ill I am. I don't know if they noticed how difficult the walk was for me. I hope not. I just don't want anyone to witness my obvious frailty. Am I daft?

We sat outside at the pub as it was a nice sunny day. I ordered gammon steak, chips and a coke, but I couldn't eat them, even though I thought I had an appetite. How disappointing. I was a bit embarrassed by the whole episode. I cannot eat, walk and I can't breathe properly. They must have thought I was a lost cause. However, it was good to see them and have a chat; that at least was a great tonic for me. But all too soon, I thought it was time to get back to the hospital. I felt cold, weak and not well at all. They took me back to the ward and to my room. When they left, I dozed off for a while.

Just before I went to sleep, I decided to write down my current medicine. It keeps my mind active to do these sorts of things. That's why I record stuff like bloods and OBS. It's boring for anyone else but it helps keep my mind active, here goes:

For rash	Betamethasone Valerate 0.1% cream
For itching	Urerax syrup 12.5ml
For anti-sickness	Metoclopramide x qtr. tablet Levomepromazine 25mg
For mouth ulcers and sore throat	Difflam liquid
For antifungal	Noxafil (Posaconazole) 5mm 3 times daily (very expensive, but helps stop invasive fungal infection).

I also recorded some information about blood that I was given:

> Blood transfusions are given when the body does not have enough RED blood cells.
>
> A bone marrow test detects immature cells present (*Blasts*).
>
> White blood cells are part of the immune system and protect the body against infection. They are larger than red blood cells but fewer in number and if an infection develops, they attack and destroy the bacteria, virus or any other organism causing it.
>
> White blood cells are mainly made up of six types:
>
> | | |
> |---|---|
> | Neutrophils | 58% |
> | Monocytes | 4% |
> | Lymphocytes | 4% |
> | Bands | 3% |
> | Eosinophils | 2% |
> | Basophils | 1% |

Complicated stuff and although I am one of those people who would prefer not to be given a detailed analysis of my condition and treatment up front, it is important that I take some interest in what is wrong with me and what medicine I am receiving to help me fully recover.

Saturday 13th August

It has been 46 days since my 1st chemo treatment began. I slept well last night although I didn't feel that great this morning. My appetite was slowly improving and I was even eating some hospital food. No offence, catering, as they have been most helpful towards me and my dietary requirements. My rash has improved too. No visitors today. Neutrophils are down to 0.06

so I am now neutropenic and confined to my room for some considerable time. During the day, I looked out through the small porthole window of my door. It was very quiet outside on the ward; I couldn't see anyone walking about. I felt like a caged animal.

"Please, someone, let me out. I'm the keeper!"

Sunday 14th August

Chris arrived this afternoon on her way back from her break away. It is always a tonic for me to see her. We chatted about her visit to our friends. She seemed to be more relaxed today. She stayed for a while but looked a bit tired, so I suggested that she went home earlier than usual. I felt sick anyway and was not particularly good company. After she left, a nurse came in and gave me an anti-sickness jab, which helped. Oh, and neutrophils were down to 0.3.

Bacteria fighting

Monday 15th August

01.00 am. Yes, that's right, one in the morning. The night nursing staff were keeping a regular eye on me. OBS were taken. Everything seemed to be okay apart from the nurses' night time visits, which I shouldn't really complain about. I slept well when I was allowed to. I was awake at breakfast time about 8.00 am.

Blood pressure

The doctor arrived at about 10.30 am and performed more standard observations, including my SATS which read 99% on air. This is a reading that is carried out in hospital as a regular patient observation called SP02 Oxygen Saturation. Ideally, the SATS reading should be 100% and not below 90%. The reading is the percentage of your red cells that are carrying oxygen and it depends on your age, height, weight, whether you are an ex-smoker. They say that if SATS are below 93% then the patient needs oxygen therapy. As my ability to breathe was to become an important indicator in the coming weeks, here is a new smiley to show how well (or poorly) my breathing was:

Ability to breathe

My isolation could last for weeks so I must be patient. I must wait until my neutrophil counts go up to 1.0 before I can get out of hospital for a while (one day at a time). Nothing more to report today.

Tuesday 16th August
I had a reasonable night's sleep apart from yet another early morning nurses' check. This time it was 00.45 am. Nothing else to report until Susan came in at 11.25 am and weighed me: 83.9 kg. Doctor Robbins closely followed her.

Neutrophils 0.1 and my blood pressure was low.

Bacteria fighting

Doctor Robins has ordered two pools of platelets and one unit of blood. My appetite has improved but I am still under-weight. When I first began my treatment, I weighed 14 stone 10 pounds and I am now 13 stone 2 pounds. I was too fat anyway, but it still worries me. I am drinking more fluids, which is even more important it seems than food. The catering manager came to see me again today about food hotness; by the time my meal gets to me it is not always very warm, which can't be good for my health. You must feel sorry for the nursing staff as they have to wait on us patients with our food as well nurse us, which in my view is counter-productive, but no politics today. I felt okay, although it is very hard for any long-term patient to stem the boredom. Sometimes I think it's best not to think at all, just sleep. But that's not me really, so let's forget that scenario, it's not good advice anyway.

I do feel that more could be done for the long-term patient's emotional state of mind, even if it is to have a free television in the room and maybe a couple of pictures from home on the wall, or a piece of familiar furniture. Maybe a visit from a counsellor, anything to stop you thinking the dark and negative thoughts that occur occasionally when you are unwell or on your own for any length of time.

Chris arrived at 3.00 pm and left at 7.00 pm. She seemed to be a bit low herself. Maybe she could do with some counselling. She is alone probably more than me for most of the time. At least I get daily visits from doctors and nurses. After Chris left I watched some television. At 9.45 pm I decided it was time for sleep. Goodnight, Mr Diary.

The Angel Bees of Onslow

Wednesday 17th August   My Birthday

Happy birthday to me. Happy birthday to me. At 8.00 am, Costa Colin the Tea man arrived and gave me a welcome cuppa. I did mention that it was my birthday as he was on his way out of my room, but I don't think he heard me. Oh, well. I had breakfast.

Blood pressure

My mouth ulcers have gone at last. The doctor popped in to see me at 10.45 am. Texts and phone calls from my four children, friends and family began at about 9.00 am and continued throughout the day, which was great. Chris arrived early afternoon with lots of birthday cards and gifts.

My presents were taking me some time to open, read and digest. Then while Chris was in the powder room, in came the nurses headed by Jincy, with a large chocolate birthday cake. They were all singing happy birthday. What a lovely surprise; I wasn't expecting that. Chris must have wondered what was happening as they were all stood around my bed when she returned. The nurses were the candles on the cake - their presence lit up the room. There was Shay, Sarah, Jincy, Carol (sister in charge) and Toni. What a lovely bunch my Onslow Angels are. Of course, I shared the cake with everyone. After the nurses left, Chris and I settled down again. I opened and read the rest of my cards.

Chris then read them, before lining them up like soldiers on the window sill.

> I am suddenly very tired and it is getting late. Chris and I said our goodbyes at about 8.30 pm. It's now 10.30 pm and I am going to settle down for the night as I am also getting writer's cramp as I record the day's events. I am another year older and guess what, I am still here, happy and eager to get to my next birthday. I wish it was tomorrow. Goodnight Mr Diary.

Thursday 18th August
After yesterday's excitement and a reasonable night's sleep, I woke up this morning feeling completely rubbish. I couldn't write too much as I was not in the mood. The doctor arrived at 9.55 am. OBS were stable. I was disturbed again at 1.45 pm by Susan. She wanted to weigh me. I didn't particularly want to get out of bed but I had to. My weight was 84.8 kg, an increase of one kg in two days. Back to sleep. I was woken up again by Doctor Robbins at 4.30 pm. Trimethoprim was attached to my drip by a nurse during the doctor's visit. I believe this is a strong antibiotic for bladder infections. I just had to lay there and let the potent medicine flow into my veins. At 11.00 pm, a nurse called the doctor as, guess what… I had spiked a temperature of 38 degrees and that's quite hot. The doctor arranged for the nursing staff to take blood cultures and the night nurse gave me some paracetamol and a bit of sympathy, which I seemed to need at the time. Poor me. Goodnight, Mr Diary.

Friday 19th August   7th day of isolation
It was only 1.00 am in the morning when Afsa the night sister came in. She is a very experienced, kind and sympathetic nurse. She noticed that I was unwell. I had a severe headache, felt sick and was burning up. She took my temperature. It was still quite

high at 37.5. She was here again at 2.00 am. My temperature was back up to 38 degrees. I couldn't sleep. I decided to sit up in bed and began to write. I was just trying to take my mind off how I felt but it was no good and I soon gave up. I found it too difficult to concentrate as I felt too ill. I eventually dozed off. After a short while I heard a knock on the door but I couldn't see who it was. Then I saw Pete's head peering through the porthole window. He seemed to be hesitant to enter so I beckoned him in. He told me that he was going home today and just wanted to wish me well. We chatted for a while about his plans for the foreseeable future including going on holiday to his native Wales in September and his trip to Spain by car. We agreed to keep in touch. We wished each other well and he left. The doctor visited me again at 10.35 am and between him and the nurse, they took my OBS.

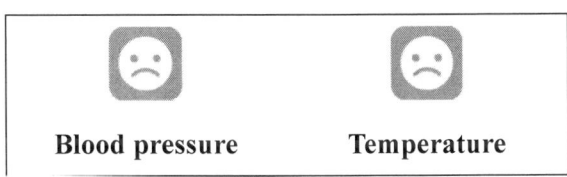

I had D again. I felt woozy and I was itching all over. I was exhausted. All I wanted to do was sleep. The nurse came in again at about 11.45 am and I told her that I had a sore throat as well.

She was very sympathetic and said, *"You are going to have another blood transfusion and two pools of platelets soon, probably tomorrow."*

At 6.00 pm the nurse was back and took my temperature which was 37.9.

> **Blood transfusions**
>
> Blood transfusions contain mostly red blood cells and a few platelets. These improve anaemia when counts are low but to prevent bleeding, platelets are also needed. When you have leukaemia the leukaemia cells prevent you producing your own blood cells and the chemo does this too. So when the counts are low, transfusions give blood and platelets for support, improving anaemia and minimising bleeding.

Saturday 20th August

I had to go for a CXR (Chest Radiograph X-Ray). The doctor visited me and didn't seem very happy with my condition. He told me that I would have a blood transfusion later that evening. Chris arrived and sat beside me. She read a book while I catnapped for most of the afternoon and early evening. A nurse came in and asked Chris if she would like a cup of tea at about 7.45 pm, which she gladly accepted. She left for home shortly afterwards. I began having the first of my platelets half an hour later and that was followed by the blood transfusion. It seems that my HB (haemoglobin) is low. All I wanted to do was sleep although I knew that I was going to be disturbed later. My temperature was taken at 9.00 pm, it was 37.9. The activity continued around me into the early hours

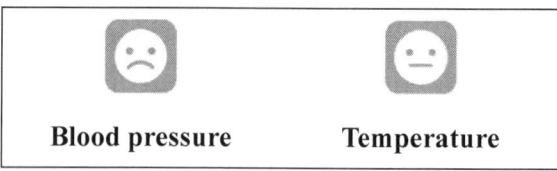

Sunday 21st August

Busy bees were outside, as the early shift had arrived and the night shift were going home for a well-earned sleep. The nursing teams get together for a handover between shifts. I had overheard the sister in charge on occasion going through her notes from her shift and all the staff present seemed to listen intently and take it very seriously as she went through the patients' notes one by one. Colin came in and left me a cup of tea. It was about 7.30 am. At 9.00 am I was given another blood transfusion. OBS were stable.

Blood pressure

BP98/59. At 11.45 am the nurse came back with the second unit of blood. Sorry, Mr Diary, the day was a bit boring. I did go for a chest X-ray though and my appetite had returned, just a bit.

Monday 22nd August

I had a good night's sleep and I felt okay. My haemoglobin was still low which meant that my red cell blood count was lower than it should be. I may need to have another blood transfusion soon. I cannot get out of this room and it is beginning to get on my nerves. More questions are making their way into my head regarding my recovery and future. How many more chemo treatments will I need before I am in remission? Maybe after the 2nd/3rd courses of chemo are finished, and I have had another bone marrow test, we will know more. I don't know, we must wait and see. I have total confidence in my doctors to do their best for me. The rest will be down to me, how I cope with the stress of it all and of course the side effects of the treatment. Sometimes I really struggle. So, I remind myself when I can to keep positive, which is sometimes difficult when you are in isolation, cocooned in a room that you cannot walk in and out of even though it is unlocked, and you are alone with only yourself to talk to. Long periods of isolation when you are ill can have a negative effect.

Sometimes when I feel too sorry for myself I get my Quotation book out. Here's one,

> *Grasp your opportunities no matter how poor your health, nothing is worse for your health than boredom.*

If my chemo goes to four sessions, 11th November 2011 is when I should get out of hospital as an inpatient for good. We must wait and see. Chris is visiting again today. She is getting very lonely at home on her own. I worry about that sometimes. One thing is for sure, both of our lives seem to be based on a day-to-day existence now. Planning anything too far ahead is not an option, judging by the way I feel. There seems to be no point in thinking too much about seeing my grandchildren growing up and getting married. That scares me. I want to get better. I want to see the sun rise every day. I want to get out of here. Please God help me find a way. Everything in my life has changed. My usual positivity is slipping away. This is purgatory. The reality of living on borrowed time seems all too real. I think you only realise this when you go through an experience that has such a life-threatening type of trauma. I must learn to handle it better. I will just have to deal with it. That's enough Tel boy, snap out of it. This is a struggle that you *must* overcome. I just wish I felt a bit better than I do now. Like they said at Houston command centre when things went wrong with Apollo 13:

> *Failure is not an option.*

Just thinking negative thoughts like this is making my headache worse. So, what's the point of moaning? Something that a very senior nurse said to me not too long ago comes to mind,

> *Sometimes we have to make you ill in order to make you better.*

I believe this to be true. What is the point of complaining about being ill, when people around you are trying their best to make you better with the best treatment available?

> *If a golden nugget was to fall onto your head, would you really complain about having a headache?*

I should appreciate things more; especially what others are doing to help me behind the scenes. Doctors, nurses, and all NHS departments, and of course family and friends, especially those closest to me. I owe it to them to pull through this ordeal. Sorry, Mr Diary, I will do my best to think positive thoughts from now on. Self-pity doesn't do anyone any good, does it? But sometimes you can't help it. Everyone on the ward can see how I look but they can't see how I feel. I know I should let someone know but I don't want to burden them further so I have to man up.

The doctor arrived at 11.15 am. Bloods checked.

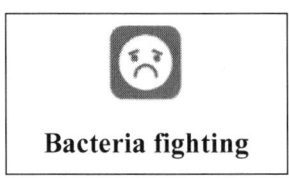

My appetite has improved. I am still on antibiotics.

At 3.00 pm, Doctor Robbins came in and said, *"I may stop the antibiotics on Wednesday and I will be looking to book you in for a bone marrow test next Tuesday 30th August."*

As I was feeling sorry for myself today, I took a mobile selfie of me looking glum with my bald, pointy head and big nose.

...looking glum with my bald, pointy head and big nose

Tuesday 23rd August
A different day, a different attitude. I have had a great night's sleep. At 9.25 am, Susan came in. How lovely to see her. She managed to get me out of bed to weigh me. 83.3 kg, that's 13 stone 1.6 lb. That's a loss of 6 kg or 13lbs in just over three weeks. Whoops. Is it my fault? This chemo leaves such a horrible metallic taste in my mouth and it also makes me feel sick, so I don't eat. Evidently, chemotherapy does not affect everyone in the same way though. We are all different.

Wednesday 24th August   12th day of isolation
Guess what, Mr Diary, my neutrophil count is now 1.6. Well enough to go home for a while maybe?

Bacteria fighting

So, I am no longer neutropenic. Will I get out today? The doctor arrived at 9.30 am. OBS were taken.

Blood pressure

Well, it seems that I am not getting out of hospital today after all, maybe tomorrow if I'm lucky. My platelets are still a bit low and I must have my last dose of antibiotics tonight sometime. I have not spiked a temperature since 19th August, which is great news.

The catering manager came in again today at 4.35 pm regarding the meal service and whether I could eat a bought-in steak slice, cremated of course. So, I agreed to try it but I just couldn't eat it, it made me feel sick. At 10.00 pm I was given the final antibiotic dose and that was that for the night, time to sleep.

Thursday 25th August   25th day in hospital

At 01.00 am, the night nurse gave me another antibiotic dose. So, the one I had at 10.00 pm last night was not the last one, oh well. When I woke this morning, there was a hive of activity out on the ward and then all around me. Nurses in and out from 7.30 am onwards. At 10.00 am in came a team of doctors headed by Doctor Louise.

"You can go home today," she said with a smile. I felt as if I

was going on a surprise holiday paid for by the hospital. Home, what a wonderful word, especially as I had my guardian angels blessing to go there for a while.

The nurses took some more OBS. They usually double up with checks on you if you are going home for a while.

Blood pressure

The PICC line was clean. At 11.10 am, the doctors returned and confirmed that I would be going home. But I had to come back Sunday 28th August for a blood test and get ready for next chemo session. I have now been told officially that I must have a bone marrow test, which is booked for next Tuesday, 30th August. At 11.55 am, Sister Carol came in and said that the Pharmacist would be up shortly with my medicine request for when I am out of hospital. I phoned Chris with the good news. She is on her way to pick me up. Yippee, I am going home. Finally, bloods were taken

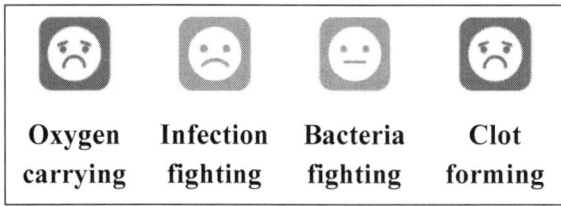

| **Oxygen carrying** | **Infection fighting** | **Bacteria fighting** | **Clot forming** |

Good results I was told, although they didn't look that great to me. Good enough to get out of here though. The pharmacist has brought up my medicine to take home with me. Chris picked me up at about 2.45 pm and off we went.

It's always great to be back home, sat in your favourite chair, sleeping in your own bed, looking out onto your own garden and eating food cooked by your nearest and dearest. I love it. I am so pleased to be here once again. We both settled in for the evening. I even watched the soaps. I had been watching them in hospital - there wasn't much else to do, especially when I was ill and in isolation, apart from write my diary – and they helped me sleep. I didn't read much either, as I found that far more tiring than writing. So, my days were filled with sleeping, being ill, feeling sorry for myself, then trying to be positive, and writing about it.

While I am out of hospital I have decided that there will not be too much to report, as I would be too busy having a good time. I was in bed by 10.30 pm. It felt so good being home again. I have really missed it.

Friday 26th August

I woke up early this morning and I had that happy feeling again. I seem to be getting more of these feelings lately, especially when I receive good news from the doctor, and all the time I am at home with my family. I haven't a clue what it all means or where it really comes from. Maybe it is because the sun was shining this morning. Whatever it is, I like it and I am not complaining.

I am still occasionally getting happy childhood flashbacks of when nothing much mattered except climbing trees or counting the spots on the ladybird that I kept in a matchbox together with a leaf for it to chew on, just in case it got hungry. Or watching frog spawn turn into tadpoles. Or scrumping apples, pears and plums from a nearby orchard. Or going on long walks into the countryside with my mates, usually into an imaginary world of adventure, swapping duplicate cigarette cards on the way. The list was endless, the experiences timeless, almost forgotten, but now they are back again. Is this a new beginning for me? Or the re-emergence of a time thought lost forever? Or have I finally lost the plot? I just don't know but it feels good all the same. Good memories have always inspired me, which reminds me of another early episode in my life.

It involved my one and only brush with the constabulary. I was scrumping pears. I must have been about six or seven years old. I was an expert tree climber in those days. The older boys used me to climb a tree, get amongst the fruit and shake the bounty off and into their greedy waiting arms. It was a condition if I wanted to be in their gang. On one occasion, a pear tree laden with plump, forbidden fruit was hanging over a very grumpy person's garden fence. I was lifted onto an overhanging branch. Unfortunately, the grumpy person spotted the tree shaking and the pears falling. The older boys ran off. I jumped down from a great height and ran hell for leather. I thought I had gotten away with it but the grumpy person recognised one of the older boys who in turn received a visit from the local bobby later that day. The older boy, one David Cleverson, decided that as the junior member of the gang I could take the blame even though I was just a pawn in their syndicate of crime.

He ratted on me. So now sixty odd years later I have decided to get even and name and shame him as the ring leader. There was a knock on our front door that evening. I was in bed. I heard a stranger talking to my parents and I was eventually called downstairs to get a telling off from the Bobby, although I think the policeman and my parents knew that I was just a scapegoat and I was let off with a caution and a smile. It's strange how solitude stirs fond memories.

You've been grassed up sunshine

But let's get back to the present. Lately, I am beginning to believe even more that we are all so privileged to be here. I read somewhere that God created heaven on earth and I for one believe this to be true. Perhaps our world is an oasis amongst an uninhabitable desert of the known universe and we are guests of the creator. Perhaps our world is God's five-star self-catering holiday destination for those he thinks deserve a break, who knows? It's just a thought. I wonder what our creator thinks of his guests these days?

I discovered that I had some sort of faith quite recently. I was alone lying on my bed in room 17. I felt particularly poorly and sorry for myself that day. I felt, dizzy, sick, unable to breathe properly and so weak with the D that I had difficulty getting out of bed and to the toilet just a few feet away. I remember sighing deeply and pretended it was my last breath. I closed my eyes and put my arm up into the air and imagined God was about to take hold of my outstretched hand to lift me into his heavenly kingdom.

Almost immediately, I pulled my arm down again and said under my breath. *"No, I am not ready yet."*

My heart was racing, I thought to myself, *"That was too close for comfort."*

I sat up and began to concentrate on my surroundings just so I could get back into the world of the living. I don't want to let myself think that way again.

Sorry about that, Mr Diary, that thought just came into my head and I wanted to share it.

Am I going mad?

5 Another rest

My chat with Lola

Chris is truly an angel. She has been saving up £2 coins, and we have a refund from our utility company because of an overpayment (what's new). So anyway, she said that as a surprise, and after I have had my bone marrow test next Tuesday, we can go to Devon to one of our favourite haunts: Topsham, near Exeter and Sidmouth. So, on Wednesday the 31st, we will be on our way to sunny Devon.

Saturday 27th August 2011 **10 weeks since diagnosis**

Just a lazy day today doing nothing, apart from a brief visit to Sacha's house. When we arrived, we were warmly greeted by Immy and Lola (aged seven and five respectively). Chris was in the kitchen chatting to Sacha while I was on the settee in the lounge drinking a cup of tea, closely flanked by the two children. After a while, Lola looked at me in a curiously thoughtful way.

She leant towards me and whispered, *"Grandad why have you got no hair now? Where has it gone?"*

Now Immy seemed interested. I wasn't expecting this and it caused an emotional lump in my throat. I put my arms around them both and pulled them even closer to me, just to give me a bit of time to think.

I replied, *"I have an illness that you can't catch, but sometimes the medicine that is going to make you better makes your hair fall out for a while, that's why I wear a cap. It keeps my head warm until my hair grows back, which will be very soon."*

They both seemed reasonably satisfied with my answer. Immy got up and went into the kitchen and returned with a few more biscuits to go with my tea. Lola started to do some more colouring in her picture book. I took a moment to watch them playing innocently at my feet and hoped that they were going to stay beside me until I left, and they did. We stayed for another hour and then went home to get ready for my hospital appointment the next day.

The Queen of all the Bees takes me away

Sunday 28th August
We had to get up early and go to hospital for 10.00 am. On arrival, we were seen by Sister Jincy. Usual OBS and bloods were taken. My PICC line was clean, my rash had improved and my temperature was normal.

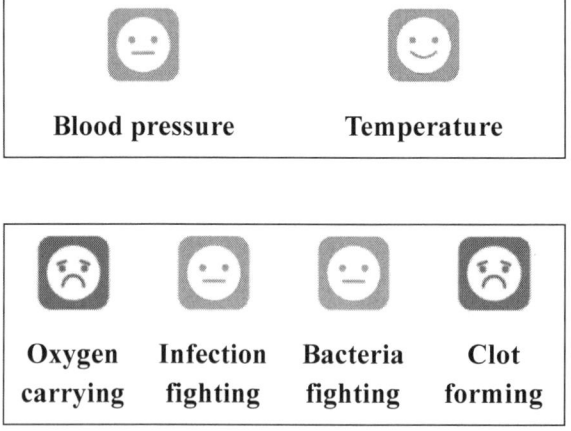

Monday 29th August
Nothing much happened today, just chilling out at home.

Tuesday 30th August
At home again today. But I had to go back to the hospital to have a bone marrow test that afternoon. When we arrived, we went to see Sue Flaherty, who performed the procedure. Yet again, although it was not particularly pleasant, Sue made the whole experience bearable. What a professional! When we left the hospital, we stopped at a pub and had an early evening meal. When we got home I rested while Chris packed our bags for our weekend in Devon.

Oh, I forgot to mention: the chest X-ray verification from 20th August was back showing a shadowing on my left lung but we are going to Devon tomorrow anyway. The shadow will have to wait. No need to tell Chris; we are going to have a welcome break and that's that.

> ## The Shadow
> The shadow on my lung was due to an infection, which was followed up by Dr McAlister to ensure it returned to normal, it did.

Wednesday 31st August
It took us about three hours to get to Devon. We booked into the Exeter Arms then went into Exeter town where we had a browse around the shops. Chris bought me a jumper in M&S. Afterwards, we made our way to the pretty town of Topsham on the estuary of the River Exe. One of my favourite places is the Quay Antique Centre. It is a riverside warehouse at the end of the village with 9,000 sq. ft. of space spread over three floors. It has a tremendous assortment of antiques and affordable bric-a-

brac, and the estuary views are fantastic. The main reason I go there is that I always seem to find prints of my favourite artist Sir William Russell Flint, and guess what, I found one called *Models in an Italian Courtyard*. Great stuff. Chris bought it for me as a belated birthday present.

Topsham is bustling with quaint shops and coffee shops with a difference. Once we had finished looking around, we made our way from the Quay to Darts Farm, which is on the way out from Topsham and towards our hotel. Darts Farm used to be just a farm shop, but now it seems to have everything from fantastic locally grown food to a deli, butcher, fishmonger, greengrocer and cider maker, as well as a restaurant and a multitude of posh shops. That's why we go there. We had a bit of lunch and a pot of tea. We spent a few pounds shopping and then we made our way back to the hotel where we relaxed for a while before having dinner. That was it for the day. We went back to our room and sat on the bed, had a cup of tea and a biscuit, watched a bit of television and we were both asleep before 9.00 pm.

Thursday 1st September

We had breakfast at 9.30 am. I felt tired, but okay. We decided to make our way to yet another one of our old haunts, Sidmouth with its 240-million-year-old red cliffs from the Triassic period. We love to visit anywhere on the Jurassic coast. We parked the car and walked through the town with its narrow streets and quaint shops. One shop we always go into is a clock shop called Pure Indulgence. It has an array of modern, tastefully designed timepieces, from watches to grandfather clocks, and they all sound different as you meander through the shop; if you manage to be in there when the clocks strike the hour you will hear a symphony of wonderful chimes. After that, we made our way to the seafront and walked along the coastal path to Jacob's ladder, which is a nice viewpoint. We then came back down to the seafront, bought some fish and chips, and sat down on a bench for a while before setting off again back to our hotel at around 4.00 pm. We rested in our room for a while before a spot of dinner in the restaurant. We then returned to our room for the same routine of watching television and just chatting about our day before we finally hit the hay.

Friday 2nd September
It's Hayley and Joe's wedding anniversary today. After breakfast, we made our way to meet them and their young family. They were staying in Salcombe, not far from Dartmouth. It was a chilly day (I seem to feel the cold more these days), but we enjoyed a nice day out. We ended up having a great early evening meal of homemade steak and ale pie at the Seven Stars pub in Kingsbridge before we said goodbye and headed back on our long journey home.

Chris, me and Baby Daisy on Salcombe beach

Saturday 3rd September
We didn't do much today, just prepared for the big day tomorrow as I am due back at the hospital for my 3rd session of chemo. I also felt as if I had a cold brewing.

No beds so treatment delayed

Sunday 4th September
We made our way to the hospital late afternoon only to be told that there were no beds. Part of me was relieved and part was concerned. The Ward Sister said that they would let me know when to come back, although I had to return for a blood test on the 7th September. So, with that news, we left the ward and went to a pub near the hospital for a drink.

When we arrived home, it was quite late. Chris decided to go to bed and I decided to stay up a while to chill and reflect on the day; although I wasn't looking forward to going back into hospital because of what I knew what was going to take place regarding treatment, the delay made me feel vulnerable. I sat there for a while and for some reason another memory from long ago came into my mind. Why, I don't know. Being turned away from having a bed to sleep in reminded me of when I was fifteen back in 1963:

> It was a Bank Holiday weekend and I had been invited to go away camping for a couple of days to Clacton-on-Sea by a friend who was used to doing exactly whatever he wanted to do. I had never been away on my own with just a mate before so my parents had to give their permission. Luckily, they liked and trusted him and he had transport and a tent, which helped the situation, so they gave their blessing. His mum had already booked

the campsite, which was just a few miles outside of Clacton.

My friend's name was (and hopefully still is) Terry LeFonze. He lived in Harold Hill just outside Romford and was a fully-fledged, stylish Mod. These were the days of mods and rockers, although contrary to public opinion, we were not all mindless thugs out to cause trouble as most people thought at the time. Two girls in the telex room at work were also stylish mods. I remember going into their office one day and they were both wearing ankle-length herringbone skirts and hush puppies, and both had the latest mod hairstyles. They were true trend setters. They both smiled at me as I shyly asked them for whatever I had come in for. One of them remarked, *"You know, if you weren't so old fashioned and got some up-to-date clothes, you would make a great mod"*.

Well that was it; from then on I was determined to be a mod. I bought a Blue Beat hat and a parker for my scooter, which I didn't yet own. The parker and hat was all I could afford. Terry, on the other hand, had spiky blond hair and all the latest mod clothes, as well as the latest in cool mod transport: a bright, light-blue BMW. He was also a good-looking and confident bloke.

On the day of our adventure, we set off early. It was a boiling hot day and eventually we arrived at our destination. We noticed some scooters parked outside a café in the town and decided to go in and have a cup of tea. Unfortunately, some rockers turned up and all hell broke loose. So rather than get caught up in the violence, we decided to make a hasty exit.

We got into the BMW and drove off to spend the

remainder of the afternoon cruising up and down the seafront, looking for girls who we thought would jump all over the three-wheeler to get at us. Yes, that's right, Terry's BMW had three wheels; it was in fact a BMW Isetta Micro, better known as a Bubble car. Unfortunately, we were mistaken about the girls. Obviously, the local women had no taste, so we parked up and bought an ice cream. For some reason, Terry went to the storage compartment of the vehicle only to discover that his mum had forgotten to pack the tent! Why he didn't pack it himself was beyond me. While we were pondering our next move, a thought crossed my mind. I turned to Terry and said, *"Where are we going to sleep tonight now?"* Terry looked somewhat puzzled and said, *"No problem, we'll go and find a Bed and Breakfast. There are thousands of them here."* So off we went knocking from door to door but without much success.

We only knocked on the doors that said 'vacancies', but for some reason we met with 100% rejection. Was it my parker or my hat? Terry's bright green jacket or red trousers? Maybe it was the BMW. We just couldn't understand why our money was any worse than anyone else's. Full of rejection, we got back into our chariot and drove to the seafront.

We parked the passion wagon and strolled down onto the beach. It was getting late. We were fed up, hot and knackered. We sat on the sand for at least two hours wondering whether we should give up our crusade of pulling the best-looking women in Clacton, go home with our tails between our legs, and make up a yarn about having the whole of the Essex female population fighting to get at us. Or rough it for the night and hope we got lucky and have a real tale to tell our mates when we got home; that would make them envious. Before we knew it, it was about eight or nine pm and we were hungry.

There was a fish and chip shop nearby so we went inside. There were two girls standing in line. They smiled at us and we smiled back. That was it, we were in! I bought some chips and a Telfer's steak and kidney pie and the chip man threw in a bag of scraps for free. (Scraps were the bits of batter left over from the fish.) Terry was more confident than me and began to chat the girls up. It turned out that they were staying in a nearby holiday camp that was full of old people in their 30s and their kids so they were looking for a bit of excitement away from the camp. Brilliant! *"What a stroke of luck"* we thought, *"we're just what they want..."*

Obviously, Terry got off with the better looking one even though he was a foot shorter than me and six inches shorter than his new companion, whose name was Mo. She was tall, slim, dressed in fashionable clothes and pretty. But they were well suited as he had the chat, the clothes, and more cash than me and of course he owned a car, even though it looked like Humpty Dumpty on wheels. But he hadn't packed the bloody tent or his sleeping bag and he wasn't sharing mine. My new companion's name was Dulci; she was shorter and not as well-groomed as her mate, and very plain with a few spots dotted around her face. But who was I to be choosy? I think at the time we were well suited and I was at least grateful to be in her company as I hadn't been in female company romantically since Christine Earwaker dumped me the previous year. I remember that she was a nice, friendly sort of girl and she let me hold her hand as we strolled aimlessly along the beachfront. Of course, I let her share my chips and scraps, although I kept the pie for myself!

Luckily, I had my sleeping bag; the girls had noticed it and I now believe it was the real reason that they stuck with us. The light was beginning to fade so we walked along the beach. Terry and I were still anxiously wondering where we would end up sleeping the night and whether the girls would get fed up and want to return to their holiday camp. We then came across a cave entrance carved out in the cliff face with another small opening about twenty feet above it. We made our way into the cave and started to explore. The cave was like a tunnel that went up and then around; it was quite a steep climb. We ended up above the cave entrance in the second opening. From inside, it reminded me of a picture frame, with an ever-changing view of the sea. We all surveyed our surroundings and the girls thought it was warm, dry and cosy.

"The tide was coming in fast..."

As the tide was coming in fast, one of the girls said, *"this is the perfect place to sleep for the night. It's so romantic!"*

Well that was it, romance was looming and the women were going nowhere as by now, the sea had almost reached the cave entrance. They were trapped by the sea, romance and two likely lads from Essex and so it was a perfect end to a not-so-perfect day. We had a bed, a girl each, and mine was magically becoming prettier as the evening turned into darkness. More stars than I had ever seen before lit up the clear, moonless night sky.

Unfortunately, I had to do the right thing and hand over my sleeping bag to the girls. Obviously, we would have preferred to be in the bed with them but that wasn't to be; there was no room at the inn for either of us.

We laid there, the four of us, looking out to sea through the picture frame opening. It was a clear night and we all saw our first of many shooting stars. On reflection, it couldn't be more romantic, could it? There is something fascinating about stars, there is no right or wrong in them. They are just there looking down on all of us.

Although Terry and I were cold, we were at least allowed to snuggle up close to the young ladies who were by now tightly tucked up back to back in my sleeping bag with no room to maneuverer except for their arms, which they kept free to give us a consolatory cuddle and a bit more warmth. We were separated from them only by a layer of polyester and duck down. Our parkers and Blue Beat hats kept us nice and warm but we pretended to be cold, just to get some sympathy from the girls. It didn't really work, so we resigned ourselves to the situation and it wasn't long before we all drifted off into a deep sleep.

I was woken suddenly. I didn't know what time it was but there was a presence, a figure dressed like a penguin with glasses and a pale face looking down on me. In fact, there were two of them.

"Good morning" one of them said smiling. *"It's a lovely morning, isn't it? Did you sleep well?"*

"Yes thanks", I replied.

Then as quickly as they appeared, the penguins left. The experience was surreal. I remember looking out of the cave opening to the beach below just after they left but there was no sign of them. Perhaps it was a dream. I am not sure what we did for the rest of the morning but Terry and I decided to go home. We said goodbye to the girls who were staying on in Clacton. Unfortunately the BMW broke down on the A12, so we had to thumb it home in the hot sun.

After many hours, I finally arrived home and my mother cooked me a most welcome meal, which I couldn't finish because I fell asleep! When I finally woke up both my parents wanted to know how my weekend went but I don't think I told them the truth.

My father asked, *"Did you meet any girls?"*

"No."

Then my mother asked, *"What are those purple marks on your neck?"*

"I fell over."

Then my father said, *"You fell over on your neck?"*

"Yes," I replied indignantly.

At the time, I thought that they believed me. Why wouldn't they? After the interrogation I went to bed and got the best night's sleep that I'd had for a long time. Well for twenty-four hours anyway. But I still think my cave bed was the one bed that will always be my favourite bed of all time, even though it was made of rock.

***

My recollection made me smile to myself and strangely helped me relax. I was ready for bed. I have no idea why that fond memory found its way into my mind but I am glad it did.

Monday 5th September

I had a text from my friend Barbara, *"Just checking to see how you are. Okay I hope, love Barb."* I replied by saying that I was doing okay and going back into hospital soon for my third chemo session.

She texted back, *"Take care of yourself I will see you as soon as I can."*

Barbara is very special to me, as is her family. They have all been good friends of mine for many years. As I also mentioned back in July, one of her daughters, Debbie, who I was privileged to know, died aged ten over forty years ago, from leukaemia. Debbie is still in my thoughts today. So, I must get through my illness somehow. When I do, I will put this experience in writing and dedicate it to her everlasting memory.

Wednesday 7th September

I had to go back to the hospital for a blood test today. The results were:

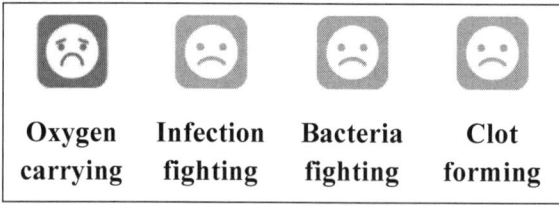

I was beginning to get a bit on edge about going back to hospital for my next batch of chemo. I don't know why, but I felt more apprehensive this time around.

Friday 9th September

Still at home pottering about the house. Chris and I are spending the weekend with her family before returning to hospital on Sunday 11th September. I was still not looking forward to it but a family get together would be just the tonic I needed before starting my 3rd chemo course. But first, we went to Ikea in Bristol. It was very busy when we arrived. Chris bought a few bits for the kitchen then we went to the restaurant where I treated myself to Ikea's famous Swedish meatballs. We finally left the store and made our way back to Hayley and Joe's., where we were warmly welcomed as usual. Oliver was playing with his toys in the lounge and Daisy spent most of her time sitting on one or other of our laps. We had some dinner and chatted until bedtime, which in my case was about 9.30 pm. I was exhausted. It's tiring stuff this cancer lark.

Saturday 10th September

Chris and Hayley went food shopping with baby Daisy this morning, while Joe and I watched over Oliver. When the ladies returned, we relaxed in the garden for the rest of the day and evening, just chatting. There were never any moments of embarrassing silences, which was great for me. But it must have been difficult for the family seeing me so underweight and with no hair. But I wasn't too self-conscious, although I can totally understand what some people in the same boat might feel, especially around strangers. Darren popped in with Angela and their toddler Lucas. They were just as friendly as usual and always make me feel like one of their own.

6 The good news and the bad news

I have been randomised

Sunday 11th September 2011   17 days of freedom
This was the day I had been dreading. I have had seventeen days of freedom and now finally the hospital had a bed for me. Of course, Chris has been dreading this moment as well, but if it is bringing me closer to the end of the treatment that will put me on the road to a complete recovery, I say bring it on. Brave words, as I am actually scared stiff. In the meantime, we were still at Hayley and Joe's. The whole family took Chris and me out to the Tawny Owl pub for Sunday lunch. It was a great send off. Thanks, everyone. When the two of us arrived at the hospital, Chris came in with me this time. I settled into my room. She left after about an hour. We were both very upset. This time, our goodbyes felt a bit final, I don't know why. Maybe it was because we had both got used to being together again.

The doctor appeared soon after Chris left, followed by a nurse who took some blood samples. The doctor noted that I had a cough and a bit of a cold. He examined my chest. I felt weird and peculiarly uneasy that I was alone again in a room which was not of my choosing in a place where I didn't want to be. Everything was quiet outside and I couldn't sleep. I just sat there on the edge of my bed for what seemed an age, staring out of the window into a fog of nothingness. I knew what to expect but I just couldn't get motivated. Was this dark mood of mine a premonition of a more sinister development this time around? It wouldn't be long before I would need all the strength that I had. Both mentally and physically.

Monday 12th September

It was 9.45 am. I was in my room sitting on my bed and I had been thinking about my last three weeks of freedom since I woke up. Today is the first day of two sessions of chemo. Bloods have been taken:

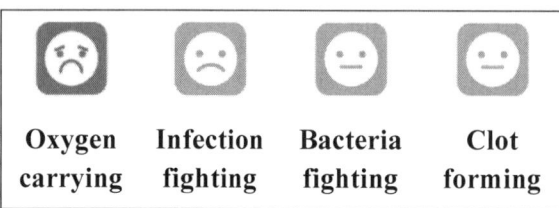

| Oxygen carrying | Infection fighting | Bacteria fighting | Clot forming |

The doctor arrived and examined my chest, which was clear. He also checked my PICC line, it was clean. Everything was good. At 3.45 pm, Doctor Robbins called me into a waiting room and told me that I have been randomised to have three courses of chemo and not four. Did he know something that I didn't? He explained to me that there was no evidence that four sessions of the AML17 trial that I was having were any better than three. They don't know whether they are over-treating patients by giving them four treatments so they are testing the efficacy of the fourth treatment. I had been randomly selected to have just three treatments. But I trust my doctors to do the right thing for me. Doctor Robbins also mentioned that mouth ulcers and diarrhoea are common with my treatment; don't I know it.

Chris arrived in the afternoon while I was receiving my first chemo session and stayed with me until early evening. She still cannot get used to being at home without me. The night sister was here at 10.00 pm and gave me my second daily dose of chemo, so no more Mr Diary today. Goodnight.

| High-dose Cytarabine | 4 hours x2 |

Tuesday 13th September

Sorry, Mr Diary, but I woke up feeling absolutely rubbish. The usual stuff: headache, tired and, guess what, the dreaded big D was rampant. This was getting monotonous. The white coat brigade came in at their usual time in the morning.

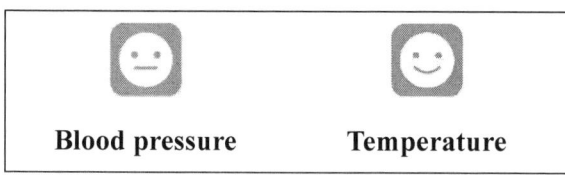

| **Blood pressure** | **Temperature** |

For some reason, the doctors were a bit concerned that I might spike a temperature so they were keeping a bit of an eye on me. Observations were taken every four hours after that. I was beginning to think that they knew what was going to happen to me before it did. Let's hope they are ready with their response when, or if, something nasty does materialise.

Sometime in the afternoon in between naps, I saw a head bobbing to and fro through the porthole window to my room. It was Pete. He was just as hesitant as he was the last time I saw him when he was discharged back in August. He eventually came in.

"How are you mate? I've heard you haven't been too well", I answered.

"I am ok mate", he replied. *"I just wanted to see you and make sure that you are ok"*.

We chatted for a short while then he left. It was good to see him again fit and well. I didn't have any more visitors today, just a few texts from people wishing me well. Looking around my room, I wished the walls were a different colour; a few nice Russell Flint pictures would help. I finally went to sleep at about 9.30 pm due to chronic boredom.

Costa Colin and Atish

Wednesday 14th September
It was just after midnight when I had my first visit of the day. It was the Night Sister that came in to check me over. Everything was okay. The visits continued throughout the night and so I didn't get much sleep. It was also my second day of chemo. The doctor arrived after breakfast and, yes again, OBS were taken:

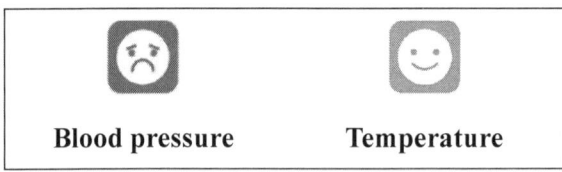

My PICC line was checked and was fine, my headache had gone. But for some reason, I was right off my food again. Costa Colin brought me in a cup of tea. He is the ward's housekeeper. Colin is not a man of many words or even a smiley face, but he is always a welcome distraction, regardless of his demeanour. He and his trolley full of delicious beverages can be seen at various times of the day on the ward beginning just before breakfast.

Another unsung hero on the ward is Atish. He has the title of HCA, which I believe is a Health Care Assistant. Atish is a joy to have around if you are a patient. He is always smiling. He is compassionate and nothing is too much trouble regarding the patient's wellbeing. He will tackle any job no matter how basic. On the occasions when I have had a mishap, if you know what I mean, he made sure that my embarrassment was kept to a minimum.

He just says, *"Don't worry, I am here to help."*

I am going on about him a bit but he deserves praise, apart from being a Man Utd supporter.

The rest of the day was uneventful apart from another four hours of chemo that evening.

High-dose Cytarabine	4 hours x2

Thursday 15th September

I was up early. I had D yet again. Colin came in at about 7.30 am. I only managed to drink half a cup of his tea. The doctors arrived at about 9.30 am. OBS okay, although I couldn't remember what they were. All I knew was that I felt a bit under the weather. There was a rash around my PICC, possibly due to a plaster allergy. Jincy came in around lunchtime and mentioned that I was going to have my last bout of chemo later that night.

At 4.25 pm, Doctor Louise was here on her evening ward round. She was accompanied by, Doctor Robbins and Doctor Rayman. They were talking about letting me out again for the weekend, probably Saturday if my blood counts were okay. But I must come back in for bloods to be taken every day that I was out of hospital. No Chris today. I finished off some diary entries then watched television until I was ready to settle down for the night.

Good news

Friday 16th September **Last day of Chemotherapy**

I felt okay today. I was prowling about. I had some breakfast cereal and a cup of tea. The doctors arrived for their morning visit. OBS were stable, apart from an ulcer on my tongue. Still on chemo, the third day now, and hopefully home tomorrow for the weekend if I am lucky. Doctor Louise had a smile on her face today. She told me that I was in remission and my prognosis (a medical term for predicting the likely outcome of one's current standing) was good. Well if it's good enough for her, then it is good enough for me. Wow! This was the best news I have had since Christine Earwaker agreed to be my first girlfriend when I was about fourteen years old and I started washing my hair, neck and feet for the first time! That's when my mother realised that there was a girl in my life. I often wondered how she knew. Doctor Louise must have had the bone marrow test results back from the lab at the Royal Marsden Hospital. That extra feel-good feeling had returned. I was so grateful to everyone concerned that I was in remission. I was going to tell everyone the good news. Doctor Louise, I could kiss you! I must say I am beginning to see another side to my very serious guardian angel. I had that strange feeling inside again that happens so very rarely in your life and usually just only for a moment. I was truly happy.

High-dose Cytarabine	4 hours x2

Saturday 17th September

I was going home. I was still not sure why they were letting me out. Perhaps it was a reward but hey-ho, away we go. I was up and dressed and pacing the room. Colin gave me a welcome cup of tea (did I see him smile?). My neutrophils were good enough to leave the hospital for a short while - 1.7. I was packed and ready to receive my discharge letter. I had a visit from the pharmacist regarding the drugs that I must take home with me, an endless supply, as you can see below. At 2.50 pm, my bloods were done:

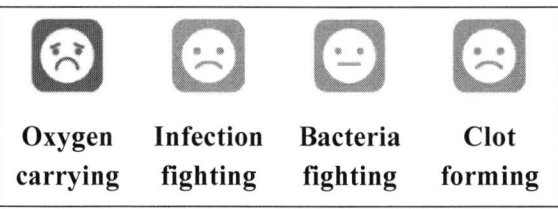

| Oxygen carrying | Infection fighting | Bacteria fighting | Clot forming |

The Pharmacist went through the medication that I had to take home with me, quite an extensive list:

Posaconazole	an anti-fungal drug and very expensive I am told	3 times a day
Aciclovir	an anti-viral drug	5 times a day
Metoclopramide	for stomach problems	once a day 8.00 am
Omeprazoe	for indigestion problems	once a day 8.00 am
Clexane	injection to thin blood and stop clots	once a day

Forceval	a vitamin and mineral capsule	once a day 8.00 am
Maxidex	eye drops to stop eye inflammation	4 times a day
Nystatin	mouthwash for mouth thrush	once a day 8.00 am
Levomepromazine	to help stop nausea	8.00 am and 8.00 pm
Hydroxylamine	syrup for rash	3 times a day
Betamethasone	cream also for rash	as needed

TOTAL COST .... I don't know, but I am now wondering. The *Posaconazole* alone costs £600-800 a bottle. I wonder how much it costs the NHS per cancer patient? If one in two of us get cancer in our lifetime, no wonder the NHS is creaking at the knees.

Jamie was playing football just over the road at the Surrey University ground, so I decided impulsively to take a stroll over there in the afternoon. It was the first time that I had ventured anywhere out on my own since I was diagnosed in June. I stayed and watched the game for about half an hour. Getting back from the football ground was a more arduous task. I was tired, breathless and I had to walk up a steep incline. But I enjoyed getting out of hospital and seeing him play. I miss that. I remember thinking that I wouldn't find it easy to make that journey again for a while. Chris was waiting for me in my room.

We made our way home, together with my discharge letter and copious supply of drugs. I was exhausted. I dozed on and off on the way home. Chris made us some supper and it wasn't too long before we both went to bed for an early night.

Sunday 18th September
After a daytime of relaxing on Sunday, Chris packed my things and we made our way to the hospital at about 7.30 pm for a blood test and possible re-admission if my neutrophil counts were too low to return home. Sister Jincy took some blood, then we waited for the results. She made us a both cup of tea while we waited. After about an hour, Jincy told us that the results were okay enough to stay out of hospital overnight. But I must return tomorrow afternoon at 4.00 pm to be re-admitted. We treated ourselves to a pub meal on the homeward journey, then relaxed for the rest of the evening.

Monday 19th September
In the morning, Chris went to work as usual and returned home at lunchtime. We made our way to the hospital mid-afternoon and went straight to my room and unpacked. It wasn't long before Sister Carol came in and took some more blood and carried out the usual observations of blood pressure and temperature. Doctor Louise came in to see me at about 6.00 pm on her evening rounds. Chris stayed until 7.00 pm.

Tuesday 20th September
I must be neutropenic as my neutrophil count was under 1, at 0.8, so the boring bit had already begun. I must stay in my room now until my counts go down to zero then back up again enough so that I can finally get out of here. I can't wait. But that could be another four weeks of solitude. I must think of more ways of dealing with this - four weeks is a long time to be locked in an unlocked room. I must come up with some new ideas to keep my brain active.

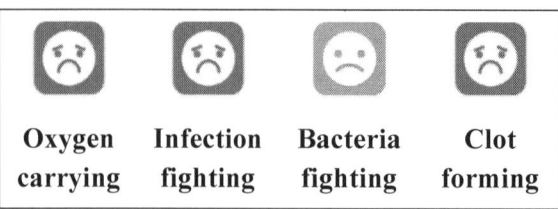

I was weighed in at 85.1 kg. Jincy came in to tell me that I must have a blood transfusion soon.

Wednesday 21st September
Just after midnight, the duty night sister woke me and put the blood transfusion on flow. She then carried out the usual OBS before letting me sleep. I was awake again at 6.15 am. Colin came in and asked if I wanted tea; I declined. I tried some cereal and some water at breakfast. I still had a bit of a cough, which was beginning to trouble me. After breakfast, the doctor arrived with Susan the dietitian. He confirmed that I was neutropenic. Susan weighed me and noted a 9% weight loss in three months. She also advised me that Chris should not bring in any more inappropriate sandwiches. I suppose a Wimpy burger is out of the question. In the afternoon, I had a text from my director at work, Dan Burge. He wanted to know the visiting times so that he could come and see me.

Early evening, I had some supper, a cheese sandwich, which I couldn't finish. Then I received another text from our friends in Somerset, Maureen and Paul. They had just heard the news about my being in remission and said, *"Great news must get together again as soon as you are able."*

Cancer gone!! And good genes to boot

Thursday 22nd September — **Three months since diagnosis**

In the morning, the registrar arrived to examine me and said, *"Everything is good and you are doing well."*

Chris walked in after lunch and we chatted for a while. An hour later, Doctors Louise, Robbins and Rayman were here. They all had their happy faces on.

Doctor Louise said, *"All the cancer has gone and your genes are good."*

This was the final confirmation that must have come through from the Royal Marsden and meant that the last bone marrow test must have been clear of any immature cells. Chris was just as delighted as I was. Of course, being delighted, relieved and grateful was an understatement, to say the least. We were over the moon with the news but could not put into words what it meant to us. The emotion I felt was indescribable. How can you describe the ultimate emotion of being given your life back? The other reason that neither of us was jumping for joy was that I was still ill and we hadn't reached the end of the journey. But this news was a massive boost for both of us.

Doctor Louise was stopping the eye drops from today and they were going to wean me off the antibiotics as soon as possible.

I said to Doctor Louise, *"Perhaps we can now plan our next year's holiday to Cala San Vincente in Majorca."*

"Why not, it sounds nice," she replied.

All being well, we will be staying at the Molins hotel, which sits on the edge of a small bay in the north of the island. We love it there. It is quiet and beautiful. We became engaged there in 2005. I have been dreaming of this holiday for a while. It has been one of my incentives to encourage myself to get well as soon as possible. Chris left at about 7.15 pm and it was not long after she left that I started to get texts from people.

My sister Linda, *"Fantastic news we are so pleased."*

Barbara my old friend, *"Oh I am so pleased. Just let me know when it's time to celebrate and I will be there."*

And my eldest son Nick, *"Excellent news dad. We should go out and celebrate when you get your appetite back."*

I am now on my own and it's quiet outside - time for me to reflect on this momentous day. I still can't take in today's wonderful news; I should feel more elated, shouldn't I? However, for the first time in a while, I am starting to think about the future.

Something nasty is brewing

Friday 23rd September
After breakfast, I was up and dressed. Doctor Robins then arrived and examined me. I told him that my cough was becoming worse and I was coughing up yellowy green phlegm. He prescribed some cough medicine and he said that the team were going to keep an eye on my chest complaint and that I was going to need more platelets soon. In the afternoon, Susan said that she was going to order a steak slice from the staff restaurant for me. No visit from Chris today. My steak arrived at 6.00 pm but I couldn't eat it. I was feeling a bit sorry for myself. Only because I couldn't shake off this damn cough. That evening I

had another text, this time from my brother Paul:

"Flipping brilliant bruv, you have brought a tear to my eye."

That's nice, goodnight, Mr Diary. He didn't say Flipping.

Ability to breathe

Saturday 24th September

I had been coughing on and off all night. At 4.00 am, the sister arrived, gave me the once over and took my temperature, which was higher than yesterday. Colin came in early morning with my usual cup of tea before breakfast. I was sitting up on the side of my bed as I couldn't cough laying down. After breakfast, a nurse again took my temperature, 37.8, higher than earlier. In the afternoon, Doctor Robbins paid me a visit. He was considering giving me antibiotics if my cough persisted. I was still coughing at 6.00 pm and Chris was giving me the cough medicine provided. I managed to eat a sandwich and Scandishake at dinner time. She left about 7.00 pm. A couple of hours later, I got another visit from the doctor. He listened to my chest and said, *"It is clear." I was surprised at this because my chest felt really bad; however, I was not going to argue.* All I wanted was to sleep but I was struggling because of that persistent cough.

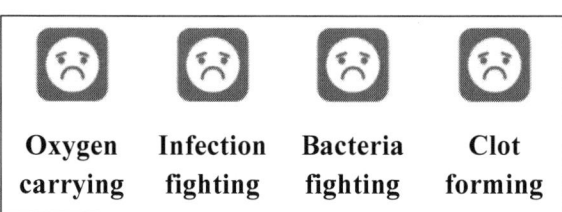

Sunday 25th September

I felt unwell for most of the night and called the nurse at 2.30 am. I was on saline solution and antibiotics so I had hardly any sleep due to the frequency of the changeovers. At 6.00 am the doctor (on call) came and took blood cultures. I felt sick, dizzy and had the mother of all headaches. My cough was getting worse by the hour. He examined my chest.

"It sounds okay," he said. You could have fooled me.

My temperature was back to normal.

Staff Nurse Betty arrived and gave me some paracetamol. The nurses seemed to be in and out of my room constantly. At 9.30 am, the doctor visited. My cough had worsened and my temperature was back up to 37.8. Something is brewing and it isn't a nice cup of tea.

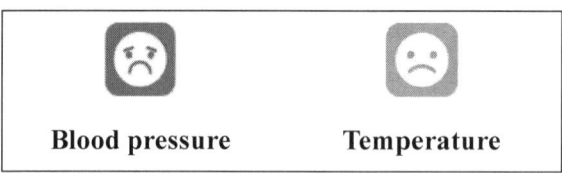

Blood pressure   **Temperature**

He examined my chest again and said, *"I can hear a few crackles,"* and guess what, it wasn't Rice Krispies.

At 10.00 am, the nurse came in for a urine and sputum sample (nice), followed by the angelic sister Sarah who attached the first of two units of blood on flow. It was 4.15 pm when the doctor returned. My temperature had spiked at 38.2. They were carrying on with the blood transfusion even though I had a fever. The antibiotics also continued. At 4.30 pm, the nurse was back with yet another unit of blood. My temperature was 38.9 and rising. The rest of the evening was the same as the daytime. I had had enough. My body felt like a furnace and my head was pounding. There seemed to be no let-up with treatment, so I couldn't sleep.

Monday 26th September
A really, really, bad day.

I hadn't been well for most of the night and didn't get much sleep either; from 6.30 am the nurses were in and out of my room all the time. They were constantly putting fresh bags of drugs on flow, the contents of which were finding their way into my veins via my trusty PICC. After breakfast, Doctor Louise arrived. My temperature was 37. She noted that I seemed to be very lethargic although my OBS had improved from yesterday. Half an hour later, my temperature was taken again by Betty. This time it was 38, which was quite high.

Ability to breathe

The antibiotics that the team are using are Gentamicin (a broad-spectrum antibiotic for severe infections), Teicoplanin and Meropenem (affectionately known as Domestos). That seems quite a mix. The micro-consultant Doctor Day has also been consulted regarding my blood culture findings and he will let Doctor Louise know the results as soon as possible. I am not too sure what that was all about but I will find out.

The doctor came back in to see me just after midday, to say that I was to have platelets sometime later and he would also let me know the Micro results from Doctor Day as soon as he received them.

At about 1.00 pm, I sat up on the edge of my bed again as I felt dizzy. I didn't know what to do with myself. Sitting up was much better for my cough than lying down. But I wanted to lie down because I was so tired. An hour later, Betty came back in, gave me some oxygen and took my temperature again: 38, still high. Later in the afternoon, a bag full of platelets was put on flow, to be followed by even more antibiotics. My BP was a bit low (104/56). Early evening my temperature was up to 39.1 and still rising. That's a bit too warm, isn't it?

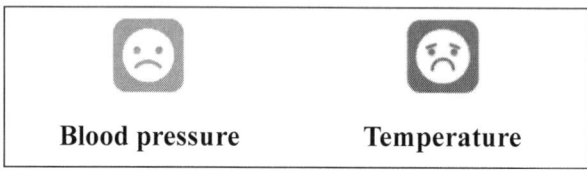

Bloods have been taken and recorded.

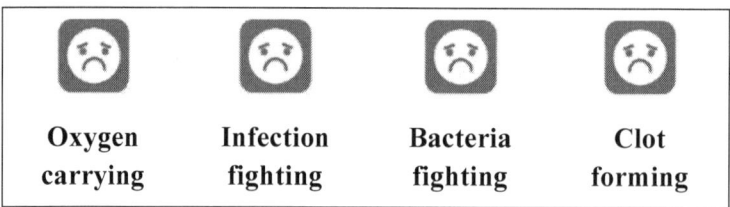

The doctor and nurses are keeping more of a watch over me. That's it. I have had enough today. Goodnight, Mr Diary.

My Antibiotics	
Meropenem	Teicoplanin
Clarithromycin	Tazocin
Gentamicin	Ambizome
Vancomycin	

Sister Sarah helps hose me down

Tuesday 27th September   7th day of isolation

It was just after midnight and I was sitting on the side of my bed, coughing hard and unable to sleep. My head was spinning and banging at the same time. I had my diary beside me with pen in hand but it was no use; I couldn't write anything down. I just didn't know what to do with myself. The angel bees came in to see me every fifteen minutes or so, mainly to administer additional bags of antibiotics to my PICC line. I felt very ill and extremely irritable. The night sister came in and took my temperature. It was 39.1 and I was on fire. *"What is wrong with me now?"* I thought.

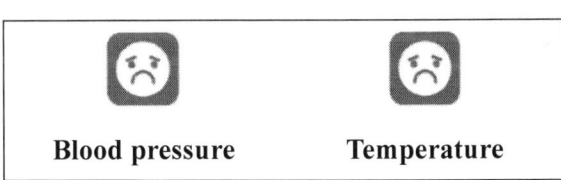

| Blood pressure | Temperature |

My blood pressure was down to 84/44. It was 3.00 am when the doctor arrived. This time my temperature was 38.6 and I was shivering. I think this is called a Rigger. I slept for a while until 6.40 am when the doctor was back again accompanied by a nurse. My temperature was down a little to 37.9.

"How are you?" asked the doctor.

"I feel ill but a little better than last night.", I replied. He seemed to be satisfied and left soon after.

After breakfast, Doctor Louise came in to see me and told me that I was still neutropenic. She examined me while the nurse took my temperature, which was 37.4; I must be getting better but I still have to stay in isolation until my immune system has reached an acceptable level.

An hour later, Susan arrived, but I didn't feel like talking about diets or be weighed so she kindly left me in peace. Mid-afternoon, Doctor Andre popped in. He told me that the results of the blood cultures were not clear. They didn't know if the problem was from the PICC line or blood, so repeat cultures had been sent. In the evening, my temperature was up again to 38.3. I still felt very hot and was sweating profusely.

And my cough was getting worse. When the doctor examined my chest, he said that there were a few added sounds. I remember thinking, *"as long as it isn't a harp playing"*. At 8.30 pm, Sister Sarah came in to see me. She gave me some paracetamol and requested a sputum sample. She helped me to wash as I felt too weak and lethargic to do a decent job myself. I didn't have any choice in the matter anyway. I think she had already decided that I needed hosing down. Although she is angelic looking, I don't think you would argue with her once she has made up her mind; she is definitely a no-nonsense type of lady. I settled down after my refreshing wash, feeling slightly better. Later that evening I was given two pools of platelets. Just before Midnight I was still awake and exhausted.

Before I drifted off to sleep, I reflected on Sarah's hose down earlier.

It reminded me of a story that my uncle Les once told me of when he was a boy growing up in the east end of London in the 1930s. It involved the poorest and dirtiest boy in the street, one 'Gutter' Manning. His real name was Billy. He got his name because he would always play in the gutter where all the dirty water used to flow along those dreary, narrow streets. The story goes that he was not allowed inside my grandparents' house to play unless he had a bath in the family's 'Bungalow' tin bath, a ritual of sorts that took place once a week.

First up to be cleansed was my auntie Maud (13) the eldest who bathed herself. Then she bathed my dad (6), followed by my uncle Les (4) who was the youngest. Finally she would wash Billy 'Gutter' Manning (6) who sat in everyone else's dirty water but it seemed to satisfy my grandma. Then the boys all played happily together for a while in the house before going back out in the street to get dirty again. Everyone living in the street was poor but the children were happy because they didn't know they were poor. It was all quite normal. Perhaps Billy's family were the poorest of all so couldn't afford a bath. If they did have one, they never seemed to wash Billy in it.

Yet again a story from the past that made me smile did the trick; it took my mind off my current situation. Fond memories and pleasant stories are medicine for the mind.

Burning up

Wednesday 28th September

At 2.40 am, the night sister came in to see me and changed my antibiotic bag over. I still had the dreaded D but she was pleased that I had not spiked in temperature anymore. I was still having platelets and strong antibiotics though. In fact, I don't know what they were putting into me now, and the way I felt, I didn't much care. I was sure that they were all doing the best for me but all this stuff that was being pumped into me made me wonder how my body managed to cope with it all.

I dozed on and off all night until about 7.30 am when the tea trolley appeared. I didn't feel too bad but I declined Colin's cup of tea. Thanks anyway, Colin. I didn't want any breakfast either. At 9.35 am, I was sent down for a CT scan to look for any signs of lung disease. I had to puff into a tube and it reached only 8 on the scale. This appeared to be of some concern to the person who performed the scan.

In the afternoon, my temperature was the highest yet at 39.2. Hotter than ever.

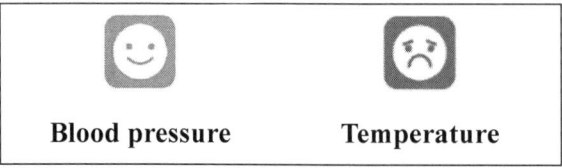

How much longer could my body cope with this? Blood cultures were taken again. The ward sister gave me some paracetamol and codeine and then informed the doctor of my spike in temperature. The micro consultant (who analyses the blood cultures) had also been notified. When the doctor arrived, he examined my chest and there were still a few crackles present. A nurse took some more blood. The doctor tried to contact the micro consultant three times, but there was no response. An hour or two later, the doctor came back and took my temperature again. It was still high, despite the strong antibiotics given to me so far. They are going to add another antibiotic, Clarithromycin, to my intravenous cocktail to help fight the bad bacteria in my body. Chris arrived later in the afternoon. She had a calming influence on me as always, especially when I was surrounded by the constant medical mayhem. She sat beside me trying to act normally by reading a few paragraphs of her book. She got me water when I needed it and helped me up so that I could go to the toilet when the D was rampant which was most of the time while she was there.

One last unit of blood was put on flow at about 7.00 pm. I gave the nurse a stool specimen (nice) as requested. Sister Sarah informed me that that the stool sample was important because they need to see if you have an infection in the bowel which is more pronc to be a bug called *C diff*. I was at risk because I have had broad-spectrum antibiotics as well as all of the chemo chemicals. *C diff* symptoms can range from diarrhoea to serious and potentially fatal inflammation of the colon. My God, the things you must do or experience when you are ill, it's not nice, for me, Chris, or the staff. I also received a welcome text from my Director at work, Dan Burge.

Dan is a lovely young man in his thirties. He himself has a family member who has had cancer. So, he has empathy and compassion for anyone who may be suffering in the same way. He is doing all he can to help minimise any financial burden that I currently may have. Even though I have only worked for his company (Benchmarx) for just ten months, he has organised, together with our MD Chris Larkin, who has it seems the same compassionate qualities as Dan, for me to be paid in *full* until I return to work. You may not know it guys, but this gesture is helping to save my life, and my wife and I are eternally grateful.

Anyway, I must record Dan's text for posterity:

"Terry, the system has stopped paying you sick pay. I have organised for you to be paid but I am afraid you will not get the money until probably Monday or Tuesday. I am sorry this has happened. I am in Guildford Monday lunchtime, so will be along to see you about 3.00 pm if still okay with you."

What a star, and what a great company to work for.

A critical time

Thursday 29th September
From midnight, the nurses were in and out checking my condition and changing over bags of antibiotics and blood. At 4.00 am, a doctor arrived and noticed that my temperature had risen yet again. Further OBS were taken and the night sister put more bags of antibiotics on flow. I don't know what time that stopped. The visits seemed to last for ever.

I eventually slept, until Colin came into my room in the morning and offered me a cup of tea, which I gladly accepted. I didn't know what the time was. I did try to make the effort to say hello to him, but he was on his way out at the time and I don't think he heard me. He probably wouldn't have answered anyway. After breakfast, Doctor Louise arrived. My temperature was still high. I had been doing my best to be positive, but I was tired and fed up with getting the big D all day and night. Maybe it was time to get my quotation book out again. Here's one, Mr Diary, that I have always done my best to live up to,

Life has 2 rules:
Rule 1: Never Quit
Rule 2: Remember Rule 1

Later in the afternoon, Chris arrived. Doctor Louise and Doctor Rayman followed soon after. I still had antibiotics on flow. Doctor Louise has confirmed that I have a severe pneumonia as the CT scan indicated. SATS were at 90%, meaning that my breathing was very poor and I needed to be on oxygen.

Ability to breathe

The doctors noted that they were going to remove my PICC if I kept spiking a temperature. They also said that if I did not start responding to all of the antibiotics soon, they were going to consider PCP (Primary Care Provider), which is some sort of critical care. Whatever way you want to look at it, it is not good news. Early evening, the nurse came in and took my temperature; it was the highest yet at 39.3. My body felt like a furnace. Bloody pneumonia.

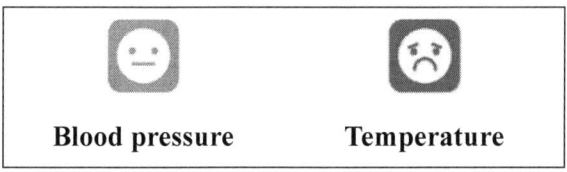
Blood pressure   **Temperature**

Unfortunately, the big D was still hanging around. Chris had been helping me get to the toilet even though it was only a few feet away from my bed. At one point during the afternoon, I didn't make it. How embarrassing. This is the second time that Chris and Atish have had to do a bit of auxiliary work (my apologies to you both). I always do my best to be independent in these situations. But today I was all over the place. Both Chris and Atish didn't seem to be embarrassed at all. They just mucked in (excuse the pun).

I have felt a bit depressed lately. I am useless. I cannot even breathe properly or get to the toilet unaided. The Gates of Hell are well and truly open today. Chris left for home at 7.45 pm. My treatment continued for the rest of the evening. I tried to think of good times gone by or some wonderful plans for the future but I just couldn't concentrate enough to conjure any up. I just didn't have the inclination or the mental energy to do it.

Friday 30th September

At 1.40 am the night sister came in and asked, *"How are you feeling?"*

I replied sheepishly, *"I still have an upset stomach and I am not eating, just drinking Scandishakes and water, and my head is pounding."*

She was very sympathetic and gave me some paracetamol for my headache. I eventually managed to sleep. At 9.50 am, Susan came in and weighed me at 88.3 kg. That's a weight gain of 3 kg. She puts this down to excess fluid and is recommending that I be fed by tube. NO THANK YOU.

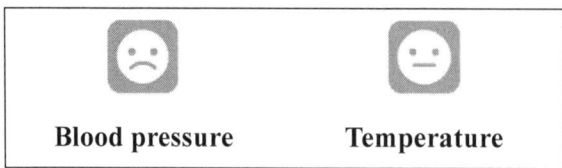

I have had bad D for the last twelve hours. The doctors have noted that the *Outreach* nurses are aware of my current condition. If there is any more deterioration, they are waiting in the wings to take over if required. I believe that the outreach people are a critical care team of specialists that give one-to-one care to an acutely ill patient. They are from intensive care.

In the afternoon, the medical team were going to switch to or include another anti-fungal biotic over the weekend. At various times throughout the evening, the nurses were checking in on me and taking various OBS. That was it for the day, I just wanted to sleep.

Saturday 1st October
It was midnight. The night sister came in and sat beside me. I was aware that I was being closely looked after. I was feeling awful, so the sister bleeped for the doctor on call. Eventually, he arrived and examined me but was not overly concerned even though I was not feeling well at all. I was sitting up in bed continually coughing and it was hurting my chest. It was also time for another blood transfusion (no rest for the wicked).

In the morning, I was still sat up on the bed and drinking a lot of water, which was a good thing. But no food, except Scandishake and Forceval. I had been dozing on and off all morning and I was very tired. There were plenty of interruptions keeping me awake, including this cough which was worsening and causing me to have a feverish headache. I was dizzy and disorientated. I couldn't snap out of it.

At midday, the doctors were back again. OBS were stable, my rash had gone and the D was slightly better as well, so that's all right then. To be honest I was still up and down like a yo-yo. I was not feeling myself and I was coughing far too much for my liking. My breathing wasn't very good either. I was having anti-fungal treatment again via the drip. Early afternoon, Chris arrived. I was getting a lot of sympathetic looks from Chris and the nursing staff. I kept dropping off to sleep. No dinner this evening, just Scandishake and sleep. Poor Chris, she just had to sit there and take it all in.

Sunday 2nd October

The day of rest. Well for me anyway. Chris has a well-earned day off. Just as well as the grotty, grouchy me wouldn't have been much fun to be with. I did manage to say hello with a smile to anyone who ventured into my room. Sunday is generally a quiet day, in this ward anyway. My OBS were stable. My blood results arrived at midday, and for anyone who is interested, here they are. Four glum faces!

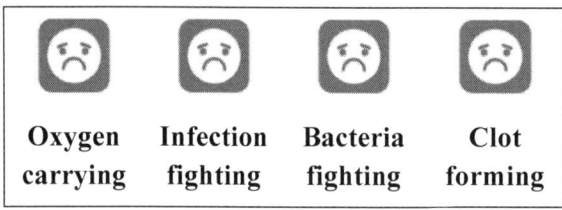

Early afternoon, I began the first of two units of blood. Nothing much more to report today, Mr Diary; it was boring. To be honest, I slept through most of it anyway.

Monday 3rd October   13th day of isolation

For some reason, I thought that I would be out of hospital today. Well that was the original plan when I was trying to work out when my chemo would be completed and my neutrophil counts would be high enough to finally go home. But I had not reckoned on getting pneumonia. I had planned to go to the South Sands Hotel in Salcombe, Devon for a few days' convalescence, recommended by my old mate Carl Williams. We were going to meet him there today. I was going to ring him and tell him that we would not be there, but Chris had already told him why we wouldn't be able to meet up on this occasion.

I got out of bed at 8.00 am and had some water and a biscuit. I felt hot and bothered. Mid-morning my temperature was very high at 38.8. This pneumonia was really getting me down.

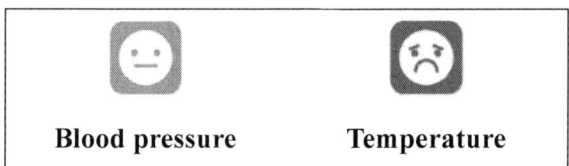

The Sister came in at midday to let me know me that I was to have platelets today and some more antibiotics. Soon after, a nurse arrived and took some bloods. I dozed off for the rest of the afternoon until early evening.

Early evening, my temperature was still over 38 but at least I was no longer neutropenic. Blood results for the day were:

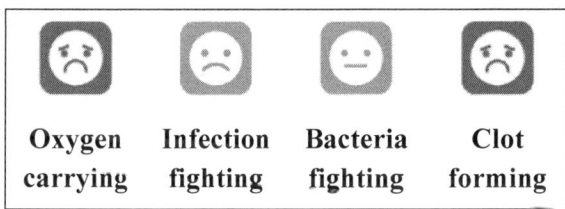

It's now 9.30 pm, I am lying on my bed. It is very quiet. Just the odd muffled noise from outside on the ward. Footsteps, voices and drug trolleys being wheeled from one room to the next. I am looking around the room. There is a sink next to my bed on the left, with a mirror above it. Beyond that is the entrance to my ensuite, which I have so much difficulty getting to now. In front of my bed, the wall, which is painted magnolia, has a small picture of a landscape on it. To the left of that is the inner door to my room. Beyond that is the outer door to my room. To the right of me, there is a window which looks to the car park below where I saw Immy and

Lola looking up and waving to me when I was neutropenic back in July. The wall behind me houses some welcome oxygen equipment. Boring isn't it? It is at times like this that all four walls feel like they are closing in on me. Surely this must be worse than being in prison. At least criminals get to go outside their cell every day. I mustn't complain too much. I know the isolation is necessary and it is for my own good. But it gets to me sometimes. Now all I want to do is sleep. But there is no rest for the wicked; the nurses were in and out with antibiotics and platelets throughout the evening and into the night.

Tuesday 4th October

I felt lethargic for most of the day. I could hardly get to the loo in time. When I eventually got there and sat down, I could hardly get up again. It took all my strength and several attempts to do it, even then I couldn't stand upright. Where has my strength gone? All I seem to do is sleep these days. I was told that I was going to have more platelets during the day. Early this morning my OBS were taken, they were stable, and my cough seemed to be improving, which meant that the antibiotics and antifungal treatments were finally beginning to work.

Evidently, my potassium level is 2.7, which is quite low. Maybe it was because I was experiencing too much D. At noon, Susan the dietitian came in. She thought I was asleep as I remained still. I heard her talking to Jincy about my fluid intake or lack of it. The swelling on my leg has returned. My bloods today were:

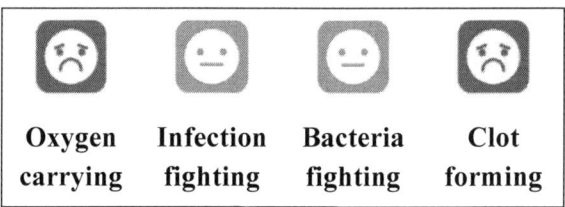

Late afternoon, the doctor examined my chest. He said I was a bit wheezy. Nothing much more to report except that Chris looked tired when she visited today. I told her to go home after about an hour which she reluctantly did. I read for a while, watched some television and then dozed off again.

Wednesday 5th October
I felt rubbish again today. It really was a struggle for me now.

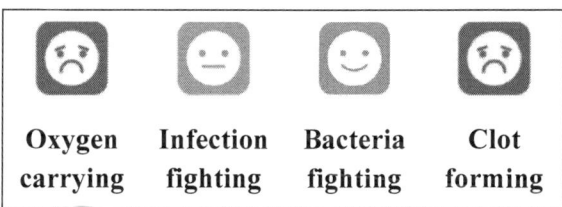

It seems my hypokalaemia is worsening (deficiency of potassium in the bloodstream). I am now on frusemide for my leg swelling. I managed to eat some lunch, a sandwich and a Scandishake. I also managed to drink lots of water, which is a good sign. No visit from Chris today. In the afternoon, I felt slightly better than I did in the morning and I was even talking more to the doctors and nurses. I had to provide a urine dip which instantly showed no protein present, which I can only assume is good news. No dinner for me this evening, just sleep. The nurses woke me up throughout the night to take OBS or to administer more antibiotics.

Thursday 6th October

Colin came in early this morning I accepted a nice cup of tea from him. I even dipped a jammy dodger in it (the best dunking biscuit in my view). I ate some cereal at breakfast and chatted to Atish and the nurses. When the doctor arrived, I mentioned that I was still having problems eating food, although this morning was an exception. My cough had also improved. The medical staff are keeping a watchful eye on my potassium level. Susan the dietitian visited in the afternoon and she told me that my weight was three kg less than a week ago. She thought it could be due to the resolving oedema (fluid retention). I told her that I was making a concerted effort to eat more and I was also drinking Scandishake and taking Forceval capsules. Chris kept me company when she arrived later but I slept for most of the afternoon and evening.

Friday 7th October

I was sitting on the chair beside my bed reading and occasionally looking out of the window. I felt really tired. I didn't get much sleep last night as I spent most of it sitting up rocking myself back and forth, coughing and bringing up brown phlegm. Late morning, I was taken down for a chest scan. When I came back the D was rampant again and I think I had the sorest rear end in England.

I was still sat in my chair at noon when the physio came in to take some respiratory observations and to show me how to do some very useful breathing exercises, although I already knew how to do most of them. I used to do similar exercises when I was a boy because I had developed severe nervous asthma when I was just seven years old.

This pneumonia lark has really taken hold of me. I have never experienced anything like this before. I felt much less in control of the situation. It sounds crazy but it felt worse than having leukaemia. It's also worse than having asthma. At least with asthma, you can control the situation almost instantly these days with an inhaler. No such luck with pneumonia. That seems to be a much slower process. But, when push comes to shove, you can't beat a bit of self-help, can you? So, the exercises are here to stay. At least until I am fully recovered.

Saturday 8th October
Doctor Louise arrived sometime after breakfast.

She examined me and said, *"You seem to be breathing better today."*

I replied, *"Yes I am, but I have a pain across my chest, I think it's due to my constant coughing. I am still having difficulty taking deep breaths."*

She seemed to concur and was quite sympathetic. Doctor Louise has added more potassium with fluids to my treatment. I also took some paracetamol for my worsening headache after she left.

Ability to breathe

I received a text from my friend Carl Williams who I was supposed to meet in Salcombe: *"Take care mate. Will be thinking of you."*

We must meet them there one day. Maybe next year.

Chris arrived in the afternoon but I kept dozing off so it was not much fun for her. I drank as much water as I could, but I couldn't eat anything. I don't know what time Chris left, or who came in to see me. All I know was that nurses were in and out. I hadn't a clue what they did, or what time it was. I was in and out of consciousness throughout the day.

My wake-up call

Sunday 9th October   2 weeks on antibiotics
The Night Sister, Afsa, gave me paracetamol and codeine. There was also a new batch of fluids on flow. It was so uncomfortable and restrictive being attached to this bloody 6-foot pole that followed me around like a pet dog wherever I went.

She stood over me and gently put the palm of her hand on my forehead and said in a sympathetic voice, *"How are you? How are you feeling? You are on fire, aren't you? We can't do any more for you. We have given all the antibiotic drugs available, just don't strike up another temperature."*

Well, that was a bit of a wake-up call. That's when I finally decided to stop feeling sorry for myself and make even more effort to overcome my illness. What's past is past. Best not dwell on negatives. It's the future that counts so let's get on with it. I will keep enjoying life until the Almighty comes calling and it is out of my hands. After yet another a sleepless night, I was up at 8.00 am. I drank some water and I tried to eat some cereal. SATS were 90%; the lowest yet. I couldn't breathe properly so I was using the oxygen provided.

Ability to breathe

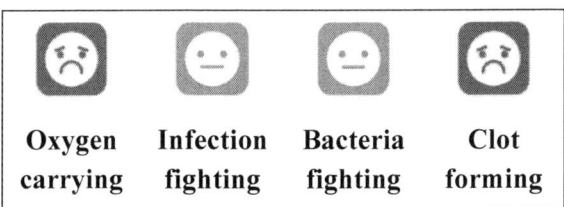

| Oxygen carrying | Infection fighting | Bacteria fighting | Clot forming |

In the afternoon, the nursing staff noticed how lethargic I was and sent for Doctor Louise. When she arrived, she confirmed that they were giving me all the antibiotics they had available. So, it's up to me now, isn't it?

No visit from Chris today. She is having a well-earned day off. I managed to eat a sandwich and drank a Scandishake; it is tasteless, but it is my food substitute now, and together with lots of water, is keeping me alive. I watched some television for the rest of the evening and eventually drifted off into a deep sleep.

Monday 10th October   21st day in hospital

Colin came in with the usual cup of tea with some orange juice and a cracker for breakfast. Soon after that, the doctor arrived and examined my chest; it was still sore but the phlegm was lighter, which I can only assume was a significantly better sign. I was then wheeled down for another chest x-ray. In the afternoon, Chris and I were chatting when Doctors Louise, Robbins and Rayman came in. I was still coughing but breathing slightly better. They are going to arrange for me to have a CT scan. Doctor Louise told me that my counts were recovering.

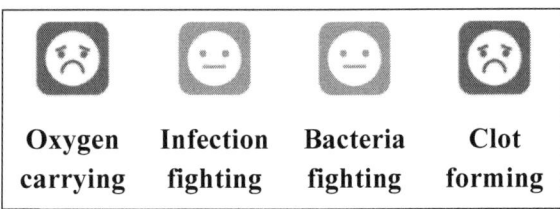

| Oxygen carrying | Infection fighting | Bacteria fighting | Clot forming |

I was still dropping off to sleep most of the time. Chris went down to the coffee shop and brought up a snack and a coffee for herself. I had some raspberry sorbet that was in my little fridge. Chris left at about 7.00 pm. I slept when I could, although there was the usual administering of drugs by the nursing staff which disturbed my sleep. I was used to it by now and hopefully they were doing me good.

Susan the diet

Tuesday 11th October
Colin came in at about 7.00 am and I greeted him with a *"Good morning Colin"* which he seemed to ignore yet again but grunted something on his way out. Never mind, his presence first thing in the morning was enough to make me feel like it was a good start to the day. I felt quite perky today. Perhaps it's because I could sense getting out of hospital very soon. My OBS were stable although I am still on oxygen.

The doctor examined my chest and said, *"There are just the occasional wheezes."*

So, that's progress then. Later in the morning, Susan the dietitian appeared. She took my weight and noted a loss of another kilogram in the last week. I told her that I regularly drank Scandishake and was occasionally eating the odd breakfast cereal. I also mentioned that I was drinking copious amounts of water. I had even ordered an omelette for my evening meal. This seemed to please her. She is a young lady that puts a lot of effort into her work. She is a very conscientious, thorough and caring Macmillan Dietitian and it is always a pleasure to see her even though she is like a dog with a bone sometimes. But that is a good thing I think.

12.30 pm. The doctors now have written verification regarding the results of my HRCT scan, it reads:

> There is a persistent extensive consolidation in both lower lobes (of the lung) which has become more confluent (flowing together) of both costophrenic angles (between the ribs). There is relative sparing of the mid zones with further bilateral apical consolidation which is unaltered.

Basically, it's a severe pneumonia, but we already knew that, didn't we?

Counting the days

> I am sat leaning forward in my chair which is next to my bed, looking out of the window from time to time but not seeing anything in particular because I am feeling sick and dizzy again and I am still struggling to breathe. It seems one minute I am okay and the next minute I am back to square one. I must not let the medical team see me like this, I will not be able to go home next week if they do. I know I shouldn't hold anything back from the people who are making me well again but I don't think I can cope with being in this room any longer. It is affecting me more mentally than physically.

It has been 117 days since I was first told that I had leukaemia, 105 days since I began my chemo treatment, 18 days since I developed pneumonia, and 19 days since my guardian angel consultant Doctor Louise gave me the best of news ever, which was that all the cancer had gone. I owe it to everyone including myself to stay cancer free from now on.

I was alone for most of the day, apart from the nurses frequently buzzing about around me. I was dozing off more than usual so I didn't take much notice

In the evening, Sister Afsa came in and asked, *"How are you feeling?"*

I replied, *"I am okay but tired and I can't breathe properly without oxygen, but I am better than yesterday and I can walk from my bed to my inner door and back without any help now."* Afsa was sympathetic as usual.

Wednesday 12th October

It's early morning and I feel a bit better today. I am walking around my room, looking out of the window and taking in the view for the first time in ages. I am beginning to feel better about my surroundings too. The difference is that today I feel better in myself. I even notice the sunlight bouncing off the magnolia walls. For the first time in a while, I can see and hear the birds outside. Is this the turning point in my recovery process? I must try to get out on to the ward again and maybe walk up and down a few times, although I might need some help.

Morning bloods were taken and SATS were 95%, which is an improvement.

Ability to breathe

At 11.45 am, the blood results were back. They didn't seem to match mine. Well spotted whoever that was. It has been recorded as an incident. Where were my blood results then? In the afternoon, the doctor called in to take further OBS. They were stable. I attempted some breathing exercises during the afternoon. I also did my best to walk around my room. I just about managed it but it took most of my strength and, without the aid of the oxygen from behind my bed, all of the air I could muster through my lungs. But I did it. I didn't want to do much else after that. So, that was it for the day.

Thursday 13th October

I was sat up in bed, coughing heavily at 8.00 am. I did manage to eat some breakfast though. I felt as if I was getting much closer to the final hurdle regarding getting out of here. Just one last concerted effort to push myself over the line was all I needed. I was beginning to think about the next chapter in the life of Tel. The transition from being ill to achieving a complete recovery. I knew I was putting on a brave face, for the doctors/nurses. But I must make more of an effort. I must keep up my walks out on the ward, even though I didn't feel like it.

By 9.00 am the doctors and nurses had been in to see me and my bloods were pending. I had been weighed (78.1 kg). That's a loss of 6 kilograms in the last two days, which seems a lot to me. I think it was mostly fluid. Still a very low breathing rate. Later in the morning, Susan was here chatting about eating well during chemo. She gave me a Macmillan booklet to read when I get out of hospital. Blood results were:

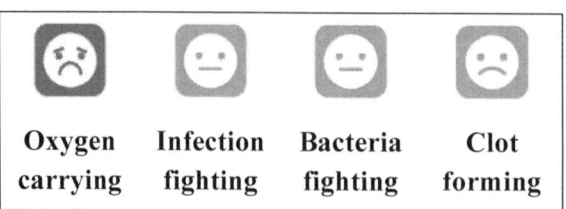

Later in the afternoon, Doctors Louise, Robbins and Rayman arrived. They all thought I looked well. I felt like crap but I wasn't about to tell them that was I? I wanted to go home ASAP!

"The Respiratory Team are going to review your case today or tomorrow," said Doctor Louise. *"We are trying to get you out of hospital and home early next week."*

Home! That's great news. Chris was here to hear this latest development and I think she was just as happy and relieved as I was. After Chris left, I had a cup of tea and relaxed on my bed watching TV until it was time to go to sleep.

My walk with Sarah

Friday 14th October   25th day in hospital
The doctors arrived in the morning with the ward sister. I told them that I was improving each day. I was still coughing, but not as bad as before.

Doctor Louise examined my chest. It was okay, but I still couldn't breathe in or out properly without discomfort. The doctors want me to become more active. Me too, but I am still a bit hesitant and very conscious of the fact that my breathing is well below par and would be detected by my carers if I tried to walk too far. I wanted to appear as fit as possible so that I could go home. In the afternoon, Sister Sarah, one of the ward's senior nursing angels, came into my room and asked me to do something without it sounding like an order. Well it was an order, but given in the nicest possible way.

She said, *"Come on, let's go for a little walk outside on the ward."*

Oh dear, maybe I spoke too soon. Have I been rumbled? I got up and walked slowly towards Sarah and the outer door of my room. For the first time, I felt as if I was 100 years old with half a lung. I was walking out and into unfamiliar territory, unsteady, breathless and unsure of myself. I felt vulnerable, a fish out of water. She looked at me in a sympathetic, knowing sort of way as I grasped hold of her now outstretched hand. She held onto my arm and reassured me with a smile, as we very slowly walked up and down the ward. I was aware of people looking at me. I didn't like it. I felt embarrassed, feeble, but it had to be done. My frailty was finally exposed for all the world to see. Sarah then took me back to my room.

She said, *"Well done you, we will do it again tomorrow."*

Sarah's message was clear: it was a gentle test regarding my mobility. I must stop feeling sorry for myself and put in far more effort to improve my current situation if I want to get out of here next week. Later, the Respiratory Team arrived. I knew whatever they and Sarah reported to my doctors would go towards deciding if I go home next week.

The truth is, that I had already decided that I must get out of here. Apart from the pneumonia, the worse thing for me was the isolation. I couldn't take much more of it. I was about to explode mentally. I don't think I could cope with any more time in hospital. It's been long enough and is having a negative effect on my mental state.

Perhaps there should be counselling for long-term inpatients as a matter of course. Maybe it could be included as part of your daily treatment. There could also be some form of counselling for your immediate family, especially while you are in hospital and in isolation. What about them and the suffering they go through? There probably is help somewhere, but when you are poorly you don't necessarily think about searching for it.

The Respiratory Team seemed to be satisfied with me even though they know of my restricted mobility. SATS were 93%, which was not ideal but on the cusp of being acceptable. They are meeting with Doctor Louise soon. Later in the evening, OBS were taken. That was it for the day. Things are looking up.

Ability to breathe

The Special Onslow Angel Bees

Saturday 15th October   **Three weeks since onset of pneumonia**

Visits are less frequent on the medical front for me now. I have been walking around my room this morning just to get some more air into my depleted lungs. I even managed to walk outside onto the ward where Toni the staff nurse spotted me. Toni is another one of the special Onslow Ward angel busy bees. She came over to me and decided to help me walk up and down the ward. I managed it twice this time which was fantastic progress from yesterday. I also felt less conspicuous today. I was managing to take deeper breaths as well. I could feel my lungs working like mini bellows. But I wasn't going to kid myself. I still have a long way to go. Toni eventually took me back to my room and we chatted for a while. I must say that this nurse has shown me some extra caring qualities. I don't know much about nursing but surely this young lady should go far in her chosen profession. She seems to have a natural intuition of doing the right thing at the right time, as far as patients are concerned anyway. She just makes me feel better, like Sarah, but I have no real favourites, they are all wonderful caring individuals, Jincy, Carol, Shay, Atish, the doctors, Sylvia the receptionist, even Costa Colin. Everyone on Onslow Ward has something special to offer. Today Chris and I are supposed to be at my friend's 50th birthday party in Norwich. Never mind, I will help him celebrate his 51st.

In the afternoon, the doctors paid a visit. I think they seemed satisfied. No Chris today.

Sunday 16th October
The day of rest. But I was more mobile today. Sunday is usually a quiet day and today was no exception. I am still on IV fluids as I am dehydrated. I told the doctor that I really want to go home. Even though I could hardly draw breath, at least I can work on that at home. I was eating well though. I hope I can go home tomorrow, fingers crossed. It's all down to the Respiratory Team and Doctor Louise, my Onslow Consultant guardian angel.

Monday 17th October

9.00 am. Doctor Louise arrived.

She asked, *"How are you?"*

I was eager to answer. *"I am feeling much stronger now."*

She knew I wanted desperately to go home. It has been 21 days since the antibiotics for my Pneumonia began. SATS today were up at 98%, that's much better.

Ability to breathe

My cough is also much improved, but I am still as weak as a kitten. In the afternoon, Doctors Louise and Rayman were here once again. I asked Doctor Louise for a sick note for when I get out of hospital. She knew I was angling for a positive response regarding my discharge and said that she would sort it out for me. Chris was also here and was busy getting my bits and bobs together ready for home. That's right Mr Diary, I am finally going home tomorrow subject to Doctor Louise having a meeting tomorrow morning with the Respiratory Team, but she was as hopeful as was I. Later on, the nurse arrived to change my PICC dressing, during which I had a text from Barb Binfield:

"Terry take care, don't let anyone come near you. We all carry germs and when you are better you can mix, please take care see you soon all my love Barb."

Goodbye Onslow Ward

Tuesday 18th October   **A Massive day for me**

This news just in: I am going home today for good! I have had some of Colin's tea and ate some breakfast. I chatted to anyone who would speak to me, in my room or out on the ward, which was next to no one, as most of the staff were busy with their patients as usual. 10.00 am, my final OBS were taken. I have been told that I must have a chest x-ray in 6 weeks' time.

> I am dressed and ready to go. It's about midday I put my head outside my door once again. Everyone is still busy on the ward. I seem to be invisible to them now. *I wanted to shout "Hello anyone, it's me, you used to look after me when I was sick." "You all made me better." "Better still you have all saved my life." "I just want to say thank you to you all."* I cannot really explain how I feel. I am suddenly about to leave all my thoughts, emotions and experiences of going to hell and back over the past four months behind me in room 17. It is surreal. I am screaming inside, *"Hello everyone, anyone, I am going home for good, isn't that great? I have survived and its thanks to you guys." Does anyone want to say goodbye?"*

The ward staff were still concentrating on the priorities of the day which were, *sick patients!* What else? And guess what, in their eyes, I was *not sick* anymore. But I felt like I wanted the celebration flags to be out and the staff to be lined up to say goodbye to me for the last time. I thought that I was special, just like anyone who had successfully cheated death or beaten a deadly disease. Who was I kidding? To the system, I was no one special, just a statistic.

I sound ungrateful. But I *am* grateful, eternally so. It has been a long, difficult, life-changing few months, but a massive leap in the right direction. I am almost cured. Now I must take the next even bigger step away from the people that I have come to rely on since 14th June 2011. They have saved my life and all I want to do now is embrace them before I go, but I cannot. Everyone seems to be preoccupied. I will just have to shout *goodbye* or wave as I walk out. It doesn't seem right somehow, for me anyway. How can they see things from my point of view unless they have gone through the same as me? Maybe it's just another day at the office for them. I don't know, I hope not.

Sarah, Jincy, me, Betty and Atish

7 Home at last

Extended family

To me, the hospital staff feel like my extended family. We have shared what for me was a lengthy and terrifying experience. I had come to rely on them and put my life in their hands, with a bit of self-help as well of course. So, saying *goodbye* should be a two-way street, shouldn't it? But it does not feel like that right now. They *have* been successful; in their eyes, their job is done. But surely if you are about to go on a five-year journey alone, your family would spend some quality time with you before you go. Even if it was just for a minute, just to show that you are not forgotten. Perhaps the NHS have overlooked this kind of care. Maybe they cannot afford it. Maybe they do not see long-term inpatients as part of their family. Maybe they do not think it is a necessary requirement. Perhaps there are no trained staff ready and waiting to attend to a patient's *emotional* state of mind when they are discharged. But if someone who had been working on the ward for a long time was to leave, wouldn't the rest of the team take the time to say goodbye properly? Forgive me if I am being a bit presumptuous, but I think they would. So why not treat a long-term patient in the same way?

This is, of course, not a criticism of the wonderful team who have been looking after me for the last four months. It's just an observation that maybe the NHS could look at and consider implementing, with an extra trained staff member perhaps. Don't get me wrong, I am glad to be out of hospital and going home. I just feel that I am leaving something important behind, but I don't know what.

It's 2.30 pm. That's it. I'm off, discharge letter in hand, medication in my bag and sick note received. My road to full recovery is about to begin. The next stage. The next part of my story. The next step. Am I ready? I don't know what lies ahead, all I do know is that I feel more cautious about my future life. But I am so grateful that I am still here. I want to appreciate everything that before my illness I took for granted and savour it one day at a time. Now I must get through the next five years. That's right, five more years until the system finally discharges me. Five years of frequent blood tests just to see if my cancer has returned. Five years in the grips of uncertainty. Five years until the danger has passed in the eyes of the NHS and they see me as an 'Unremarkable Man'. So, I must learn to live again, more so as each day goes by. I will face this journey head on in the most positive manner that I can. But it is the unknown, so bear with me. I don't want to just survive, I want to live. So, goodbye Onslow. My parting message to all the Onslow angels and doctors is:

Those who help save just one life helps save the world entire.

Maybe now is the time for me to share *Christine's Letter in* which she tells, in her own words, what it has been like for her over the past few months.

Christine's letter

One of the saddest things I remember about the time that you were ill, is seeing you having your hair shaved off in the barber's shop in Harmanswater when you were at home for a weekend. I didn't want you to see me cry. I tried to hide it from you because it must have been hard for you. It finally sank in that you really did have cancer, as I watched the barber remove the last patches of hair that was left on your head. I thought the barber would not charge you as it only took him a few minutes to do it. But he did.

I would leave work most days at 1.00 pm. Then I would make my way to the hospital, only to see you laying there weak just watching television or asleep. I was not allowed to bring you any food. So, you ate next to nothing, as you were not eating anything that the hospital provided and you just got thinner and thinner as each day passed. You even lost your Beetle Belly which you are now getting back.

Sometimes I would cry all the way home after visiting you. Sometimes I would be okay. Going home to an empty house every day for months wasn't much fun. Most of the time I would sleep downstairs on the settee. For some reason, I didn't like to go upstairs on my own. The only good thing was that I could watch the soaps in the evening without you moaning. My family and my friends Maureen, Paul and Carole would ring me plus your brother Paul and your Uncle Les. Some weekends I would stay with Hayley, my daughter. On one occasion, I went to Maureen and Paul's house in Somerset for the weekend and stopped off at the hospital on the way back home on the Sunday. I went to a barbeque at Carole and Paul's on another occasion.

My mother would phone me and offer to come and stay. But I didn't really want to have company by the time I got home from the hospital and sorted myself out. I just wanted to lay down on the settee, collect my thoughts and watch television. I didn't want to have the responsibility of having to worry about someone else. Although it was kind of her to offer.

One day, I went to see you in hospital and you needed to get to the toilet. You didn't make it. The result was unpleasant. I don't know how I wasn't sick but I wasn't. I had to clean it up with paper towels.

I remember bringing you a small fridge and television for your room, as there was nowhere to keep your drinks cold on the ward. I also brought you in an electric razor, not that you needed it very much as all your hair on your face was gone and thankfully your nose hairs had disappeared completely. I remember when you first phoned me at work and told me that the doctor had just told you that you had leukaemia. I thought you were pulling my leg and told you to shut up. But you were telling the truth. I didn't know what to do when you told me that. I just had to get out of work and come and see you. I couldn't take it in. How could you go to hospital for a pain in your kidneys, to be then told that you have leukaemia?

One weekend before your treatment began on a Saturday morning when you were let out for a while, we went to Birds Hill golf club to have breakfast. Before we went in we sat in the car while you spoke to your sister to give her the news. Then we went and had our breakfast but we both got upset at the thought of you having to spend five months or so in hospital.

***

On the way home I once again contemplated my future. What is in store for me and Chris? I don't know for sure. I have been told that in my case it is normal to allow five years before the doctors give the all clear and you are deemed cured. I have decided to keep my diaries going until the five years are up, although not in so much daily detail. I also hope to be doing as many normal things as possible and that would be far too boring and repetitive to record.

Well, this is day one. Only 1,827 days to go before a full recovery.

From now on, most of my recovery will be down to me. I must prepare myself by having a positive attitude, proper diet (if I can), exercise and get on with normal everyday living, but at my own pace.

When we arrived home, I felt kind of odd as I took those first unsteady, breathless steps from the car to our front door. Once inside, I made my way into the lounge and sat down on my favourite comfortable chair. Chris went into the kitchen to make me a cup of fresh filtered coffee. I put my feet up and slowly took in my surroundings. Momentarily, I felt like a stranger in my own home. Chris joined me after a short while. She switched on the television and opened the lounge windows. The first thing I noticed was the sound of birds singing and the leaves falling from the trees opposite. It was still bright and warm outside. I walked over to the open window, leant forward and gulped in as much fresh air as I possibly could, as I felt the need to exercise my depleted lungs. In and out, in and out, as many deep breaths as I could take. Before I turned back into the room,

I became uncontrollably overwhelmed with emotion. That truly happy feeling had returned once more. At last, I am home for good.

Wednesday 19th October 2011 onwards   **19 days to first blood test**

Chris went to work as usual. I was at home, alone again for the first time since June 14th 2011. I got up and dressed. It was quiet outside. I am aware of just how weak I am still. My brain seems to be adjusting to my new kaleidoscopic world as well as my fragile body.

I was beginning to become aware the things around me that have always been there. I have just not taken the time in the past to notice them. Things that I would normally take for granted, I am seeing for the first time since my childhood. The natural world around me; above me the sky ever changing in colour of blues and greys, beneath my feet the grass seems greener, the reddish-brown leaves falling from the branches of the trees beyond my back garden and drifting to the ground. Was it my illness, the trauma, the drugs? What is it that is responsible for me having these feelings and occasional emotional flashbacks. Why have I developed these heightened senses that have renewed my vitality for life? Why do I have this overwhelming sense of guilt for being a survivor? Maybe I still need to heal emotionally. Only time will tell.

The tree at the top of the hill

I spent the first few days at home exercising my weakened lungs. As I mentioned earlier, the last time I remember doing this at any length was when I was a boy and suffered from nervous asthma that began when I was just seven years old.

In those days, the 1950s, I used to suck a yellow pill when I had one of my many bad attacks. Although the pill worked as far as my breathing was concerned, the after effects were horrible. I would become completely lifeless for some considerable time. My heart would pound and beat rapidly for at least half an hour. That would be that for the day, no more running about for me. Sometimes, especially when people could see me having an attack, I would get so frustrated and embarrassed; I would take matters into my own hands and run as far away as possible from the sympathy of concerned onlookers.

Where I lived at that time (Collier Row near Romford), there was a cornfield opposite my house in Firbank Road, and next to the field a hilly country lane that led to a tree with a flat top standing proudly at the summit. I used to play in the cornfield with my mates in the summer and make camps from the corn that the farmer left behind. We would mess around and lay in our camps and watch the skylarks singing as they hovered high in the sky overhead. Sometimes, when I had these asthma attacks at home, I would run breathlessly over the road, into the lane and keep running until I reached the tree at the top of the hill. I remember not being able to feel my legs working while running but I still managed to put one foot in front of the other. My lungs seemed like they were going to burst out of my chest. I would cough and nearly choke as I was spitting out phlegm as I ran. But I used to keep going until I reached the tree at the top of the hill. I remember collapsing exhausted in a heap when I finally got there. I was puffing and panting, my eyes misty with tears of fear, frustration and joy all at the same time. But I could breathe again, even though the mixture of tears and the gasping for breath made my whole body shudder. I had won. I had beaten the attack through my own sheer persistence.

I remember resting under the tree canopy and looking back to where I started my run far away in the distance. I was feeling a great sense of accomplishment, although I did not fully understand the importance of what I had achieved at that time. But I now know that I had the willpower and mindset not to give up, even though my body and lungs were telling me to do so. I had learned to succeed in the face of adversity without anyone's help. There was no better feeling once I had reached the summit; I was a winner, an achiever, without even knowing it. I would sit there for a while, listening to the mysterious call of the cuckoo far away while watching the wildlife scurrying about me. Were they accepting me as just another innocent creature who had strayed onto their turf, were they oblivious to my presence, or did they sense my obvious non-threatening vulnerability? There were rabbits, squirrels and all sorts of insects and birds. This was my idea of heaven. It still is.

I remember one time, after a similar run, a solitary robin perched itself on the end of my shoe as I sat there resting against the trunk of the tree. Its friendly face and liquid eyes seemed to invite me into its world. There was just him, me and my feeling of self-fulfilment. I hated getting those asthma attacks. But I loved the way I felt when I finally reached my destination. I kept up my breathing exercises from then on. Eventually, after I left home for good, my asthma attacks ceased. I am sure the breathing exercises helped, as did leaving home. I have always done my best to rise to physical and psychological challenges. Being this way has helped me through some difficult times, especially as I made my way along a relatively tough, unguided and sometimes brutal childhood and a somewhat naïve, uncharted, early adult life path. But that is a completely different story which I must tell one day. My father was born in the harshest of winters, and as far as I was concerned, he never thawed.

The tree and its surroundings were my sanctuary in those days. I even carved my name on the trunk with a sharp stone, bonding the tree and me forever. It was where I could go and be alone with myself and my thoughts to dream of a happy and healthy life without the disability of illness and hardship. It was somewhere to escape to and be surrounded by lifeforms that seemed to accept me without judgement and didn't threaten me in any way. This was where I could chill out and create my own world from up high on the hill where the air was pure and I could breathe fresh life into my stale, diseased lungs. Where I could listen to the wind and birds singing without interruption. Where finally my asthma attacks and troubles disappeared as if by magic.

***

The rest of the month of October 2011
I have not written too much in the diary for the remainder of this month. I contacted work just to let them know that I had been discharged from hospital and when I expect to start back, which should be about the beginning of December. Well, that's my plan anyway. I was also slowly coming to terms with the fact that my life going forward needed a bit of adjustment, at least for the

near future. I don't know what is in store for me. Who does? But I am doing my best to search for the daylight that I know is at the end of the tunnel.

While I was spending time during October planning this and that, negative thoughts did occasionally creep into my mind. For example, I was going through my wardrobe one day and decided to have a clear out of my unwanted clothes. Instead of thinking *"I will get rid of this and that and buy some new gear"*, I hesitated and thought that I wouldn't buy anything yet as it could be a waste of money. I think they call these thoughts dark moments. Or is it the Gateway of Hell opening again? I soon snapped out of it, although negativity is still lurking there somewhere.

Tuesday 25th October

Today I had to go back to hospital to have my PICC removed. I thought it was going to hurt but it was completely painless. Thank the Lord for that. It's another sign that I am on the mend. That thing has been attached to me for the last one hundred and twenty-five days. Without it, I wouldn't have been able to receive the treatment necessary to enable me to be in the position I am today. It has been another weirdly welcome and constant companion of mine since June. But today I can say goodbye to my two-pronged wiry friend as my treatment has ended and Mr PICC and I must go our separate ways. In the nicest possible way, I hope we never meet again.

8 Recovery

Planning ahead

Wednesday 26th October to Sunday 6th November 2011.

I have been keeping myself occupied with planning short-term goals as well as long-term goals. Chris and I are looking at holidays for next May as well as next November. The May holiday I must book soon. It will be to Cala San Vincente, the Hotel Molins. I remember telling Doctor Louise back in September that I was planning this holiday. Unfortunately, my mind was distracted from such pleasurable thoughts as I had to concentrate on other priorities. Our other holiday will be to Tenerife for a bit of winter sun. Then, of course, there was to be the Christmas holiday that Chris and her family have planned to have in a farmhouse in Herefordshire. Well, that's the pleasurable goals sorted. My future health goals remain obscure, but I will persevere. My appointment with Doctor Louise is looming, I don't know why this hospital visit is playing on my mind, but it is.

Monday 7th November   First blood test

I arrived at the outpatient's half an hour before I had to see the doctor so that bloods could be taken and analysed. Eventually, a nurse showed me into an anteroom where I had to wait until Doctor Louise arrived with my results. It seemed like an eternity. I could hear her speaking in the adjoining room, either into a Dictaphone or to the nurse, I couldn't tell which. Were they talking about me? All I did know is that it made me feel nervous, as I could hear almost every word. My hands were sweating. I sat bolt upright when Doctor Louise finally appeared with her notes.

"How are things with you?" she said.

I replied, *"I am okay, and yourself?"*

She went on to say, *"Your bloods are fine, I will see you again in three weeks' time after your next bone marrow test."*

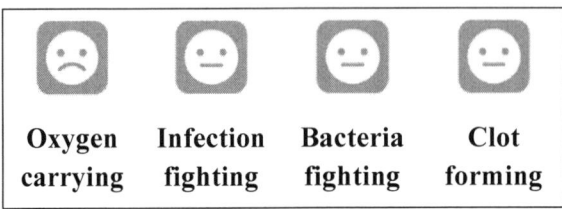

| **Oxygen carrying** | **Infection fighting** | **Bacteria fighting** | **Clot forming** |

I don't think I heard her finish what she had to say as my mind was too busy digesting the relief of not hearing the words that I had been dreading since leaving hospital, *"It's come back"*, which would have been a whole new ball game as far as treatment and recovery was concerned.

She continued, *"I want you to have a course of warfarin until the end of January 2012, I will send a letter to your GP just to bring him up to speed."*

Afterwards, I went to see Susan. She was as thorough as ever. I weighed 83 kg, a weight gain of 5 kg since the 13th October. She gave me advice on diet and exercise as well.

I made myself busy for the rest of the week with domestic chores and breathing exercises. But generally, I took it easy. I was still reeling with Doctor Louise's good news and wondering whether she or anyone knew how much it meant to me.

But as the next hospital date drew nearer, I was becoming increasingly edgy. What will the chest doctor say? Will the bone marrow test show that I am still clear of unwanted cells? I don't know. I must wait and see. Let's be optimistic, let's be positive. What if?

Tuesday 8th to Tuesday 15th November
Nothing to report except my breathing is improving. I am keeping busy doing normal day-to-day things although just a bit slower than I used to.

Wednesday 16th November   Bone marrow test
Chris came with me to the hospital. The bone marrow test was my first appointment at midday. Sue, the specialist nurse, greeted me on the ward. We made our way to the anteroom where she carried out the procedure. This time it was not too bad; maybe I am getting used to it.

This is the fourth time that I have had this procedure. Now all I must do is wait until the results come back from the Royal Marsden where they analyse the bone marrow. So that's another bit of unwelcome waiting time that I must endure. But I suppose it is better to be safe than sorry.

My second appointment was at 2.00 pm, but first I had to have a chest x-ray and get weighed. This time my weight was up another couple of kgs. This appointment was with the chest consultant. He asked me how I was. Of course, I said that I was fine even though I was still weak and breathless. But I was better than I was a week ago, so that's progress in my book. He told me that my chest x-ray was clear and he was happy with my progress. Well that was enough for me and I left the hospital in a more positive frame of mind.

You will notice that there are less daily diary entries from now on. That is because, just like most people, I am getting on with doing everyday ordinary things most of the time. Obviously, when something comes up that is worth a mention, I will let you know Mr Diary.

Sweaty hands again

Monday 28th November **Bone marrow test results**

I must admit that, although I have been keeping myself busy with short-term plans for social events and getting ready for my return to work, I have been a bit on edge for the last few days yet again. Mainly because I was going to receive my bone marrow results today at my outpatient appointment with my consultant, Doctor Louise at 9.30 am.

Chris and I arrived early so that my bloods could be taken. We had a coffee in the canteen before I was ushered into the anteroom to wait for the doctor to see me. Yet again I had sweaty hands during my wait, but Doctor Louise soon appeared with a smiley face, which is always a good sign.

"Bloods good," she said. *"Also, the bone marrow test result from the Royal Marsden shows once again that there is no evidence of MRD."*

That means (no cancer cells in the blood). But I read in the notes later that they are not going to resume the cytogenetic study unless requested. I will leave that decision to my doctor.

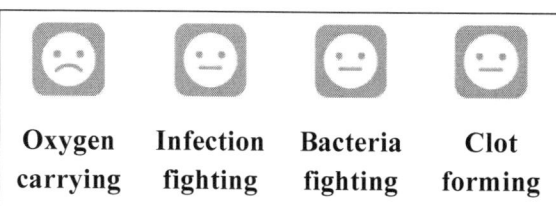

I now know that I must have another bone marrow test on the 14th February 2012. As I have said before, the bone marrow test and subsequent results are the only true way of knowing whether there are any leukaemia cells left in my body. That means I must wait for another 93 days before the results at my next clinic on the 29th February 2012. But the sense of relief I felt today when my doctor gave me the news that I was still in complete remission was fantastic. We wanted to celebrate. I am a firm believer that you should reward yourself if you have been given good news, or you have achieved something. So, that's what we did. It was only a glass of wine that evening at home but we did chink glasses and smile a lot. Happy days.

You may have wondered, Mr Diary, why I am making such a fuss about welcome news. Or stressing about the possibility of unwelcome news. Well, the reason is that my cancer has a nasty habit of returning within the first few years. The tension I feel and the negative uncertainty that I experience a few days before and on the day of my blood test results is all consuming. I can't help it. But when I hear those words *"bloods good!"*, the overwhelming sense of relief is indescribable.

> Waiting for my doctor to give me my blood results makes me feel like I am the losing gladiator in a Roman arena who is waiting for the thumbs up. Receiving the thumbs up makes me feel like the

victor who lives to fight another day.

Back to work

Tuesday 29th November   42 days out of hospital
Today was to be yet another momentous day for me. I went to see Dan Burge at my company's head office in Leatherhead for my back-to-work interview and start date, which is to be the 5th December 2011. When I arrived, the staff and Daniel welcomed me. Dan is the guy who ensured that I was paid when I was in hospital, for which I and my family are eternally grateful. I wanted to let him and everyone concerned know that in person, even though I had already sent a letter of appreciation to my MD the week before.

I am to be working closely with Daniel during my convalescence or back-to-work period, which will be two -three days per week initially. While I was there, the managing director Chris Larkin came into Daniel's office to see me.

He asked, *"How are you feeling Terry?"*

"Take your time Terry, don't rush about, just take things easy and if you get tired just go home. Welcome Back."

I was not expecting any of this. If I had any doubts of just how kind people can be, I am in no doubt now. My faith in human nature is growing by the day.

Interestingly, both Dan and Chris have experienced close family members being diagnosed with cancer. So, they have some empathy with my situation. It is very reassuring when someone truly understands what you are going through, during and after treatment. I could feel their genuine warmth towards me when

I was speaking to them.

I did say in my letter to the MD that if it was not for my wife, doctors, nursing staff, family and friends, and without doubt my company's generosity, I truly believe that I would not be here today, so thank you everyone concerned.

The rest of the week I spent preparing for work. As a special treat, we are going to visit our friends Maureen and Paul in South Cheriton, Somerset. We used to live near them in Sturminster Newton, a small market town just over the border in Dorset.

Paul – my editor

Saturday 3rd December   9 days to next blood test
We made our way to our friends last night and spent the day resting in their beautiful home. We had arranged to celebrate my discharge from hospital by having dinner at our favourite eating venue in Dorset, Plumber Manor near Sturminster Newton, a famous country house hotel run by the local blue bloods, whose roots go back to William the Conqueror.

Maureen and Paul are true friends, they are considerate and thoughtful to the extreme. I have only known them since 2004 but they welcomed me as a friend from day one.

> Maureen has been friends with Chris since they were young children, when they used to put snails under the flaps of stamp machines dotted around the town so that unsuspecting people got more than their stamps when they lifted the flap. Chris has also told me of her fond memories of chasing each other around with a blob of dog poo on the end of a stick! I can just picture it. Maureen is a real lady now, smart, elegant and she has a posh voice. But I always get pleasure of reminding her of her tomboy urchin childhood playing with Chris, which she takes in good spirit.

We had a lovely relaxing stay which took both our minds off my medical upheaval. Just what the doctor ordered.

Maureen and me at Plumber Manor

Monday 5th December to Saturday 10th December

My first day back at work involved taking a 38-mile round trip to Reading where I was welcomed and looked after by the local manager Dave Gurling and his staff, Narinder, Andy, Paul and Anthony. Everyone is being so nice and sympathetic towards me. I enjoy being made a fuss of, but I knew that it would not last forever. I had better get used to standing on my own two feet sooner rather than later.

Apart from a few appointments to my local GP, everything has been routine. Chris went to Longleat on Sunday 11th with her son Matthew. I decided to stay at home and relax, as tomorrow I have another clinic appointment at the hospital with Doctor Louise for one of my frequent blood tests and general check-up.

Monday 12th December   Blood test

The appointment with Doctor Louise was at 11.30 am. She had a junior doctor with her and was showing her the ropes. Doctor Louise is going to let my GP know that she wants me to be on warfarin until the end of January 2012. My blood counts remain stable and I have a good chance of staying in remission (I hate that word). Surely there is a better phrase that can be used. Like, *cancer free*, or *no evidence of cancer*.

We also discussed the unlikely possibility of a relapse and maybe getting ahead of the game by finding a donor, usually a sibling, in the unlikely event of needing a bone marrow transplant. I took this discussion in my stride at the time but it was going to be something that would play on my mind. Perhaps I was not as brave as I thought. Those dark thoughts were to return later the following year.

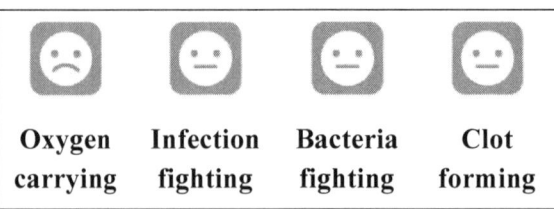

| Oxygen carrying | Infection fighting | Bacteria fighting | Clot forming |

I must say that that I still dread the build-up to my hospital appointments. I am still somewhat moody and apprehensive two to three days before I attend them. The sense of relief when you are told that your blood tests are fine more than compensates for any apprehension. That very happy feeling is becoming ever more frequent, and a celebratory cup of tea, or whatever reward you feel like, is a must.

> This reminds me of another one of my all-time joys, which was seeing my son Jamie born. He was the only one I was allowed to see born of my four children, as the rules were different in the days before he came onto the scene. I remember standing in the delivery room at Cliveden Hospital, Taplow, donned in a green gown and mask attempting to give some sort of comfort to his mother, who was going through the sort of pain men can only imagine. I remember hearing the nurse whose task it was to deliver Jamie saying, *"nearly there, nearly there"*. For some reason, I repeated what she had just said to his mother. I was just a bystander, a hopeless, helpless echo but what else could I do? I was transfixed, rooted to the spot. I was totally in awe of all woman probably for the first time ever. Suddenly, the nurse said, "I can see the head". None of us knew whether it was a boy or girl at that point. To my amazement, almost immediately, Jamie's head turned and he looked up at me. Whether he saw me or not, I was the first person to make eye contact with him as he entered the

world. This was the moment that I can never forget. It was a moment of wonder, a miracle and of pure joy; a rare, indescribable feeling that will stay with me forever.

My tick tock check

Saturday 17th December — **6 months since diagnosis**

We are staying at my son Damien's house overnight in Bournemouth and exchanging Christmas presents before travelling on to Yeovil on Sunday, where we are also staying overnight, before going to my annual routine appointment with my consultant cardiologist Doctor Tim at his Sherborne clinic on Monday 19th. After a stroll on the beach on Sunday morning with Damian, Nicola and Scarlett, Damian treated us both to lunch. Then we made our way to Yeovil and the local Travelodge.

Monday 19th December — **32 days to next bone marrow test**

The doctor was late but I didn't mind too much. Doctor Tim is a quiet Welshman who has an air of confidence about him. He never seems to smile. Maybe he does when the Welsh beat England at rugby or when he is windsurfing down at Preston near Weymouth.

Long story kept short: I have a heart defect called *Left Bundle Branch Block* (LBBB), which means that the left ventricle of the heart is a bit uncoordinated with the right ventricle. It was discovered by accident in 2007. I had been to South Africa on holiday and when I returned I had a dull ache in my calf muscle. To be on the safe side, I went to the doctors to get it checked out.

I was sent to hospital by my GP for an echocardiogram because there was a possibility that I had deep vein thrombosis. But the test came up with LBBB, a heart defect. It sounds worse than it is and yes it did cross my mind when I was in hospital with leukaemia whether the chemo would affect my heart condition, but everything seemed to be fine. I am sure that my doctors were aware of my condition and took it into consideration before and during my chemo treatment. Everything went okay at today's appointment. So, afterwards, we made our way home as we both had to be at work the following day.

Visiting Barbara and Debbie

Wednesday 21st December   **9 weeks out of hospital**

After working for just the morning, I went to visit my friend Barbara whose daughter Debbie died of leukaemia many years ago. I just wanted to wish her well and show her that I was on the mend.

I also hoped to get her permission to lay some flowers on Debbie's resting place at Hitcham Church near Burnham. Barbara seemed to be pleased to see me and said that it was okay to visit Debbie. During our chat, I mentioned that I was writing a book about my cancer experience. I asked her whether she would she be upset if I mentioned Debbie as well as herself and the rest of her family in my story.

Her reply was, *"Of course, you can. I talk about Debbie every day."* She went on to say. *"I won't get upset about you writing about her. I only get upset when for example, I might be washing up and sometimes a particular washing up liquid smell reminds me of her standing in the kitchen beside me helping out. Or she used to buy me liquorice Pontefract cakes out of her pocket money and since she died I have stopped eating or buying them."*

We chatted on for about an hour and exchanged Christmas cards before I made my way to the church.

I had to remind myself where Debbie's final resting place was. I took a long slow walk around before I found it under a tree. There were already some Christmas messages and potted flowers at the foot of the tree. I stood there for a moment. I knelt and read the messages. They were from her sisters Denise, Kerry and Kirsty, and another whose name I couldn't make out because the writing had been smudged by recent rainfall. Their words touched me deeply and I began to get upset. I found myself speaking to her. I muttered under my breath, *"Sorry Debbie."* A feeling of guilt came over me as I imagined her little face looking up at me from below, just how I remembered her all those years ago. I was thinking, *"Why her and not me."* Life isn't fair, is it? I left the flowers and said goodbye. I kept looking back. Fleetingly, I imagined her standing by the tree waving to me as I made my way out of the churchyard. I got into my car and drove home.

Chris was there. We had some lunch. She was obviously aware that I was still upset.

Eventually, she said, *"Are you okay? How is Barbara?"*

I answered, *"She is fine."* and we finished our lunch in relative silence.

That afternoon we made our way to Sacha's house to drop off more Christmas presents for her, Wayne, Imogen and Lola because I will not be able to catch up with them during the festive season. It was lovely to see them. While we were there

I couldn't help thinking that it was just a few months ago, when I had pneumonia, that it had crossed my mind that I may not ever see them again. Although I never actually thought at any time that leukaemia was ever going to be a death sentence, I had the horrible feeling that the severe pneumonia could be. It was only a passing thought, but it felt real enough at the time. So, it was extra special for me to see and talk to them at this happy time of year.

Family Christmas past and present

Thursday 22nd December
We were getting ready for our arranged Christmas family holiday in a large country cottage in Haorwithy, a small village on the River Wye in Herefordshire, from 23rd to the 28th December. Christine's family are going to be there. The family have decided that they will celebrate the festive season the same way every other year at least. Great stuff. I love these sorts of family get-togethers. They bring back fond memories of Boxing Day all-day family affairs at grandma Oakley's back in the 1950s and early 60s:

> In those days, the whole family used to attend; aunties, uncles, mums, dads, great grannies, granddads and lodgers. At any point during the day, there could be up to 30-40 people in their house at one time. Neighbours and other well-wishers just turned up unannounced and walk in through the back door. Even the man from the Prudential, who was a regular visitor, would have been welcome. Everyone was given a beer or a glass of sherry when they arrived. Or if the ladies and older

children were lucky they were offered a Babycham, or a glass port and lemon, and a sausage roll and mince pie.

The Boxing Day festivities would really begin early afternoon and go on to late at night. The adults would fill a carrier bag full of Christmas presents for each of the children. One grandchild was elected each year to help hand them out. The bags would be placed under the tree, ready to be handed out at an allotted time in the afternoon. It was total but organised chaos. Food and drink were plentiful throughout the day. Later in the evening, more food arrived from the kitchen. Chicken, ham, corned beef, cheese or paste sandwiches and homemade pickled onions, followed by jelly and blancmange, trifle, Nan's rock cakes, jam tarts and if you were lucky, a Victoria sponge.

After the men had their fill, they used to smoke big cigars and the ladies would pass around boxes of chocolates, usually Black Magic. The children would play games or watch some television. Robin Hood, Ivanhoe, Wagon Train and Wyatt Earp used to be my favourites. The adults used to play the card game Canasta as I seem to recall because my auntie Florrie didn't know how to play anything else. Also, grandad used to fill the balloons with flour and the adults used to burst them in the evening after a few bevvies.

At suppertime, my favourite was bread and beef dripping (I liked the jelly at the bottom) and a glass of milk. That's if the milk hadn't gone off, as Nan didn't have a fridge in those days.

I don't know how my grandparents managed to fit everyone in as their house was only a small semi-detached council house in London Road, Romford. I don't know how they we able to afford such a day and feed everyone either, as no one had any spare cash in those days. I think the adults collected coupons throughout the year. No credit cards in those days. My uncle George used to save Kensitas cigarette coupons to buy Christmas presents. He used to smoke at least forty a day, so it was always his present that was the biggest and most expensive.

Boxing Day at grandma Oakley's 1959

Back: Cousin John, Grandad and Grandma Oakley, cousin Beverley, Auntie Sylvia (obscured)

Front: Cousins Peter and Jane (bottom left), brother Paul (bow tie), cousins Helen and Yvonne, cousin Michael being held by sister Linda, me, Great Grandma Sheba Barret

Ladies...   **...Gentlemen...**

Grandma Oakley, Aunties Flo, Joan and Margie, my Mum (Beryl) and Auntie Sylvie

Back: Uncles Leslie, Frank, George, Frank, George and George. Front: Frank (lodger) and grandad Oakley

...and children

Back row: Helen, Linda, me and Peter
Front row: Brother Paul, John and Yvonne

Back to today. We set out early and met Hayley en route. When we arrived, we explored the nooks and crannies of the lovely house, which overlooked the river below. The views were stunning. Then the ladies set about putting up the Christmas tree and decorations. Almost everyone else will be arriving on Christmas Eve, each couple bringing a certain amount of food and drink to last us all throughout the festive holiday.

It was almost tea time. The decorations were up. The Christmas tree was glittering with lights, baubles and a star was shining down on us all from the top. Joe and I had piled logs onto the open fires and lit them. The food and drink had been put away. The bedrooms had been allocated and the children were happy. We decided to take a walk down the hill to the local pub, the New Harp Inn, where we had a meal and early Christmas drink before returning to the cottage.

> It is about 7.30 pm. Everyone except me is in the kitchen, chatting and preparing food for Christmas Eve. Little Oliver and Daisy are in bed. I look out of the window in the lounge. The rain is beating hard against the window pane. All I can see is the blackness of the night. I turn around to face the array of presents piled up in a dark corner of the room.
>
> I soon forget the wintry air outside and find myself sitting in a comfortable armchair next to the roaring fire. I am mesmerised by the flames curling and swaying, flickering this way and that way. How grateful am I. It's such a great feeling just to be here enjoying this moment. I thought it would never happen but here I am, alive and well amongst loved ones the day before Christmas Eve 2011, thanks to the Almighty, medical science and some very special people.

The others soon join me and we settle down in front of the fire to enjoy the rest of the evening, eating some of Christine's homemade sausage rolls and drinking a few glasses of prosecco. We chat about the day and the events yet to come. We are all very excited, happy and content.

Saturday 24th December 2011   Christmas Eve

After breakfast, Chris, Hayley and Grandma Marian went to the local supermarket armed with their final shopping list, while Joe and I looked after Oliver and baby Daisy. Next to arrive was Darren, Angela and Lucas. Then Joe went to pick up his dad (another Joe) from the railway station early that evening. The final guests, Matt and his partner Gemma, were not going to arrive until Christmas Day. So, everything was set.

It is now early evening. The children are all very excited. They have left out food and drink for the reindeer and Father Christmas. Soon after they are tucked up in bed, we all gather in the lounge, the log fire burns brightly. Additional presents are laid on top of the already huge pile, eagerly waiting to be opened. Everyone has a glass of bubbly in their hand. We are all fed, everyone is chatting away merrily to each other. The atmosphere is one of complete joy.

What more could anyone ask for on this Christmas Eve? Once again, just for a moment, I feel emotional as I contemplate my own good fortune. I look around at everyone in the unlit room. Their happiness is obvious to see as the flames and warmth from the open fire project long shadows over their contented faces. I try not to show it to the others but I think a few of them notice that I am having a bit of a moment, a *catharsis*, an overspill of emotion as the tears fill my eyes. They say nothing, there's just the odd glance directed my way. I sense their approval and acceptance of my vulnerability, which they seem to be happy to share.

Sunday 25th December   Christmas Day

What a great day. We began with Buck's Fizz, salmon or bacon with scrambled eggs, lashings of tea and coffee, excited children, all the usual stuff. Joe and I took charge of building up and replenishing the log fires. The ladies took care of the Christmas lunch preparation, Joe oversaw the distribution of presents, which was to be staggered throughout the day as there were so many. Darren shared the responsibility with Joe of ensuring no one had an empty glass. After the first batch of gifts were distributed and opened, we decided to go out for an early afternoon Christmas Day walk, while the turkey was slowly cooking in the oven. When we returned, we enjoyed some pre-dinner drinks before the day's main event.

Christmas dinner

From the left: Joe senior, Oliver, Marion, me, Angela, Lucas (end of table), Darren, Chris, Gemma, Matt, Hayley and Daisy

After a fantastic meal, everyone helped to clear the table and wash up so that we could continue with our festivities. It was almost the same routine every day until we left on the 28th December. Everyone had a great time. We said our goodbyes and set off home. We are already looking forward to our next Christmas holiday get together in a farmhouse by the sea in 2013. That is yet another goal that I can set myself and look forward to. I wonder whether I will feel just as emotional and happy as I do this time? I am sure I will, but let's get there first. There is still a long way to go.

Thursday 29th December

The first morning after our Christmas holiday, Chris was up early. She was busy with the laundry and preparing breakfast at the same time. I was still in bed. I looked through some of our photos of the Christmas holiday. I still felt a sense of achievement just by getting there and taking part. A special memory was having baby Daisy sitting comfortably on my lap opening her present to me. She is only eight months old and I would like her to get to know me. So, there was another goal for me to set myself.

The final two days of 2011 were quiet and non-eventful. Chris and I did see the New Year in with a glass of bubbly. She said that she was glad to see the back of most of it and I was just glad that I was here to see the New Year in.

Daisy opening her Christmas present to me

Sunday 1st January 2012 **11 days to next blood test**

The year of the Water Dragon, according to Chinese astrology, and you will not be able to stop luck coming to you throughout the year, apparently. I was born in 1947, the year of the pig. Pigs don't have to do any farm work, they just eat, drink and sleep in their pen; mmm, that's uncanny.

Countdown to cure

I don't know about anyone else but I am not usually one to make New Year's resolutions as I would probably break them. I do believe though, in making short-term and long-term goals that are important to me. I don't make many and I rarely write anything down as I think if they are important enough I will endeavour to remember what I must do to achieve them.

It has been one hundred days today since my haematologist first told me that all my cancer was gone. That was back on the 22nd September 2011. So, my long-term goal is to reach my outpatient treatment all-cured date, which will be in September 2016.

> That's approximately one thousand seven hundred and twenty-five days from today. Or two hundred and forty-five weeks. Or only four years, thirty-seven weeks more to go.

After entering all the hospital appointments, blood and bone marrow tests into my new diary, I struggled to add some short-term goals, as currently I am living my life almost one day at a time. Too much planning gives me the jitters and makes me feel uncertain about the future. But the busier I get, the more positive I feel. I constantly do my best to motivate myself by asking, *"When was the last time I did something for the first time?"* and then doing my best to act accordingly. I am getting close to the first hospital appointment of the year and yet again I am on edge. I had problems sleeping the night before my hospital clinic on the 11th.

Wednesday 11th January 2012   Blood test

Chris came with me to the hospital. The appointment was at 3.00 pm. We arrived early for the blood test then waited as usual for my turn to see the doctor. Yet again, I could hear muffled voices speaking in the adjacent room. I put my hand over my ears until the doctor appeared. It was a lady registrar this time. She noted that my energy levels were improving and my blood test was fine:

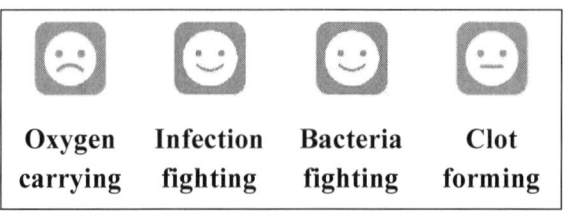

What a relief! Maybe I shouldn't get so nervous about these blood test results. But I still can't help getting the jitters a day or so beforehand. I am doing so well. Most of the time, I am not even thinking that I have ever been ill. But the last thing I want to hear is, *"It has come back."* It still feels as if all your birthdays have come at once when the doctor gives you the thumbs up. There is no getting away from the constant reminders of my medical situation in these early stages of my recovery. Maybe the memory of having cancer or any other serious trauma never leaves you and you just have to live with it. I don't know, it's still early days. All I really want to do is forget all about being ill and move on as quickly as possible and enjoy my life to the full again. And more importantly, release Christine as soon as possible from the same burden of worrying about whether we have a long-term future together or not. Sometimes, I wish I could fast forward time but I must be patient. I am sure we will get there but patience was never one of my virtues. It's a good job Chris has it in abundance.

I had to visit my GP on the 16th January and then there was also the wait until my next hospital appointment. The rest of January ran smoothly. My breathing was much better and I am putting on weight, thanks to plenty of Mrs B's home-cooked comfort food.

I am working five days a week now. It was my decision, not my employers. My increased diary entries are helping me to achieve my short-term goals. There are few days now without one or two entries going in. Even the longer-term planning entries are increasing with more positive social events or tasks. My mind is mainly being occupied with work-related stuff. My company has given me a workload that allows me to pace myself without too much effort.

February 2012

I had GP appointments on the 5th and 9th, before yet another very important appointment at the hospital on Tuesday 14th, my bone marrow test day. We arrived at 10.00 am and Sue the specialist nurse yet again performed the procedure.

When it was all over, we said goodbye to Sue and then went to say hello to the rest of the nursing staff on Onslow Ward before leaving. When we arrived home, I booked an overnight stay at the Royal Exeter Hotel in Bournemouth for this coming Saturday, the 18th. It was going to be another treat for being a brave boy on bone marrow test day.

On Sunday, we had lunch with my son Damian and his family. These little breaks and family visits are doing us both the power of good so we must keep them going if we can. Mr Diary 2012 is beginning to fill, although the rest of this month was reasonably uneventful. Unfortunately, for most of the last week in February and before my hospital appointment, I kept thinking about my test results before I had even had them.

Wednesday 29th February — Bone marrow test results

Today was my clinic appointment with haematologist Doctor Louise. I was to receive my blood and bone marrow test results. The appointment was for 2.15 pm. Chris and I arrived early as usual for my routine blood test. Then we had a coffee before a nurse called me to wait in the anteroom next to Doctor Louise's office. The nurse weighed me and I waited for the doctor to appear. What would she say? What would be the look on her face as we greeted each other? My hands were sweating again. I was on edge; my heart was pounding. I heard her talking in her office. What was she talking about? Who was she talking about? Had the leukaemia returned? This might sound a bit overdramatic, Mr Diary, but that is how it is for me every time I come here. What if?

Eventually, after what seemed to be a lifetime of waiting, the doctor appeared.

She smiled and said, *"How are you? You look well, the bloods are all good and the bone marrow test results show that you are in complete remission."*

However, she went on to say that she was waiting for a *Cytogenetics* study on the bone marrow that would give her a better idea if there was any more residual disease. So now I don't know how I feel, there is still some uncertainty. I don't want to have leukaemia residuals in my body. So, Royal Marsden, please get your finger out and pass on those results to Doctor Louise so that she can let me know that everything is okay and I can have complete peace of mind again.

The Fountain Centre

Doctor Louise went on to say, *"I will see you again in six weeks."*

I then asked her, *"If I am fit enough, I would like to go on holiday abroad in May."*

She replied, *"That should be okay, but you should have adequate travel insurance that covers your medical conditions."*

Fortunately, I had a list of cancer patients' insurance companies that the Fountain Centre gave me. I was considering Insure Blue, as they were offering the best-value and comprehensive quote.

Doctor Louise also offered some cautionary advice by saying, *"A patient with similar conditions went on holiday to somewhere in the Far East when they were taken ill without the necessary medical insurance cover and they have had problems getting home due to considerable medical costs etc. which they were not covered for."*

I think the figure was £45,000 or something like that. I decided to take my doctor's advice.

I need to mention some more about the Fountain Centre. They are a patient-led service with the ultimate goal of empowering those affected by cancer to regain control over their lives. They are a central information point within the hospital for all cancer patients' families and carers. They are open Monday to Friday 9.00 am to 5.00 pm. If you are a cancer patient, a relative, or a former cancer patient or carer you can drop in anytime for a cup of tea or coffee and have a chat. There are comfortable chairs and a library. You can book various support therapies, such as massage, acupuncture, reflexology, counselling and much more. There are group discussions such as, Look Good Feel Better, Lung Support Group, Pilates and much more, but you must book. As far as I am concerned it is worth a visit. Maybe a representative from the Fountain Centre could be available to patients that cannot leave the ward. Now that would be a good idea. What do you think, Mr Diary? Bloods were:

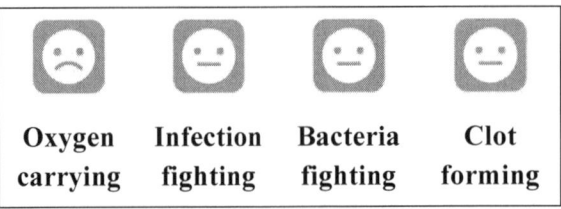

Thursday 1st March
After work, Chris and I went to the Theatre Royal in Windsor to see the ballet Swan Lake. I have had an interest in the art ever since I was shown the many exercise steps that are required for a dance routine by a former Royal Ballet dancer. This lady owned a beauty clinic in Iver, near Slough. She also taught air stewardesses deportment, which included walking up and down with a book on their head. I could not imagine being served a cup of tea in this way! It must have been difficult. Joking aside, we had a very pleasant time at the ballet. I am beginning to have more of an interest in all sorts of leisure activities that before my illness I wouldn't have given much thought to.

Monday 5th March   37 days to next blood test
I had an arranged GP visit this morning, this time with the nurse. Afterwards, I went back to work with yet another thought that has crossed my mind, and that was to phone HR for a death-in-service form. A colleague at work mentioned this recently when I was going through my contract. It turns out that I have never filled one out. My next of kin, Christine, could be left high and dry if something happened to me. So, to ensure that Chris is my sole benefactor, I had better fill in the form as soon as possible. These are the sort of things that take priority during the early stages of recovery. *What if?*

The rest of March was uneventful. I was getting into the swing of things at work, which is keeping me busy. The weekends are just about relaxing and enjoying family life again. The only physical effort for me is to increase my lung capacity by walking more.

April 2012

> Easter is here. It's Good Friday, 6th April. Ten months since I was first diagnosed and five months since I left hospital.

We are making sure that we are keeping to a normal routine. Being around family is proving to be the best medicine that both of us could wish for. We are off to see Hayley and her family for the weekend. Chris knows that seeing any of the family, especially the grandchildren, is keeping my demons at bay. She is aware of how fragile I still am at times.

Tuesday 10th April
I managed to get straight back into my work routine today and it was not until I arrived home that I reminded myself that tomorrow was yet another scheduled visit to the hospital for blood tests. The good thing is that I have not been brooding or having too many dark thoughts lately about what my blood results might be. Was this due to the family support that I was getting in abundance? Probably the main reason was that I was beginning to be more occupied with everyday normal healthy living and the less frequent reminders of my illness the better I felt about the future.

Wednesday 11th April   Blood test
My appointment was at 3.30 pm. This time I made a point of going to see the nurses on Onslow Ward after my bloods were taken. They were busy as usual. Sylvia the receptionist greeted me as I walked in. She asked about my health and found the time to talk to me for a short while, as did Sarah, one of the senior sisters in charge. Atish, the ward orderly, and Jincy, another sister, also came and said *hello*. Everyone was as

friendly as ever. They all seemed genuinely pleased to see me. After leaving the ward, I made my way down to the waiting area in outpatients and I was eventually called into the anteroom next to my doctor's office.

This room reminds me of the room that I was cocooned in for so long as an inpatient. Sparse and clinical, it has no soul. It's a room that could do with a few pictures on the wall. It needs some warmth. You certainly couldn't relax there. The room is how I imagine a cell for a criminal, but I have done nothing wrong.

I was going through the same experience I go through every time I came here. I was very apprehensive. I am just beginning to enjoy life again so please don't spoil it, doctor, by giving me bad news. The door opened and the first thing I did was to make eye contact with her, hoping to get a tell-tale look before she told me the results. I needn't have worried, she was smiling.

"How are you? Bloods good," she says. *"No problems."*

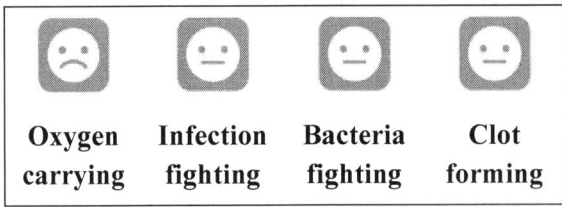

The consultation was brief but pleasant. Chris and I left, relieved and happy. As usual, we had a small celebration that evening. Chris cooked a special meal for me of homemade cottage pie and I opened a bottle of Beauchene, my favourite red wine. We were both so happy that I was continuing to be fit and well, physically anyway. I was still a little bit concerned about my emotional state. But I will get there. If I can continue to keep busy and fill Mr Diary with good and positive things, I am sure that time and God's grace will resolve everything. Nothing just happens, does it? *You have to kick doors and make things happen.*

There was not too much to report for most of April, health wise. Just the odd, scheduled GP visit. I was getting well and truly into the swing of normal healthy living. I was very busy at work and I was pacing myself as best I could. There was to be another treat in store for us later in the month. We are going to see the Lion King in London, including an overnight stay.

9 Returning to normal

A step too far

Saturday 21st April 2012 **6 months out of hospital**

We made our way by train to London Paddington and decided that before we checked into our hotel, the Park Inn in Bloomsbury, we would have something to eat in Paul's, one of our favourite patisseries just behind Covent Garden. We travelled by tube to Covent Garden. Impulsively, I decided to walk up the steps of the tube station rather than get the escalator.

I said to Chris *"I need the exercise."*

I didn't realise that there are 193 very steep, narrow and winding steps to the top. After about 40 or 50 steps, I had to stop and let people by as I was out of breath, almost exhausted.

Chris was quite concerned when I said to her, *"I feel a bit dizzy."*

So, we just stood there for a few minutes until I felt better. People had to literally squeeze by us to get through. Everyone seemed to be in a hurry. No one showed any concern. Where's the fire? We finally made it to the top after a few more stops on the way. So, it seems that I was not as fit as I thought I was. That's the trouble with people like me that naturally do everything in a hurry and have an active sports background. You occasionally have to be reminded that you are not as young as you were. I am almost sixty-five but think I am still twenty-five. Okay, lesson learnt. For now, anyway.

We had our coffee and pastry, and then wandered around the West End. We slowly made our way to our hotel and checked in. At about 5.30 pm, off we went for an early meal followed by a happy-hour cocktail in a Mexican bar in Maiden Lane, opposite the stage door of the Adelphi Theatre in the Strand. After a few margaritas, we merrily strolled around the corner to the Lyceum Theatre just a few minutes away to see The Lion King, which was fantastic. We both thoroughly enjoyed the experience. When the show ended, we took a slow walk back to the hotel, enjoying the fantastic atmosphere of the West End at night. I was well and truly exhausted, but we both enjoyed the whole London experience.

Next morning, after breakfast, we made our way back to Covent Garden. It was very quiet, probably because it was Sunday. We heard some church bells ringing in the distance. We followed the sound and discovered a small church called St Paul's in Bedford St, WC2.

It is a hidden gem, quietly tucked away behind the bustling square of Covent Garden itself. I walked into the building alone at first. For some reason, Chris doesn't really like churches but she reluctantly joined me inside for a short time. St Paul's is known as the actors' church, designed by *Inigo Jones* and built in the 1600s. The artist J.M.W. Turner was baptised here. Many famous actors had memorial services and plaques dedicated to their memory - Charlie Chaplin, Noel Coward, Vivian Leigh of Gone with the Wind fame and many more besides. The ashes of Ellen Terry, a leading Shakespearean actress, rest in a silver chalice on the right-hand side of the chancel near the altar. We were allowed to wander around the church, as there was no service at the time. As I was about to leave, I felt the overwhelming need to stay inside. Alone this time. I looked up at the altar bowed my head, and quietly thanked God for allowing me to be there that day, and to keep me and my loved ones happy and healthy. I even crossed myself after giving thanks. I don't know why I did it; I'm not a Catholic, it was just an impulsive act. This was the first, but not the last, time that I felt the need to walk into a church and thank God for my existence. Why did I do it? I am not religious and only visit churches for the usual stuff, weddings, funerals. We sat in the church gardens for a while before making our way home.

On the 23rd April, I received a text message from Pete Small, the chap I was in hospital with. I was hesitant before finally reading it. It was only to give me his home phone number. We intend to keep in touch with each other. He is raising money by jumping out of an aeroplane in aid of the Onslow Ward.

Raising money or doing something to help a worthy cause is another new thought that has crossed my mind recently. I do not intend to do anything just yet, but I will make some sort effort in the future. I think most of us survivors of extreme illness or physical trauma feel the need to do this eventually if we can, for at least one worthy cause or another. It's a form of gratitude I think. I am beginning to consciously appreciate what people do in this country to support others less fortunate than themselves, including worthwhile charities.

My awareness of everything that is good in our world is becoming increasingly heightened, probably because of my recent experience. I now have a fledgling understanding and empathy for others that are worse off than myself. I knew it was inside me somewhere and although I still don't fully understand it, I am glad that it is slowly rising to the surface.

That's another positive that has come out of having cancer. I think going through it and coming out the other side cancer free has helped make me a better person. I value life and listen more for a start and I am sure that there are more positives to come.

The remaining few days of April flew by. Immy had a birthday on the 26th, but apart from that it was just the same normal mundane routine in our house, just like I imagine most other households, and that suits us both fine.

My favourite month

Tuesday 1st May
May is my favourite month, mainly because I have always loved what Mother Nature has to offer; it was all around me in all its glory today. Warm sunshine and the smell of flowers in full bloom. The natural world has always made me feel good, even as a child. Now I have been given a second chance. My feelings of gratitude and awareness are becoming more apparent each day and my health is improving day by day. Most of my emotions seem to be the same today as they did when I was that small boy sitting under the tree all those years ago. Is that what they call Déjà vu? Is it Mindfulness? Or is it what is known as cryptomnesia? I don't know for sure. But all sorts of childhood memories, guilt complexes and heightened senses are beginning to emerge in my mind these days as I take the time to rebuild my life. Mostly good and a few not so good.

I have also been sorting out our travel insurance for our holiday later this month. It's the first time that I have had to use medical insurance. We finally chose *Insure Blue,* a cancer patient insurance company that I mentioned previously when we were considering insurance from a list provided by the Fountain Centre. It cost £92.75 for both of us for one week in Majorca. This was another reminder of a cancer patient's financial handicap but it was the best value quote and a necessary expense for us at this stage of the game.

Wednesday 9th May
Today is the birthday of another one of my granddaughters. This time it's Lola. We gave her a present and birthday card when we visited her at home in Ascot. She was so pleased to see us and was also very excited about her upcoming birthday party.

Tuesday 15th May
I have been too busy lately to even think about tomorrow's clinic with Doctor Louise. But today I felt increasingly nervous about the outcome of my next blood test.

I also booked and paid for our holiday to Cala San Vincente, Majorca. We are going on the 19th for a week. We have both been looking forward to this holiday since I was an inpatient. I just hope that my bloods are okay so that we can go. You never know. It all hinges on the results. That's the thing. You do your best to think positive, you do your best to make plans, but no sooner than you make a commitment to the future, doubts about achieving your goal creep into your mind. What if?!

Wednesday 16th May   Blood test
My hospital appointment was at 2.00 pm. We arrived early. Bloods were taken. Then we waited in the anteroom until the doctor finally appeared. She seemed happy and full of beans.

She said, *"Everything is okay."*

Once again, I was relieved. I said to her, *"We would like to make plans if possible to move to a new house, but we are a bit hesitant and slightly uncertain about my future health and it is deterring us from making a decision. I was wondering whether I should be considering the possibility of having a bone marrow donor in place should I need a transplant in the future?"*

Doctor Louise seemed to think the transplant idea was worth considering and said, *"Okay, let's get ahead of the game then. I will give you a letter to give to your siblings to take to their respective GPs to see if they are potential donors and hopefully they will be a good match."*

She didn't comment on the moving question. Bloods today were:

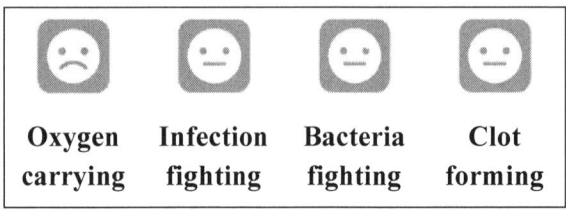

Her parting comment was, *"Have a nice holiday and I will see you in 6 weeks' time."*

When we arrived home, I wasted no time and phoned my brother and sister to say that if they were still happy about becoming donors I would send them a letter to take to their GP so they could be tested to see if they are a good match. They were both already aware that I was going to speak to my doctor about this and had agreed to have the test should it be necessary.

Another dream comes true

Saturday 19th May   39 days to next blood test
We were off on holiday. It was an early flight, 6.00 am from Gatwick. We had to be at the airport at 3.30 am! When we arrived, it was the usual hustle bustle with long waits for baggage dropping off and security checks before we eventually got airside. We had a breakfast baguette and coffee in Pret a Manger. Why people eat breakfast at that time in the morning is

beyond me, but many of us seem to do it. It must be part of the holiday experience.

We eventually arrived at Hotel Molins in Cala San Vincente. It was about midday and everything was just as I remembered it. The weather was warm and sunny and a gentle breeze caressed our faces as we stepped off the coach and into the sunshine. The small bay just behind us at the foot of our hotel looked beautiful. The sea was calm and turquoise blue. It was full of people in the shallows.

We made our way up the steps to the reception where we saw a familiar face. It was Rafael who has worked at the hotel for over thirty years. He greeted us with his usual friendly smile and offered us both a cool glass of champagne. Nice touch. Rafael had made sure that we have the room of our choice, room 601, on the top floor. The reason for asking for this room is because it is the room we occupied on a previous visit before my illness and it is very spacious as well as having the best views of the bay below.

> It feels great doesn't it, when you first walk into your hotel room after a long journey? You put your cases down and claim your bed for the holiday duration, before unpacking your suitcases and exploring the facilities and the resort. But today I feel slightly different. We walk into our room. We put our cases down. There is a complimentary bottle of champagne and a basket of fresh fruit on the small table next to the balcony doors.

> I open the balcony door and step outside to take in the sunshine, the view of the bay below and the amazing cliffs in the distance. I whisper under my breath, I am finally here. I have made it. I turn around and walk back into the room.

The dream becomes reality

There are dressing gowns and slippers laid out on the beds. I open the champagne and pour the bubbly into the two champagne glasses provided, while Chris is busy unpacking our suitcases. I am beginning to feel emotional again. So, I go back outside, I grip the balcony railings in front of me with both hands and lean forward and breathe in deeply, just to take in more of the warm, Majorcan air and the wonderful views below me and beyond. Just for a second, my mind flashes back to that terrible day when I held onto the radiator when I was first in pain at Frimley Park Hospital and all my dreams were shattered in an instant. But now my dreams are back and turning into realities one by one. I take another deep breath, close my eyes for a moment and the bad memories are gone. I say to myself again, *"I can't believe that I am finally here"*. The emotion that I am now experiencing is yet again overwhelming. I begin to cry, unable to contain my happiness. I have rarely openly cried in the past, but these days I cry easily. Is this a bad thing? Am I weak? Or am I just more mindful of the world I am lucky enough to live in?

I turn around once more and walk back into the room and sit down on the bed. I feel exhausted, mentally drained and I don't know why. Chris notices my distress even though I try to hide it from her. She immediately stops what she was doing and walks over to me and sits by my side to reassure me.

"What's wrong?" she says. *"Everything is okay now."*

She puts her arm around me and gently pats me on the back. She hands me my glass of champagne and we tap glasses.

"Here is to our holiday," she says. *"You have made it haven't you?"*

I looked up at her, smiled and say, *"Yes, we have haven't we."*

Chris is unpacked and ready to take a stroll in the sun

After our wonderful week away, I got straight back into work until the end of the month. Time is beginning to fly by, as normality takes hold of our lives once more.

Saturday 2nd June

We spent the weekend in Bournemouth. We are staying at the Royal Exeter Hotel overnight and Sunday we are spending time with Damian and his family before setting off home again.

I would not usually give anyone advice if they are going through a similar experience. But all I would say is to enjoy yourself as much as you possibly can by doing as many pleasurable things as possible, whether it is in work or play. Plan future events in a diary if you haven't already. You would be surprised how quickly it fills up. Seize the day when it arrives and enjoy it to the full. Then tomorrow will arrive sooner than you think. Make sure you don't have too much time on your hands to brood on negatives. I know you can't avoid it sometimes, but it's best not to think about them too much if they do enter your head. Whatever negative situation you come up against, do your best to accept it, look for a solution or the next step and move on from it. This is easier said than done of course. Don't I know it. But in my view, you must move on. Try not to dwell on past negative situations if you can help it.

Golfing exercise

Wednesday 12th June
Today was another milestone. It was to be the first time that I had played golf for a year. Some work colleagues invited me to have a round at Pine Ridge golf course, which is not too far from where I live. It was a warm sunny day and we began our round at about 3.30 pm. I am a keen golfer so I was excited about playing. I teed off and marched towards the general direction of where I thought my ball had landed, quickening my step as I approached. *"Is that my ball or is it a daisy?"* I thought to myself. Luckily it was my ball.

Golf can be torture, but most enjoyable at the same time. Just getting your drive to land on the fairway is like getting a hole in one. After about 12 holes of zig-zagging the fairway, rough and woodland beyond, I was beginning to get tired. By the time, we finish the 18th, I was glad that it was all over. I don't think I kept my scorecard. After a welcome cold beer and a bit of banter at the 19th hole, I made my way home. On the way back I realised just how unfit I was. I knew it was not just the lack of exercise. I still wasn't used to pacing myself in certain situations. Ok, that's another lesson learnt.

Sunday 16th June
It is exactly one year since I was diagnosed with leukaemia. It's

a strange anniversary to celebrate but it has a different significance than a normal birthday or wedding anniversary. It felt like I was celebrating something like the end of a battle and yet it also felt like Chris and I had achieved something extra special. We did celebrate on our own at home by opening a bottle of prosecco and a tin of Roses chocolates. We have already agreed that we should celebrate any good news. I celebrate every day when I wake up in the morning, open the window, smell the air and hear the birds singing. Every new day is a celebration to me.

Saturday 22nd June
We spent the weekend at my brother Paul's house in Tonbridge. His wife Christine is sadly going through cancer treatment herself. We tried to keep off the subject of her illness while we were there. Perhaps in hindsight, it would have been better to speak about it openly if she brought the subject up. She is still suffering somewhat and I am well and truly on the road to recovery. But I didn't particularly want to be reminded of what I had gone through myself and I didn't really want to hear how difficult a time she was having. I know I was being selfish but being confronted by cancer patients that are not getting any better still makes me feel uneasy. I also have a guilt complex when I see people with cancer and I am cancer free. It was a delicate situation. But we managed to enjoy each other's company as best we could.

Wednesday 27th June — One year since chemotherapy started
It was my hospital clinic day again. Chris was with me. I was hoping that my doctor had received a reply from my brother's and sister's doctors regarding a tissue match. I was more concerned with those results than my own blood results. The doctors call this test HLA (*Human Leukocyte Antigen*) *typing*. It

measures how closely the tissues of one person match the tissues of another. So, ten out of ten would be nice. We must wait and see. I wonder what percentage is acceptable?

Yet again, I waited in the room adjacent to Doctor Louise's office. I was sweating as usual and my hands were over my ears so that I couldn't hear what was being said. There is nothing worse than overhearing someone talking about you when they are not in the same room.

When Doctor Louise appeared, she said that my bloods were okay but she was still waiting for my sister's results. It seems that my brother is not a match so he cannot be considered as a bone marrow donor. This poses more questions regarding bone marrow transplants vs chemotherapy. It seems that there is more success with chemo treatment, but like the doctor said, she is just getting ahead of the game and would only consider a transplant if I was to relapse. However, I do have a good prognostic leukaemia so let's concentrate on the positive. Bloods today were:

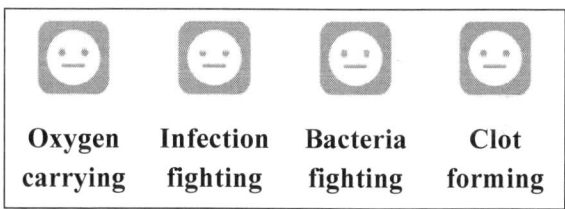

I felt somewhat troubled about my conversation with the doctor that afternoon. I later said to Chris that I had forgotten to mention to the doctor that we would like to go on holiday again in November of this year.

I also made the decision to surf the internet when we got home to get some medical answers. Big mistake. Again, I do not want to give too much advice, Mr Diary. But I would not advise any layperson to seek medical answers in this way. It is confusing and may not be specific to you as an individual and you will probably only get half the answer anyway. But I have looked online and the answers to my questions mainly about bone marrow transplants have raised some doubts in my mind as well as creating more questions that needed to be answered by my doctor. It has prompted me to email my consultant for some more advice and reassurance.

Saturday 14th July

We went to London today. We parked our car at Osterley for a daily charge of £2.50 then bought an oyster card for the two of us for £17.00. That included underground and buses throughout London. Bargain! We were going to lunch at a recommended restaurant in South Kensington, so we decided to get off the tube train at Knightsbridge, window shop at Harrods and then visit the museums.

We usually spend time walking around the Harrods food hall before buying a posh sandwich and eating it in a well-known coffee shop over the road, but not this time. We were two hours early, so we took a stroll around the V&A and the Natural History Museum before making our way to our restaurant. It is a steak and lobster restaurant; I ordered steak and Chris ordered lobster. The meal was nothing special, even though Chris had something quite exotic. After we finished, we decided to make our way back to the underground and go to Covent Garden before making our way home.

Suddenly, Chris became quite ill. Now it was my turn to look after her for a change. We took refuge in a hotel's reception area. Chris didn't look too good at all and needed to be close to the toilet. She had terrible stomach cramps which worried us both. After I felt she was reasonably comfortable, I went to find the nearest pharmacy to get some medicine to help with her obvious discomfort. After describing Chris's symptoms, the pharmacist recommended some medicine that would at least give some temporary relief. After I returned and she took the medicine, I spent the next hour reassuring her. The medicine was slowly starting to work. We then made our way home. At last it was me that was providing some help and reassurance. It was roles reversed for a change and that felt good.

The rest of July went well. Work was steady and I was getting stronger, physically and mentally, as each went by.

Wednesday 8th August   Blood test
Hospital clinic day today 2.15 pm. Same thing. Bloods and an uneasy wait for the doctor to appear. Everything was still okay. My blood test results were satisfactory:

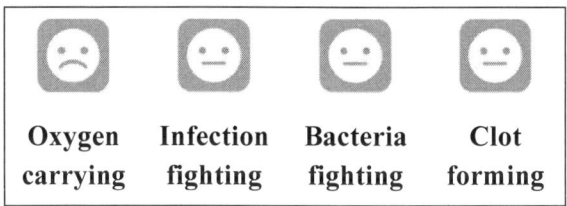

However, there was a mix-up with the form my sister filled in regarding HLA typing, so I still had to wait for those results although, as I said previously, the typing is just precautionary. The good news was that I do not have to come back to hospital for two months. That means more time to focus on planning and positive living.

Friday 17th August
Just another day in the calendar for most people, except today was my 65th birthday. I can draw my state pension now. I remember thinking even before I became ill that if I were to snuff it before I drew my state pension, I would be more than miffed. Especially after paying into it for the last fifty years.

We are going to visit our friends Maureen and Paul in Somerset for the weekend. This time last year I was not even sure if I would be able to celebrate my 65th birthday. On one occasion, when I was feeling low and very sorry for myself, I imagined briefly seeing my epitaph showing the dates of 1947 to 2011. But it only lasted a microsecond. I soon dismissed any such thoughts and concentrated on the more positive outlook of getting better. Now, of course, all I want to do is to live forever.

Although I am at retirement age, I believe that to continue to work for a while would benefit my health as well as my financial situation. Working is keeping me active both physically and mentally. Health and wealth is a combination that I am working on and it seems to be okay so far.

August has flown by. Everything is good. Our routine of work and play is beginning to be the same for Chris and me as anyone else who is happy and healthy. It's just the two-monthly hospital visit that gets in the way of normal living. But even they will get less soon I hope.

September 2012
Everything went well this month. No mishaps. No hang ups. We had a nice long weekend away, including a fantastic meal out at the Weighbridge Brew House, which was a special treat for Christine. The only other thing that happened was that on the 26th September, I heard from my old hospital buddy Peter Small. He had just completed his aeroplane jump and managed to raise £1000 for the Onslow Ward. He asked me to accompany him to the hospital to present the proceeds to the sister in charge at the time, Carol Burrows, which I gladly did. On Thursday 27th, I had to have a routine blood test at my local doctor's surgery but that was it for the remainder of the month.

10 My vitals

Oh no

Monday 1st October 2012
I received a phone call from my local GP surgery and the receptionist told me that the doctor would like me to come in and discuss a recent blood test that I had.

I asked, *"Why, what is the problem?"*

She replied, *"The doctor will discuss that with you when you come in."*

I was standing in the lounge at the time and Chris and Darren were sat there listening to what was being said.

"Can you get the doctor to ring me as soon as possible please, I don't want to wait for an appointment."

The receptionist agreed and said, *"The duty doctor will ring you as soon as they can."*

Both Chris and I were thinking the worse and I was on edge. I eventually got the call from the Duty doctor.

I said, *"Can you not tell me what's wrong over the phone?"* Chris and Darren were looking at me in anticipation as I waited for the answer.

"The blood test shows that you have chronic kidney disease."

I replied, *"Chronic kidney disease?"*

The doctor went on to say, *"Make an appointment and we will discuss it then."*

I put the phone down. Chris was in tears. Darren seemed shocked and I was afraid once more. I couldn't wait for the appointment, so I went straight up to the surgery, but it was closed. I rang the surgery as I was stood in the car park pacing up and down. I had to know what this latest news meant. I eventually got through. It was the same duty doctor that answered.

I said, *"I spoke to you earlier. Is this disease serious? When you mentioned chronic and kidneys, I was shocked! I am not going to die, am I?"*

The doctor replied in a reassuring manner, *"Of course you are not going to die! It sounds worse than it is. Don't worry you are going to live for a long time to come. Make an appointment to see me and we will discuss it then. It just means that we keep a more regular eye you as far as the condition is concerned that's all."*

I went home and repeated the news to Chris and Darren. We were all relieved. We can continue to enjoy life again. It's strange, when I received the news that I had leukaemia back in June 2011, I didn't say to the doctor *"I am not going to die am I?"* so why am I saying it now, a year later about something far less life threatening? But I didn't know that at the time, did I?

After that small blip in the life of Tel, the rest of October went well. Even the hospital visit was reassuring. We went there on Wednesday 10th at 4.00 pm. Susan saw me first. She weighed me at 97.1 kg and my BMI was 31, which is classified as *obese*. This is not good and to avoid things like diabetes, we discussed a potential diet. I will endeavour to do something about that. Probably more exercise and eat less fatty foods. Doctor Robbins saw me this time. We seem to get on well. He was part of the team that looked after me when I was an inpatient.

He said to me, *"There are no signs of a relapse and your blood count is normal. You have been out of hospital for almost a year now without any problems, so we will not need to see you so often, let's make it once every three months. So, we will see you again early January 2013."*

This was great news. Twelve more weeks to help my mind adjust to living without constant health reminders. My blood results were:

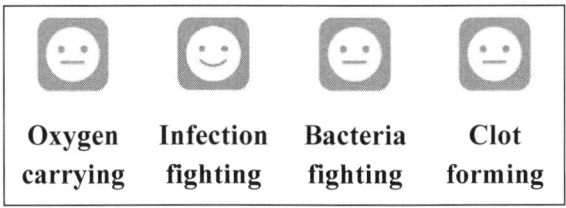

"Oh look, there's a blue smiley face!"

When we arrived home, I booked our travel insurance. We are going to Tenerife in November and this time the medical insurance will cost £103.37 for 7 days. We went to a family Halloween Party on the last weekend of the month. Life can be grand if you are lucky and have a passion for it.

Thursday 18th October — **First full year of being cancer free**

I woke up early; Chris was still asleep. I opened the window, the wind was blowing leaves off the trees beyond our garden fence. I looked down into our garden and a blackbird was shopping for its breakfast. I closed my eyes and gulped some of the fresh autumn air. I felt good; I felt healthy; I felt happy. I was experiencing that indescribable feeling again and why not; today was my first anniversary of being out of hospital and cancer free. We celebrated, of course, with a meal for two from M&S and a bottle of champagne at home that evening.

Friday 2nd November

> We are off to Tenerife for a bit of winter sun for a week today. We are creatures of habit so we are staying at another of our regular haunts, the Hotel Vulcano, in Playa das Americas.

It was 28 degrees and sunny when we arrived and it remained sunny every day while we were there. Although neither of us drink much, we enjoyed sitting at one of our favourite bars on the seafront of Los Cristianos, with a 1-euro pint of ice cold beer brought to us by our favourite waiter, who Chris has christened Scratchy Balls! I can guess why. We just sit there for ages, soaking up the sun and people watching. We also made some new unexpected friends, a young a lovely Italian couple called Milena and Simon. They had just opened a bar near our hotel and it was obvious that they were still finding their feet. So, we made sure that we gave them some custom while we were there.

When we returned from our winter's break, we both managed to get back into the normal routine of work and carried on enjoying leisurely weekends. Halfway through the month I was due to visit my cardiologist, Doctor Tim in Dorset. I wasn't particularly worried because it was only a routine appointment and we were looking forward to yet another short break away.

My broken heart

Friday 16th November
I was back in Dorchester for an echocardiogram. When it was over we went to check in at the place we always stay at when we visit the area, the Royal Yeoman guest house in Grimstone, just two miles outside of Dorchester. The accommodation, food and owners, Sue and Garry, are fantastic and it is great value for money. Sue is a regular visitor to Dorchester hospital, unfortunately, so we had plenty to talk about. She was also very sympathetic to my health situation. People generally have good intentions if they are inquiring about anyone's health. But in my case, I tend to get a little defensive about my own health when asked, as if there was something wrong with me. But that's my problem I think, not theirs. We both felt good about being in the area. We love Dorset.

Monday 19th November
I was at my second appointment with Doctor Tim, sitting opposite him in his consolation room, to discuss the results of my echocardiogram. He asked me how I was keeping while reading my notes. He didn't look particularly happy, but then he never does. I like him just the same and I have complete confidence in him.

He looked up at me and said, *"There is some deterioration to your heart."*

This news shocked me somewhat.

He went on to say. *"I can make a recommendation for you to be considered for a CRT Pacemaker Implant."*

I answered somewhat bewilderedly, *"But you said on a previous occasion that I probably wouldn't need a pacemaker for years to come. If at all."*

"Well I am afraid you may have to consider it now, but it is up to you."

All sorts of things were racing through my head. Was it the leukaemia that caused this deterioration? Was it the chemo? My now fragile heart was racing, almost thumping through my chest. You've got to be joking What now?

I managed to compose myself without thinking too much. Then just as I did that day when I was stood in front of Professor Smith back in June 2011, I decided to accept the situation there and then. I was going to put my faith in my doctor. As if I had any choice anyway. I gave a deep sigh and looked up at him. He genuinely seemed concerned, which gave me the confidence to say to him,

"Okay, what do we do now,"

"I will discuss your case at my next consultants' clinical decisions meeting on the 11th December. I think that you are a good candidate for cardiac resynchronisation therapy."

It seems that my echocardiogram on the 16th showed that I have *heart failure syndrome with moderate to severe left ventricular systolic dysfunction and a broad left bundle branch block with QRS duration of 162ms.* Whoopy do.

He went on to say, *"I will contact your haematologist and GP to put them in the picture."*

We shook hands and I walked out of his office where Chris was waiting for me. I didn't say anything to her at first. I had to think what to say and try to be positive about the news that I had just received.

It didn't take me too long before I said, *"The good news is that instead of letting my heart condition deteriorate, the doctor and I have decided to improve the situation by possibly having a pacemaker."* I continued, *"It's a bit like having an engine part that is wearing out, being replaced by a brand-new part free of charge."*

This seemed to reassure her, but I don't think she was totally convinced.

Chris then said, *"Well what happens next?"*

I told her that the wheels were already in motion and I would go onto a waiting list which is about three months long. For some reason, I felt almost relieved about this latest news, once it sank in. At least I knew that my broken heart was going to be repaired by a doctor and a system that I knew and had the utmost faith in. We were both quiet for most of our journey home; I think we were both stunned by this latest news. The snakes and ladders game of life continues; now let's get back on that ladder.

The rest of November was reasonably uneventful.

December 2012
We have been busy this month with all things to do with the festive season. We are not going away to a Christmas cottage this year. Instead, we are just distributing goodies to family members that we are not seeing over Christmas.

On Tuesday 11th I received notification that my pacemaker procedure had been approved. I also knew that Doctor Louise, my haematologist, had received a letter from Doctor Tim asking whether I was fit enough for him to go ahead. I was now on a 14-week waiting list. So sometime in March 2013, my pacemaker procedure should take place. It seems the ball is well and truly rolling. Do I feel sorry for myself? Yes, I do a bit. Would I give up, or stop embracing and enjoying life after this latest news? No, not a bit of it.

Hayley and her family stayed overnight on the 15th. On the 17th, I booked our summer holiday for next year and on the 19th December, I took some gifts to the hospital in Guildford for some of the people who had looked after me when I was an inpatient. And we spent Christmas Day at Hayley and Joe's.

So, you see, Mr Diary, I am gaining more confidence about my future. I am planning, I am working hard and when I get knocked down with occasional bad news, I am picking myself up and rising to the challenge. Sometimes I feel that I need help. Sometimes I feel alone when I fall, but that's life. Looking forward to something that we have planned is my motivation to seize the day and continue my struggle until I am completely well again. At last, I think I am beginning to flourish.

Monday 31st December 2012
We saw the New Year in just by ourselves at home. We had a glass or two of champagne, watched a bit of television and at midnight, we toasted getting through 2012 without too much drama. We welcomed in 2013, which was going to be yet another challenging twelve months with the usual highs, lows and new experiences.

2013
Welcome to 2013. This is the year of the water snake according to the Chinese Astrology Calendar. Most people who are born under this sign will experience a mix of good and bad fortune. So not much change there then. For now, I am going to look on the bright side I think.

THE UNREMARKABLE MAN

Two jailed men looked through the same prison bars, one saw only mud, the other saw the stars

We are well into the routine of normal living in our house now. This is mainly due to the less frequent visits to see my haematologist and the fact that I have not suffered any setbacks since I was discharged back in October 2011 as far as my leukaemia is concerned.

Most of January and February passed by without much drama. On Wednesday 9th January, I attended my scheduled appointment with Doctor Louise. She told me that my bloods were fine and that she had a reply about my sister as a tissue match. She said that it was a 70% match and that might be good enough. She went on to say that she had heard from my heart doctor about his plan to fit a pacemaker and thought that it was very reasonable to proceed; in her opinion I have a good chance of being cured of leukaemia. Well that's something to look forward too isn't it, Mr Diary? Bloods today looked like this:

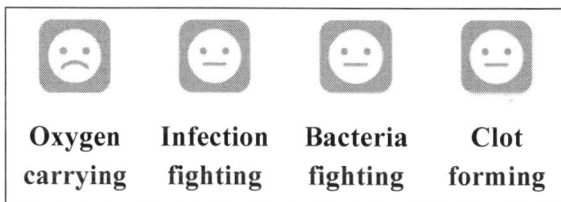

The three-legged jellyfish

It was not until Thursday 7th February 2013 that I had to attend a hospital again. This time it was an 11.00 am appointment at the Pre-Admission Clinic in Dorchester, to go through the procedure of my pacemaker implant. The purpose of the clinic is to save time on the day of your admission, by ensuring that all relevant checks have been made beforehand. Also, it would give us the opportunity to ask any questions that we might have.

The pre-assessment nurse showed us a dummy of the type of pacemaker that I was going to have implanted. I remember thinking that it looked like a small jellyfish with three legs (or leads).

I asked her, *"Is it a good one? Is it the best you can have? Will it last a long time?"*

She said, *"Yes, it is a super, super, duper one."*

Well, that's alright then.

She also said, *"One lead is a bit tricky to place in the right position as it is very close to your lung and there is a possibility that the lung could be punctured, but that is most unlikely".*

With that reassurance, I was then asked to sign a consent form. I did so reluctantly because I wasn't looking forward to this operation one little bit, although I really knew it was yet another life-saver.

She went on to say, *"I will probably see you on Wednesday 6th March 2013, which is the day that Doctor Tim will fit your pacemaker."*

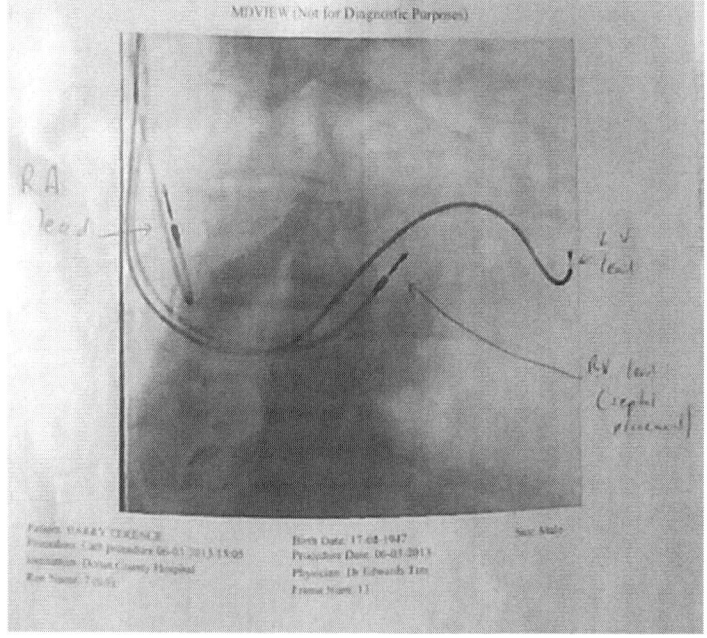

"...my actual jellyfish with three legs"

Building sand castles in the sky

We left the hospital and made our way back home, as we both had to be at work the following day. On the way, I felt a bit depressed and wondered whether I was beginning to be a bit of a liability to Chris health wise. There seemed to be no let up with one scare after another. What if she said yes, you are a liability. What would I do then? Anyway, she wouldn't say that even if she thought it. I think I know her well enough. She would always be there for me one way or another, as I would be for her. So best ignore those sorts of negative thoughts; I am sure we all get them from time to time.

But while I am bearing my soul and feeling sorry for myself, the truth is that I have always struggled in one way or another health wise. Health scares were all too frequent when I was young and seemed to get in the way of normality and happiness. It has nearly always been down to me alone to overcome life's obstacles, especially when I was a boy and a young man. Sometimes, no matter how much I tried, something would always take me back to square one again.

I felt like I was building sandcastles in the sky, trying hard to please and to be healthy but seemingly getting nowhere. That's what it is like when you are attempting to overcome something you don't really understand, especially as a young person; you feel alone. But I have become quite resilient over time and have overcome almost every obstacle that life has decided to throw my way. Although it must be said that I have not always chosen the right path to follow. I am lucky to be in a partnership where the foundations are deep and strong and with someone who would always be there to support me through thick and thin. This makes choosing the right life path to follow so much easier.

Tuesday 5th March 2013
We were off to Dorchester again today, to have my pacemaker operation. We have planned to have a few days there if I feel up to it. We arrived at our lodgings at the Royal Yeoman in the afternoon. Sue greeted us in her usual friendly way and we discussed my up-and-coming event tomorrow at the hospital. Then we set off for an early evening meal just down the road in Stratton at the Saxons Arms. After a lovely meal, we returned to our lodgings for an early night.

Me and the Welsh Heart Surgeon

Wednesday 6th March

Sue and Gary always prepare a fantastic and freshly cooked breakfast. Made to order, from locally sourced products, but today I was under orders. So, it's a little bit of scrambled egg on one piece of toast with black coffee, for me and all before 8.00 am. At about 10.15 we said our goodbyes and set off to the hospital, which was only 10 minutes away.

At 11.00 am we checked into Cardiology Reception. I was to be in hospital overnight. Chris would be on her own this evening back at the Royal Yeoman but I knew that she would be looked after. The hospital instructions also said that I was to remove any nail polish/makeup. I also had to bring with me a dressing gown and slippers, which I did, and a CD of my favourite music which could be played while the procedure is taking place, which I didn't. But more of that later.

Chris stayed with me for most of the time as they prepared me for the operation in a side ward adjacent to the operating theatre. I had to put a gown on. The usual OBS were taken. A cannula was put into place ready for the local anaesthetic. The operation could not be performed using general anaesthetic because patient co-operation was needed during the procedure. I did ask for some jungle juice or relaxant, which Doctor Tim had already agreed to let me have.

I waited and waited. I was eventually moved to a room on my own next to the theatre. While I was waiting, I did see Doctor Tim dressed in his green pyjamas and cap shuffle slowly past the entrance to my room a couple of times, head down looking like he had the world's troubles upon his shoulders. Or he was lost? I couldn't work out which. I remember thinking to myself that he reminded me of a character from the film One Flew Over the Cuckoo's Nest. On one occasion, he did look my way and we both acknowledged each other with a smile, although I think he had to pay for his. I liked him all the same and I had the utmost faith in him to do the best for me. Well, it was a bit late now if I didn't.

Eventually, at about 4.00 pm, the theatre nurses came and wheeled me into the theatre. I did not get time to take anything in. There were bright lights above a stainless-steel slab. Before I knew it, there were quite a few people surrounding me. Technicians, nurses and doctors, all dressed in their theatre uniforms of green pyjamas, masks and bedroom slippers. Then in unison a few of them got either side of me, said 1-2-3-up and hoisted me onto the silver table. They all seemed to have a specific important job to do but I didn't have a clue who was doing what. They were all very organised.

Everything seemed to be going like clockwork and with efficient speed. Before I knew it, I was on some sort of high, but it was not the jungle juice. It must have been the anaesthetic working its magic. There was all sorts of equipment around me, TV screens and leads attached to complicated equipment. But there was still no sign of Doctor Tim. Had he forgotten me? Was he lost? Had he fallen asleep somewhere? Was he in a coffee shop down on Preston Beach near Weymouth? I just remember thinking, *where is he?* Nothing can start without the organ grinder. Where was the Welsh Wizard?

Someone then asked me, *"Have you brought in a CD of your favourite music?"*

I replied in a bit of a slurry voice, *"No I haven't."*

I was then asked what sort of music would I like playing as they had a selection. With that, Doctor Tim appeared looking as dour as ever, shuffling into the theatre and towards me.

I remember saying at that point, *"Play anything Welsh. The rugby national anthem. Whatever makes him happy."*

I do remember that my remark did stir one or two chuckles. I even think Doctor Tim managed a smile under his mask. The anaesthetic must have worked as I was going in and out of consciousness. All I remember then was him pushing down just below my shoulder and saying, *"I am putting the device in now,"* and that was that. I don't remember anything else until I came around in recovery.

I cannot remember what time Chris came back, but it was early evening. She brought me a sandwich which I demolished in seconds. She stayed for a while and nurses drifted in and out to see how I was and to perform various OBS. I soon settled down for the night although I did have a bit of discomfort now and then. But I was glad it was all over. I remember thinking *"I don't want to be alone in hospital again. I have had enough of being a patient."* Then I drifted off to sleep.

Thursday 7th March
Chris arrived at the hospital at about 11.00 am. We had to wait for a while before I was told that I could be discharged. At about midday, I was given the discharge papers and we made our way back home. Chris had to drive, which gave me time to read the discharge advice notes.

The wound had been closed using sutures, which should be removed if possible by my GP or nurse after seven days. There were certain rules that I had to follow. I had to check the wound every day when I got up and when I went to bed, if there was any redness, swelling or bleeding, I should contact the hospital immediately.

For one month after the operation, I must not lift my arm up high on the same side as the pacemaker. I must not push myself up out of a chair or bed, carry heavy objects, push, pull, or even put my arm behind my back for a scratch. All this is to prevent bleeding or movement of the leads attached.

You also must be careful getting dressed and undressed as you can imagine. Everything had to be done with my left arm down by my side. Showering was also difficult, as you must keep the area around the wound dry. I am used to this, as when I was an inpatient in the Royal Surrey Hospital, I had to keep my PICC site dry for nearly five months. And we had plenty of Waitrose bags at home to do the job.

We finally arrived home late afternoon and Chris dropped me off before she went out again for weekend provisions as we have Hayley coming to visit. I am fully aware of just how much she does for me. I sometimes wonder how I would have coped without her constant support.

> How lucky I am to be in the position I am in today. Just how kind people can be continues to surprise me, especially towards those less fortunate than themselves. There are so many more people that are in a worse place than me right now and I will eventually show my gratitude in the future in some small way.

Monday 11th March

I will be off work for a few days until my wound heals, but I am keeping busy all the same. My friend Barrie Gould came to see me and we spent some time ripping each other apart with our usual dark banter but it cheered me up. Barrie tends to make intuitive visits from time to time. I think that is a trait that I share with him.

Thursday 14th March
I had my stitches out and had a welcome visit from Duncan, a colleague and friend. He came to see how I was recovering and, just like Barrie, we spent time laughing and joking with each other with a bit of work chat thrown in. I have not returned to work since my operation because I am not allowed to drive. But I have been able to work from home. Tomorrow I will be able to drive again, so it's back to work full time. March ended without anything major happening and we spent the Easter weekend with family.

Thursday 4th April
We stayed the night with our friends Penny and Les in Sturminster Newton, Dorset, before moving on to where we usually stay in Dorchester, the Royal Yeoman, as tomorrow I am having my first pacemaker check-up in Dorchester Hospital. Chris used to work with Penny at the local butchers/deli in the village when we lived in Sturminster a couple of years ago. I don't know Leslie very well but he seems like a very nice guy. Penny is a bubbly, blonde lady who used to be a teacher back in Berkshire until she met Leslie. Before too long they decided that they both wanted to get away from their hectic suburban existence to live the rural life in Dorset. We arrived quite late so we only had a couple of hours with them before we turned in for the night but it was great to catch up.

Friday 5th April
After breakfast, we said goodbye to our hosts and made our way to Dorchester Hospital for my 11.15 am appointment at the Cardiology Department, where the technician wired me up to a machine. He told me that he was about to test the Pacemaker and I may feel my heart alternately slowing down and racing. I felt like I was some sort of robot as I experienced some weird sensations. Everything was good, any adjustments that had to be made were made and I was free to go. We dropped our bags

off at the Royal Yeoman. We had a brief chat with Sue and Gary before spending the rest of the afternoon in Weymouth.

Saturday 6th April

Today we were off to visit another one of our favourite places, Sidmouth in Devon. It is only 50 minutes from Dorchester by car. We stopped on the way at the famous Otter Nurseries for a spot of lunch. We seem to do the same thing every time we visit Sidmouth and today was no exception. We parked the car. And walked into the town, meandering our way through side streets and the clock shop before walking along the seafront just to take in the beautiful view of the Jurassic coastline, its red cliffs standing proud against the sea below. We had a cup of tea in one of the numerous quaint cafes, then made our way to Topsham where I managed to acquire yet another Russell Flint print, The Sunlit Bastion, at the antique warehouse on the estuary, followed by a brief visit to Darts Farm before heading back to our digs. We had another nice chat and pot of tea with Sue and Gary before setting off again for an early dinner at the Saxon Arms.

11 Pete

Pete's bad news

Pete Small

Sunday 7th April 2013
We left Dorchester after breakfast. On our way home, we called in to see Damian and his family in Bournemouth. He invited us out for a light lunch at the Harbour Heights Hotel, a delightful art deco establishment perched on a hill overlooking the Bournemouth coastline. Nicola and Scarlett also joined us. This visit was the end of our short break away, which was perfect apart from one thing. As we all took a stroll along the beach after lunch my mobile phone rang. I took it out of my pocket and looked to see who it was. It was Peter Small. I hesitated for a second before answering.

When I did and before I could say any more than, *"Hi Pete"*,

Pete said,

"It's come back!"

My blood ran cold before I replied, *"What has?"* It was a stupid thing to say because I already knew the answer. He then confirmed what I already knew.

"The leukaemia," he said, *"My platelets are low."*

I replied, *"I am so sorry to hear that Pete."*

What I was really thinking of at that moment was myself. Will it happen to me again? If it has happened to Pete, maybe it will happen to me after doing so well. Good job I have a 70% match for a bone marrow transplant. Is 70% enough? Will I survive the treatment? For pity's sake life, give me a fucking break. All of these thoughts rushed through my mind in an instant before I stopped being selfish and began thinking of Pete again and his bad news.

I then said to him, *"Don't worry too much Pete, they will sort it. Keep your chin up and keep me posted. Ring me anytime night or day if you want to talk, but let me know how you get on."*

Pete seemed to be somewhat reassured and grateful that someone was sharing his dreadful news. Cancer can be so generous with its punishment I thought. No matter how positive you are, the reminder of a possible relapse is always at the back of your mind but you just have to deal with it when it emerges, don't you? Poor Pete, he needed to share this news with as many caring friends as possible. He needs all our best wishes, compassion and support and of course I was here to give it as always.

After I finished the call, Chris must have noticed that I was shaken up and said, *"What's up? Who was that?"*

I told her it was Pete and his news. She looked just as shocked and deflated as I did. We said no more about it and continued our walk in relative silence. Damian and his family were blissfully unaware of what had just taken place. I could not get Pete's current unfortunate situation out of my mind and it has knocked my confidence for six. It felt like I had to start all over again regarding being optimistic and positive. But if I had to, I would. And I will. We eventually said goodbye to my family and made our way home.

Although Chris and I didn't say any more about Pete's situation, we both had to rethink and rebuild our own confidence regarding my health situation after hearing his news, even though my health is now good. When you hear such unexpected negative news that could affect you personally, your own recovery process seems to take a knock. This is obviously something new that I must deal with head on from now on. It brings me back to the physiological care of people who have suffered life-threatening illnesses or traumas. And that includes their close family. They go through it as well. Don't they?

I know we all handle good and bad news in different ways. I know cancer comes in many forms and patients react to treatment in different ways. I understand that trauma is relative to the individual and recovery periods vary. But whoever you are and whatever your trauma may be, you still have to pick yourself up and dust yourself down occasionally, don't you? That can be hard to do, even harder if you are alone and especially if your recovery period is lengthy. It does not matter how tough you think you are, everyone takes a serious knock sometime or other in their lifetime. It's how you react to it that counts. That's what I believe anyway. If you are lucky you will have a very supportive family or friend, or even your peers could be enough. But it all begins with yourself. And you should never have to go through cancer or any other serious trauma alone.

Wednesday 10th April

Today is my outpatient hospital visit to see Doctor Louise, at 3.30 pm. I have been a bit on edge ever since Pete gave me his news last weekend. But I am dealing with it. I had my bloods done. Then I had a meeting with Susan. Just to go through some balanced low energy daily meal advice. After that, it was verdict time again with Doctor Louise and yet again I need not have worried, as she said that my blood results were good.

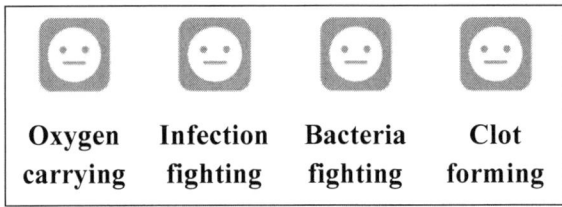

Now I do not have to go back for four months. Which was great news.

To celebrate the occasion, as soon as we got home I booked tickets to see The Bolshoi Ballet company perform Swan Lake at The Royal Opera House in Covent Garden on Saturday 10th August 2013. The rest of April passed by without any personal problems. Although on the world stage in America on the 15th April, the Boston Marathon became the victim of a terrible homemade bomb attack by two terrorists, killing three people: an eight-year-old boy and two women. They were both in their twenties and later a police officer was shot. He was also in his twenties. Twenty-six other innocent people were also injured. I mention this because it is these sorts of tragedies that bring me back down to earth and realise just how lucky I am. I seem to have a more genuine empathy towards other people's suffering these days.

Visiting Pete

Sunday 5th May
We had decided to take a trip to London today, as tomorrow is a bank holiday. We thought we would break up the weekend by going to Covent Garden. We had breakfast at Pauls Patisserie in Bedford Street, followed by a walk through to Leicester Square, then onto a bus to Knightsbridge, where we did our usual thing and bought a posh sandwich in Harrods to eat over the road in a coffee shop. We then had an interesting stroll around the Natural History Museum. We were having a fabulous time when my mobile phone rang in the afternoon. It was Pete Small. Before answering the call, I said to Chris, it's Pete. We were both hesitant. I eventually answered the call. We were walking back past Harrods at the time with the intention of finishing our London tour with a spot of early dinner in the Hawksmoor Grill in Air Street, near Leicester Square, prior to heading off home.

Before I could say anything to him apart from *"Hello Pete, how are you?"*, he said *"I am in hospital now. I was admitted on the 23rd April."*

His voice sounded shaky. I sensed his fear on the other end of the phone. He sounded desperate, afraid. He wanted some reassurance but how could I do that over the phone? An eerie silence seemed to come over me, even though the London traffic about me was as busy as ever. I felt like I was shut in a soundproofed room.

I answered, *"Are you in Onslow Ward?"*

"Yes, I am."

"Okay. I will come to see you now."

He seemed to be happy with my reply and I told him that I would be with him as soon as I could. I then finished the call and said to Chris who had already guessed what was happening.

"I think I should go and see Pete now, is that ok with you?"

There was no objection from Chris, only support to whatever we did next. So off we went by train to Osterley where we picked up our car. Then onto the M4, M3 and A3 to Guildford Hospital.

We arrived about 6.00 pm. Chris said that she would wait for me in the coffee shop at the main entrance while I went to see Pete. I walked into the ward. For some reason, it made me feel uneasy, as if I was back as an inpatient myself. I turned to my right where the reception area was. Sister Carol was there and seemed to be expecting me. Maybe Pete had told her that I was on my way. She told me what room he was in.

Before I entered Pete's room, I peeked through the window of the door just to see what I might be letting myself in for. This reminded me of the day back in September 2011 when our roles were reversed and Pete came to see me and nervously looked through the window in the door of *my* room.

> Right now, it is a strange unsettling feeling that I am experiencing. I am nervous. I must not let Pete see the fear in my face when I walk through the door to his room.

He was sat up in bed. There was a bowl of semolina on the tray over his bed, which looked very unappetising. I tried to put on a happy face. I didn't ask how he was.

I just said, *"Hello mate"* and remarked on how nice the room layout was and waited to see how he would react to me being there.

Then he said, *"You look good mate."*

"So do you. How do you feel?"

He answered, *"Not too bad"*.

He went on to say that he and his wife were going away as soon as he could get out. He told me that he was on a course of injections. Then came the words any cancer patient does not ever want to hear.

"I think I have got four months," he said. There was a fatalistic recognition in his voice now.

"The injections just keep the leukaemia at bay. They have not told me exactly how long I have got left."

At that point, he must have noticed my shocked expression. The fear that I could no longer hide was written all over my face as I felt my blood run cold. Without warning, he grasped my hand with both of his and said in a shaky voice, full of emotion, *"Whatever you do, don't overdo it."*

Now it was my turn to hold back tears, as I answered him, almost in a whisper. *"You will be okay mate and no, I will not overdo it."*

He didn't seem to want to let go of my hand. His eyes were firmly fixed on mine. It seemed as if we were as one, locked together in body and soul just for that moment in time. I waited until he loosened his grip before I spoke again. I didn't know what to say. He looked ill. His face was full of fear. He looked very frail.

Eventually, I said, *"Don't give up mate, you never know."*

I couldn't find any appropriate words that would help his

situation as I was still in a state of shock myself. His eyes fell on me again as I sat there beside him, our hands once again firmly gripped together. There was now an uneasy silence as I searched my mind for the right thing to say. But how could I? I was in a way confronted with my own possible destiny. It was like looking and talking into a mirror to myself, searching for the answer that would prolong my own life. Then a nurse walked in on her drug round. I stayed for a short while after she left – I don't know for how long – before we said goodbye to each other.

I walked out of the ward, past reception where Carol the ward sister was sitting. She looked at me and smiled knowingly. I had to force myself to smile back at her. I could not stop and speak to her like I normally would. I just walked out of the ward as quickly as I could. I was still numb with shock and disbelief. I had just experienced the reality of my own fears in Peter's unfortunate and final diagnosis. But I felt as if my body was still attached to Pete's bed by a strong elastic band that kept dragging me back to his bedside.

I rejoined Chris in the hospital cafe. She suggested that I take a seat while she fetched me a cup of coffee. It must have been obvious to her that I was a bit shaken up, although I thought I disguised my feelings quite well.

She arrived back with the coffee, sat down and said, *"How's Pete?"*

I just said, *"He told me he thinks he has got four months, he doesn't know for sure though."*

She didn't say anything else, neither did I. I thought that this was yet another new and unpleasant experience we both had to go through. I finished my coffee and we headed home.

As you can imagine, Mr Diary, Pete's news did knock me

sideways. But it didn't take me too long to readjust and get on with the business of normal healthy living again. What choice do I have? What's the alternative? I know how lucky I am to have a positive prognosis. But hearing sad news such as Pete's doesn't make it any easier. You must accept and deal with every negative situation that comes your way. Life goes on. Life is too short. Don't I know it.

Friday 10th May
I popped into my travel agent and bought some euros for a holiday in Tenerife for 10 days at the end of the month. My work was also keeping me fully occupied and stopping me dwelling on any depressing stuff that occasionally finds its way into my thoughts. Everything seems to be running smoothly and I even watched some of the Eurovision Song Contest on Saturday 18th, only because I enjoy Terry Wogan's commentary. He laughs with us about the usual unbelievable farce that unfolds before our eyes. And this year was no different. It took place in Malmo in Sweden and was won by Denmark with 281 points for a quite catchy tune. Unfortunately, our UK entry from the mighty Bonnie Tyler managed only 23 points. Oh well, it's only a bit of fun.

Tuesday 28th May
I just cannot get away from bad news can I, Mr Diary? It's just three days before Chris and I go on holiday and my brother has just telephoned me to tell me that his wife Christine has passed away. I have not mentioned this much before, but she has been suffering from cancer herself for some time. The last time we met up was last November 2012.

> It was the night before we were going away to Tenerife and we were staying at my sister's house near Gatwick. She lets us stay at her place when we fly from there. Her husband Geoff drops us off at the airport and picks us

up when we return.

My sister had arranged for my brother and his wife Christine to join us for a family get together and a spot of dinner. This was a great idea, bearing in mind that both Christine and I had been poorly. Unfortunately, she was still going through treatment. We all enjoyed the evening, although I noticed the same sort of fear in Christine's voice, as I did when I last saw Pete just a few weeks ago. As they left I found myself saying something like, *"Don't worry too much, I hope you will get better soon,"* and she replied. *"No, I won't, I am not going to get better."* There it is again. That same fatalistic recognition, something I hope I never have to resign myself to.

Anyway, that was the last time I saw her.

Thursday 30th May
We were staying at my sister's again near Gatwick. It was the night before we flew to Tenerife. She prepared a nice meal as usual. We did talk about poor Christine and how my brother would cope now that he was a widower. Her funeral was to be Friday 7th June. The day we were flying back. Unfortunately, we would be too late to attend. We had an early night as we were to be at the airport by 4.00 am the next morning. Poor Geoff, my sister's husband, had to rise early and take us, but he did not seem to mind.

Friday 31st May to Friday 7th June
We are off! We had checked our baggage in the previous evening, so we headed straight to Security where I had to show my pacemaker card. I also had to have a separate search as I am not allowed to go through the normal security screen. This was another first for me, but it went smoothly enough. We made our way to Pret a Manger for our usual 5.00 am breakfast. Our flight

was good. We arrived at our hotel, the Vulcano, in Playa das Americas. We were given a nice room on a high floor, but not much of a view. But hey, we were not going to be staying in our room all day, were we? The weather was great. The sun was shining and it was constant 27 degrees for most of our stay.

We both did our best to enjoy our week away and forget all the bad news that went before.

The local church

We know the island well. We have regular places that we go to, including a lovely seashore walk from our hotel in Playa das Americas to Los Cristianos. I also visited the church in the town square. I went inside and thanked God for allowing me to still be here, alive and in such good health too, just as I did back in April last year, in St Paul's Church in Covent Garden.

When I am away on holiday or on a day out enjoying myself and there is a church in the vicinity, I will always make the effort to go inside look around and give thanks for my very existence, I will even pray for others. *Why not*? That's another positive that has emerged from within me since I was given the all clear. I am not sure what you call it - spiritual faith, a sense of well-being, gratitude, religion - but I feel better for having it whatever it is. I am more at peace with myself these days.

The week went far too quickly for our liking and before we knew it we were back on the plane and landing at Gatwick where my sister and brother-in-law were waiting to take us back to their home where we had left our car. We went inside for a cup of tea and had a brief chat about how Christine's funeral went and how sad it was. Then we left for home which was just over an hour away. When we arrived, we unpacked and Chris was busy as usual with washing as tomorrow she is off to London to see the show Mama Mia with Hayley and Angela - an early 60th birthday present.

Saturday 8th June
Hayley and Angela arrived early and I dropped the three of them off at Bracknell station. I love these sorts of days. I knew the Mrs was going to enjoy herself and it entitled me to do the same, usually watching some sport on TV and flicking from programme to programme at my leisure. I eat chocolate and one thing I sometimes do when on my own at home for the day is watch old movies, like Seven Brides for Seven Brothers, South Pacific, or Lawrence Olivier and Merle Oberon in the classic black and white film Wuthering Heights. Usually one after the other. Normally I would have a good cry, which I did on this occasion also and I enjoyed every minute of it, especially whilst scoffing chocolate and crisps. I know shouldn't do that but I was having an indulgence day. So, while the cat was away... I picked the girls up at about 9.30 pm. They were all in good spirits and said that they had a fabulous time and the show was great. They

ate at an Italian restaurant in Soho and had a few cocktails that's for sure.

Thursday 13th June

After a busy day at work, Chris and I settled down after dinner to watch some television when I received a call from a number I did not recognise. I answered. It was a lady's voice. Quietly spoken.

She said. *"Hello Terry, I am Emilie, Pete Small's daughter".*

I knew what was coming, but I did not know how I would react. She went on to say in a very timid voice. *"Dad has passed away. He died at home on Sunday 9th June 2013. It was his wish that you would be invited to his funeral."*

I was almost speechless. I didn't know what to say. I couldn't think straight, but I had to say something.

So, I replied with the obvious, *"I am so sorry to hear that Emilie. Just let me know when the funeral is and if I can I will be there. Please give my love to your mum and family."*

With that she said goodbye and within fifteen minutes she had texted me the funeral details.

What can I say, Mr Diary? You can only imagine how I was feeling. Guilty. Shocked. Sad. Alone. Except I was not alone. Chris was almost as shocked as I was. She had overheard my conversation with Emilie. She didn't ask any questions. She was just waiting to see what I was going to say first.

I just said, *"That was Pete Small's daughter. Pete has passed away."*

Chris looked at me with a concerned expression on her face and said. *"Oh no, poor Pete. Was he at home or in hospital?"*

I replied, *"It was his wish to be at home."*

Unfortunately, we were going to be away on the day of Pete's funeral on Monday 24th June. To be honest, I am not sure that I could have faced it, but I would have gone if we were not away at the time. I think that when my time comes and I have a choice, I would want to be at home also, but not yet, not for many years to come, I hope. Poor Pete. Rest in peace mate, I will miss you. I didn't feel any sort of closure when Emilie told me that Pete had died. I thought I would but I didn't and that worried me.

On a much lighter note, on Thursday 20th June it was Christine's 60th Birthday. The family held a celebration dinner for her at her favourite restaurant, the Weybridge Brewhouse in Swindon. It was a total success and she loved every minute of it. Life goes on, doesn't it?

Christine's 60th Birthday day and my poem to her

Sometimes just by chance a priceless treasure
can be found
That was before thought myth
A mortal man should not gaze but withdraw
from his discovery forthwith
But when this treasure lives and breathes
With eyes that shine like gemstones resting
upon freshly fallen snow
There is nowhere to run, nowhere to hide,
nowhere for him to go
I am the mortal who found you, this treasure
thought lost for all time
and though I could never be worthy, will you,
be my, life's valentine

Terry Barry

For the remainder of June 2013, I concentrated as best I could on work. We were away for the last week of the month, although on the day of Pete's funeral at 2.45 pm, I did have a moment to myself and said a quiet prayer for Pete.

12 Fully engaging with life again

Cancer free for 680 days

July 2013
I have given Mr Diary most of the month off, as not much has happened out of the ordinary. This is helping me to concentrate on my future to remain healthy and happy for a very long time, or until I get ushered through the pearly gates by whoever is on duty at the time. I do on the odd occasion still reflect on my health situation. The current positives are that I have gone from four-weekly hospital outpatient visits to four-monthly visits.

This has given me a fantastic psychological boost. Although I still cannot get used to the occasional news of people that I know, mainly of similar age or older, becoming ill or worse without it affecting me. More reason to look after myself and enjoy life to the full. Everyone gets old if they are lucky. It's the ones that don't that I feel sorry for.

Before my illness, other people's bad news, health or otherwise didn't affect me as much as it seems to do now. I seem to feel other people's suffering almost as if it was my own. But I am as well as I could possibly wish for. I am getting stronger and stronger as each day passes, as I constantly keep reminding myself.

So, that's it as far as July is concerned. I enjoyed watching Scotland's Andy Murray win Wimbledon, which is great for British tennis. Perhaps the All England Club ought to consider changing its name to the All British Tennis Club from now on, who knows, it's just a thought. Same-sex marriage has been made legal in England and Wales, and the Duchess of Cambridge has given birth to a little boy.

> Oh, and by the way, I have been *cancer free* for **six hundred and fifty days.** That means I only have another **one thousand one hundred and seventy-five** days to go before my five years are up and, as far as the NHS is concerned, I am cured and unremarkable. Or only **one hundred and sixty-seven weeks** or **three and a quarter years.** Not that I am counting.

Our belated visit to the Hawksmoor

Saturday 10th August 2013

Today was our day of culture. We went to see the Bolshoi Ballet Company perform Swan Lake at the Royal Opera House in Covent Garden. We chose the matinee performance, which gave us time to have our usual coffee and cake and a stroll around Soho before the show. The performance was just as we expected, sensational. My favourite scenes were the Entrance of the Swans with Odette, and the Dance of the Cygnets. The ballerinas danced their way through their wonderful routines in perfect unison, with precision and grace. I am getting so cultured these days, what with ballet and supporting West Ham United FC.

We ended our day by having an early supper at the Hawksmoor Grill in Air Street just off Regent Street. This is the restaurant where we were supposed to go last time we were in London back in May, the day that I received the phone call from Pete Small telling me that he was back in hospital.

This time there was no sad or bad news. We were finally there and we enjoyed a fabulous meal. Afterwards, I sat back in my comfortable chair, just to take in the beautiful art deco surroundings whilst sipping my favourite cocktail. My mind drifted back to that dreadful day in May. I began to think of Pete and my sister-in-law Chris, who were no longer here to enjoy days such as this. Not for the first time, I realised how fortunate I was just to be here alive and well. But how guilty I felt for being able to enjoy this lovely day. We toasted their memory and our future just the same.

Wednesday 14th August   Blood Test

Clinic day today with my haematologist, Doctor Louise. This time I went on my own for the first time since my first outpatient appointment back in November 2011, a sign that Chris and I are becoming more confident of my full recovery. I still get the jitters sitting in the anteroom waiting for the doctor to appear, but apart from that, I am getting used to these visits. Sure enough, Doctor Louise confirmed that everything was fine and she thought that I was looking very well. Bloods were:

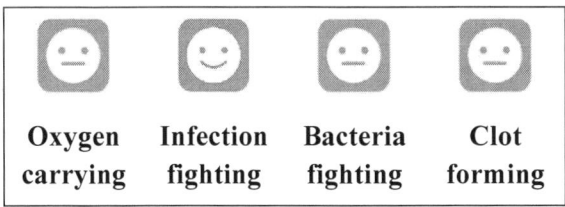

| Oxygen carrying | Infection fighting | Bacteria fighting | Clot forming |

"See you again in another four months, just before Christmas."

On Thursday 15th, I had another outpatient appointment with my new consultant cardiologist at Frimley Park, Doctor Faircloth. He had a nice bedside manner, which is what I prefer in a doctor. He was friendly, straight talking and confident. He seemed to be happy with everything. I did ask him reluctantly if my life expectancy had changed due to my heart condition, he said, *"Maybe a year or so, no more than that if any at all."* With that reassurance, I left happy with the thought that I was in safe hands regarding my ticker care.

In September, I had my annual visit to my brother's golf club, in the grounds of Hever Castle, which used to be the home of Anne Boleyn's family. It was the members' men's invitation day on 21st September. We had entered this two-man team event for the past 10 years apart from the last two years when I was not fit enough to take part. This year my brother had not played any golf due to the recent loss of his wife to cancer. He just didn't want to play. Who can blame him? So, I suppose it was good for both of us to take part in an event that we had always enjoyed and shared some success with in the past. It has always been a fantastic day out and this year was no exception.

We didn't win the tournament due to both of us playing rubbish. Although I did win nearest the pin on the 6th, which gave us both a lift. As did the general comments from other players, which were sympathetic both to my illness and my brother's recent loss, as well as being complimentary towards our golf on the day. People can be so kind and thoughtful sometimes. I have noticed this increasingly lately.

Nothing much happened in October either, apart from taking out more travel insurance to cover my medical conditions for Tenerife in November.

Thursday 7th November 2013
My first Pacemaker 'Pacing' appointment at Frimley Park Hospital. A pacing machine checks that the three leads attached to the valves of my heart are functioning properly. As I walked up to the entrance I glanced over to the small wall that I ended

up sitting on to phone and tell Chris that I had leukaemia all that time ago in June 2011. I shuddered at the thought but carried on without a second glance. The clinic was fine. I didn't have the same apprehension that I still experience every time I visit the Leukaemia Clinic. The technician wired me up to a machine. I felt my heart slowing and quickening as he put the pacemaker through its six-monthly MOT. Everything was okay. It was working fine and no changes had to be made. Great stuff.

Saturday 9th November

We are off again to Tenerife. This time, I booked the airline myself and we are staying at a friend's apartment in Los Cristianos for ten nights. We stayed again at my sister's near Gatwick the night before flying. We had a fine meal and chat before we all decided to have an early night, as Geoff was dropping us off at the airport at 4.30 am. We had already checked in our bags the night before, so it was straight to the security gates. I had to show my Pacemaker card again with one hand, while trying to hold up my beltless trousers with the other, no mean feat.

We arrived in Tenerife at about 11.30 am and purchased our bono card. This gives you reduced public transport fares and is something I recommend to all Tenerife visitors who wish to use the service. After we unpacked, we went off to get some provisions at the local supermarket. Then it was down to the seafront to have an ice-cold beer for one euro at Scratchy Balls bar.

Neither of us drink much, but as it was over 25 degrees and sunny every day, we thought we would indulge ourselves and we did every day while we were there. We were also lucky enough to see Canarian Traditional Folk dancers perform in the square down by the seafront on two occasions.

It was fabulous, as was the whole holiday. I thanked the

Almighty again in the local church in Los Cristianos after mass, on one of the Sundays we were there. This is still a regular pilgrimage for me whenever I am away. I am still grateful to be able to experience the good things in life that are all around me. I still remind myself each day that I am getting stronger, healthier and happier. There are the odd health niggles but I think that comes with age as I mentioned earlier. Providing you have a reasonable diet and get regular exercise I don't know what else you can do. Although I am still working on improving both.

Can you read my thoughts?

Tuesday 19th November to 30th November
After our fantastic winter break in the sun, we were both back at work from the 19th and straight back into the swing of things at home. I was already thinking about our family Christmas cottage holiday. But for now, I needed to focus on work and paying the bills. So, that's what we were both doing. November was over before we knew it. That's the beauty of going away late in the year. You get a bit of sun on your back and when you finally get home you are already thinking about Christmas trees and holidays again. Chris had already bought the family presents, probably back in the summer.

We both are last-minute shoppers as far as buying each other's presents are concerned. Probably because neither of us can ever get the other to decide on what they want. I tell Chris I am happy with socks or slippers, but she usually wants to wait until the New Year sales. Her logic is that there are more bargains then. Why is it that bargain buying always results in spending more than you normally would?

December 2013.
I thought it was worth a mention that the great Nelson Mandela passed away on the 5th and on the 9th I had to go into hospital for a biopsy. I had been having a bit of stomach trouble but it all turned out to be okay. It is important to me that I have potential health problems investigated sooner rather than later. This is another thing that I have learnt. Don't be backwards in coming forwards as far as your health is concerned. Especially at my age and with my recent health history. It is just not worth it. So, best nip any medical problem in the bud.

Wednesday 18th December   Blood Test
It is my leukaemia clinic day today with Doctor Louise and I came bearing gifts of Beauchene red wine and Christmas cards for various nurses, Susan the dietitian, Doctor Louise and tins of

chocolates for the Onslow Ward reception. My first appointment was with Susan. She has always been so thorough and today was no exception. She weighed me 95.6 kg, ouch! I had better become organised regarding my diet. Then I saw Doctor Louise who seemed happy with my blood test:

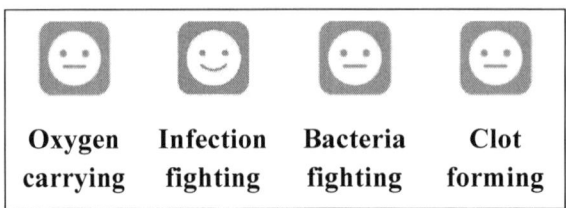

| Oxygen carrying | Infection fighting | Bacteria fighting | Clot forming |

She wished me a happy Christmas and even kissed me on the cheek! I am honoured. Then off I went to begin mine; as from today my holiday began in earnest.

Christmas in Paradise

Monday 23rd December
We were off to our holiday cottage for our family Christmas vacation. I had been looking forward to this ever since Hayley booked it early this year. The cottage/farmhouse is called Tidicombe House. It is near Barnstaple and Arlington in Devon and just five miles from the sea.

Tidicombe House: the calm before the storm

There would be ten of us again this year. We were the first to arrive with Hayley's family and the rest of the family are arriving Christmas Eve.

We unpacked our presents, put away the food and then I explored the cottage. It had a log fire in the lounge already lit. The Christmas decorations were up. There were some fantastic views of the five acres that surround the cottage. The only thing was, when we went for a walk we had to pass a farmyard just a few metres from the house.

Young Oliver pointed to an object just inside the farm gate and said, *"What's that?"*

To our horror, lying on the ground, were two dead and bloated cows. We couldn't believe our eyes! They looked like giant toy animals. Maybe that's the countryside for you. We quickly ushered the children away from the corpses and told them that the cows were not real. I thought that perhaps I should have a word with the farmer but there was no one around to speak to at the time. And there were other more pressing things on my mind, such as having a good time. Later, back at the cottage, we explored the rest of house, had some dinner and settled down in the lounge in front of the log fire to relax for the rest of the evening before the family onslaught the following day.

Tuesday 24th December   Christmas Eve

One by one, the family arrived, laden with Christmas presents, food and drink. The ladies went off to Barnstaple for some last-minute food shopping while us men folk looked after the children and, just as the last time we went away for Christmas as a family, we all had certain roles to play. My main role was to feed the flames with plenty of thick dry logs. Joe, Hayley's husband, oversaw Christmas present distribution. Darren, Christine's son was the drink replenisher, with Joe's help. The ladies oversaw the food and dinner prep and cooking, and the children just helped make the whole Christmas experience wonderful.

> There is no better feeling as far as I am concerned than right now. It's about 9.30 pm. We are all in the lounge. The fire is blazing. The lights are down. The reflection from the flames of the fire are once again casting long shadows on everyone's happy faces. We all have a drink in our hand. We are all relaxing. The presents are under the Christmas tree. The children have put mince pies and milk out for Father Christmas and carrots for his reindeer. They are now in bed, fast asleep, dreaming of the following day.
>
> I am now sitting in an armchair watching everyone as they smile, laugh and chat amongst themselves. Now their voices are just an echo. My eyes are

becoming misty as I again experience that very happy/sad cathartic contented feeling. I lean forward just to let my face capture a little more of the gentle heat from the receding flames, then lean back into my comfortable chair. What more could anyone want or wish for than a gathering such as this? At a time, such as this. With people, such as this. I don't want these happy times to end. I know they will one day, but not yet. Please God not yet.

Wednesday 25th December 2013   Christmas Day.

The children were awake very early, I could hear them unwrapping their stocking presents that have been left by Father Christmas outside their bedroom door in the early hours, which they did in the privacy of their respective parent's bedrooms. It reminded me of my own children doing the same thing when they were young. Then everyone made their way downstairs to get organised for breakfast. Merry Christmas greetings, kisses and cuddles were exchanged countless times. Joe and Darren made sure all the adults never had an empty glass of bubbly or bucks fizz. The ladies - Chris, Hayley, Angela and granny Marion - prepared the breakfast.

We raised our glasses and toasted each other, *"Merry Christmas to one and all."* Then, after a fine breakfast of scrambled eggs, smoked salmon and lashings of champagne, we all made our way into the lounge to relax. I threw some more logs on the fire that I had already lit before breakfast. There were mountains of seasonally wrapped gifts under the Christmas tree for everyone. The children - Oliver, Lucas and Daisy - were salivating at the thought of opening all the presents there and then, regardless of who they were for and as soon as possible. We decided to stagger the present opening. Some in the morning, some after lunch and some again after dinner, and that's what we did. It is a great system because there were just so many presents. Food and drink were in abundance all day. We are going to have the main event, Christmas dinner, on Boxing Day and everyone again would have a part to play.

It was brilliant, as was the rest of our five-day Christmas break. We arrived back home on the 28th December, which gave us time to adjust and get ready for work on the 2nd January 2014.

2014

This is the year of the Horse according to the Chinese Zodiac. I think the horse is deemed to have a higher ranking in society than me, a lowly pig. I disagree, but for now, I will let sleeping pigs lie.

My road to recovery has yet another year under its belt, although I have fallen into one or two emotional potholes along the way. Some were deeper than others and I am sure there are more to come. You can never fully prepare or see where and when the next pothole will appear. You must just be positive and hope that you do not fall into one. If you do, you have to find a way out of it as quickly as possible. Brush yourself down and carry on with your life's journey.

I still cannot read aloud what I have written in my diary over the last few years without choking up occasionally. Therefore, I realise that I still have some way to go before I am completely emotionally healed. But I will persevere until I am. I have already mentioned once before that your brain is a powerful tool, but it is also a fragile organ at times. Don't I know it.

Not much happened out of the ordinary for the first few months of this year as far as our lives were concerned. Chris and I just got on with things without any excitement or trauma. The world around us wasn't that exciting to us either. We had all experienced bad wet weather throughout January in the UK and someone who I had always admired passed away on the 14th March and that was Tony Benn the politician. In April, Pineau De Rae won the Grand National, Oxford won the boat race and David Moyes lost his job as Manager of Manchester Utd. Maybe he should have stayed at Everton.

Thursday 18th April 2014   Easter weekend

On the home front, I thought it was about time Chris and I had another short break. So I booked an overnight stay at The Royal Exeter Hotel in Bournemouth for £85 which included what turned out to be a fabulous breakfast. I also booked a meal in the hotel restaurant, called the 1812 for some reason, which was also a nice change. What made it better is that Chris had a discount card for the meal as well. Buy one get one free. She does love a bargain, but I am not complaining this time.

We made the most of the bank holiday weekend by staying with Damian and his family on Saturday. On Sunday we made our way to The Nelson pub in Mudeford for the best roast lunch carvery I have ever eaten. The chef is not the traditional English chef but a Thai gentleman called David. I know it's a bit boring for the reader when I go on about food, holidays and family visits and Christmas. Normal people doing normal things can be boring for normal people to read about. But please bear with me as I have not yet reached the dizzy heights of normality yet.

Wednesday 23rd April   Blood Test

It was my cancer clinic again today. After my bloods were taken I went to see Susan. She weighed me, 96.3 kg and my BMI is 30, whoops!! Still, that's one better than last time. Susan suggested once again that I must have a balanced diet. High in fibre to help reduce symptoms of diverticulosis, with which I have now been diagnosed. Also, my fluid intake should be about three litres per day. She suggested that at lunchtime I should include a bread roll and some protein. My evening meal should have low-fat content as far as protein choices are concerned. On top of that, I should make sure that I have at least 20 minutes of exercise per day. Whoops, I'm in trouble and I need to get back on track.

All of this is good advice of course. My problem is that I eat for comfort. When I am stressed I eat. When I am worried, I eat, and I don't only worry about myself, I worry about others too. Then I eat for them as well. But I know that is just an excuse for bad eating habits. I agree that a good diet with exercise is the way forward. For everyone, not just me. It's true that I sometimes eat the wrong things. Chris even hides sweets or chocolate from me. The other day I found crisps in a plastic bucket high up on a shelf in the utility room. It had a note in it saying, *"What are you looking for, piggy?"*. Well, I was born in the year of the Pig. I even found stock cubes recently hidden in a drawer in the lounge. I make a lot of homemade soup because it's healthy and occasionally I use various over-salted stock cubes. So, Chris's deterrent is to hide everything that she thinks is not good for me. And that includes salt.

I know she is doing this to stop me from overindulging and reduce the sugar and salt in my diet. But it she bought the stuff in the first place. Is this woman's logic? Next, it will be the remote control to the television hidden away in the loft. Or even the television itself, especially when sport is on. Anyway, I digress. I went for my appointment with Doctor Louise. I am still apprehensive and nervous while I am waiting for her in the anteroom, even though her news turns out to be good. I am okay and I do not have to go back for four months from now on. My blood results were:

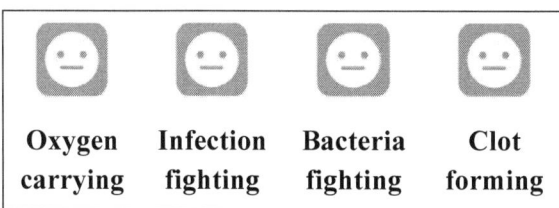

Doing my bit for a worthy cause

I have decided to do some charity work. There are so many worthy charities to choose from but I am going to start with the charity that my Company supports. It's called CLICSargent, a cancer Charity that provides vital emotional, practical and family support to young cancer patients during and after treatment. That will do for me. I had my bucket and pasting table. I will spend a few weekends outside Tesco and see what happens. I will also be abseiling down the Orbit at the Olympic Park in London on behalf of the charity, hopefully towards the end of July.

May 2014
May is my favourite month of the year. We went on holiday to the Hotel Molins in Cala San Vincente again. This time for ten nights from 16th to the 26th.

I know that we are still fortunate enough to be able to realise our dreams in some way. As I have said before, a visit to this place has always been a goal of mine. Especially when I feel a bit low; it's a heavenly place. We wake up every morning to the sound of the waves softly rolling into the tiny bay below us. We sit out on our balcony with an early wake-me-up cup of tea and take in the view. We then go down for breakfast (no queuing here) and Chris usually has champagne, fruit and there are all sorts of fresh bread. The chef will make you a hot breakfast to order while you wait. The same goes for your evening meal. There is always a selection of showcase cooking as well as a fantastic buffet selection. It's Paradise for us and I take advantage of most things that are on offer at breakfast and dinner, depending on how I feel at the time.

We are not ones for sitting around, so we either get a bus to Puerto Pollensa or walk over the small mountain range between the two resorts. It's a hilly pass really, but it makes us all feel better to refer to it as a mountain in conversation, especially if we have successfully climbed over it! We also visit Pollensa town every Sunday. Old Pollensa has its own local farmers market full of the best selection of fruit and veg you could ever wish to see. There are many arts and crafts stalls scattered about the narrow streets of this ancient town and we love it. This time we found a stall near one of the town squares that was full of interesting, old bric-a-brac. Chris had her eye on a pair of brightly covered majolica fish, which looked quite old. I noticed a man sitting in a chair reading a book behind his goods, taking no notice of his prospective clients standing before him. Then an elderly lady who was sitting with him eventually got up and came over to talk to us. I asked her how much she wanted for the fish. She pondered for a second and answered me in a broad Yorkshire accent, ten euros. She was a friendly sort and we got talking. She said that she and her partner left England eleven years ago, with no money as such and nowhere to live. They decided to move to Pollensa and they have been here ever since. They have no intention of returning to England as they love it here so much. All they do is buy and sell their wares on their market stall and just manage to make ends meet, but they are both very happy. Good for them. Not bad for people well into their 70s. Needless to say, we purchased the fishes. We forgot all our troubles while being on this holiday. We even walked from Puerto Pollensa to Port de Alcudia on one occasion; that's about 5.4 miles. I couldn't have done that last time we were here in 2012, so there's progress.

Abseiling the Orbit

June, July, August and September 2014
I seem to be planning and doing more things, as normality has well and truly returned to our lives. On 12th June it was Jamie's little boy Brandon's 1st birthday. On Friday 13th June, I booked my charity event of abseiling down the ArcelorMittal Orbit at the Queen Elizabeth Olympic Park in London. It is 114.5 metres tall, that's 375 feet in old money, or 7874 inches in angling terms. I had already opened a Just Giving page and printed a leaflet explaining why I am taking part and who my chosen charity is. I'd also booked a couple more days at my local Tesco supermarket to promote my upcoming event. My t-shirt, pasting table and bucket were ready. We celebrated Christine's birthday on the 20th June and on Sunday 6th July, I watched Lewis Hamilton win the British Grand Prix for the second time.

Sunday 20th July
I was at Tesco today in Warfield, not shopping but raising money for CLIC Sargent. I arrived at 9.30 and set up, leaflets about my upcoming abseil attempt, who I am and why I am doing it before me. My bucket was strategically placed in the centre of my pasting table, which was covered in green baize. I was ready for action!

Bucket strategically placed

I thought I would stand to one side and avoid eye contact with would-be contributors, until they made eye contact with me. It seemed to work. It was not long before people started to put money in the bucket or just wandered over to talk to me. This amazed me. One lady came over and said that her elderly mother has terminal cancer but she did not know it yet. She was going to tell her that very afternoon. She was very upset and began to cry. I attempted to reassure her by offering her a cup of coffee and a chat inside. But she was okay. My offer seemed to help her situation. She sat on a chair beside me for a while and we chatted. She left me reasonably happy and stuck a fiver in the bucket.

Increasingly, people started to invite themselves over to talk to me. I enjoyed the attention. It's great when you can talk to people for long enough in this situation. You find out so much about them in a very short space of time, mainly by being patient and listening to what they had to say.

I learned that people really do like to get things off their chest if anything is troubling them. They just need the right opening and opportunity to do it without interruption. As the day continued, so did my confidence. I didn't want it to end! The banter seemed to be doing my benefactors as much good as their contributions were doing for me and my charity. People spoke about their up and coming treatment. Some were curious about my illness and many walked off reading my leaflet.

One who did this was an Eastern European lady until she turned and walked back up to me and said, *"Is this you on the front of this leaflet?"*

To which I replied, *"Yes, it is."*

She went to the cash machine and drew out £20 and put it into the bucket and wished me well. I remember thinking, *"I could do this full time!"* I seemed to be able to engage people without really trying. All I had to do was to be genuinely interested and listen to what everyone had to say, something that comes naturally to me anyway. The day ended at 4.00 pm and I hadn't even had time to eat or drink anything. When I arrived home and counted all the pennies I had collected over £200. *"Not a bad day's work,"* I thought.

Over the next few days, more donations came in from work and family and friends also chipped in. Even Beverley, my lovely skiing dentist, contributed. I had noticed that some people were reluctant to donate even though they were not pressurised by me. It makes you feel like you are begging sometimes even when you are not.

Thunderstorms delay my descent

Friday 25th July
Today was yet another big day for me. Chris, a colleague from work Ian, his wife Michelle and I are off to the Olympic Park in London. Ian is an amateur photographer and was interested in supporting me as well as photographing the event. They travelled up to London by car while Chris and I travelled to Stratford in East London by train.

We arrived at about 5.00 pm. I was not scheduled to abseil until 6.30 pm so we strolled through the Olympic Park. It was deserted, apart from a few people walking towards the Orbit itself, which we could see quite clearly not too far ahead of us. The closer we got to it, the more awesome it looked. I have been told that 60% of it is made from recycled steel including old washing machines and recycled cars. When you get to the top of the viewing platform where I am to descend from, I am told that you can see for 20 miles on a clear day. We went over to register with the lovely CLIC Sargent staff who informed us that there was a delay as they had to stop the event during the day.

There had been a few thunderstorms and they didn't wish to put anyone at risk. So, I was not due to descend before at least 8.00 pm when it would be nearly dusk.

The event safety team called me at 8.30 pm. They issued me with a helmet and thick gloves, then hooked me up to a multitude of straps before sending me up to the viewing platform in the lift. There was still a long wait ahead, but it gave me time to take in the fantastic view of London from dusk to dark. The view transformed before my eyes: London by day and London by night. I was also able to witness the Olympic stadium being dismantled below me to my right. I was interested, more so because the stadium is going to be the home of the football team I support, West Ham United. It was nearly 10.00 pm and I was getting very close to being called to the edge of the platform by the safety team.

The person abseiling just before me was a young lady. She looked very excited and happy, until the safety guy who was making sure she was well and truly strapped in said to her, *"Stand on the edge of the platform by your toes. Hold onto the rope and lean back straight"*.

Which was into thin air, with a drop of 376 feet to *terra firma*. You can only imagine how scary that must have been for her. But not a bit of it! She obeyed her instructions, leant back and she was off, still with a smile on her face. Now it was my turn. By the way, not everyone I saw descend was as fearless as that young lady. The safety guy asked my name and issued the same instructions.

He said whilst smiling, *"Terry you will be fine, we will make sure you get to the bottom safely."*

He obviously noticed that I was a bit apprehensive and, to be frank, when I stood on the edge and I started to lean back, I felt like chickening out. But it was too late. I was in mid-air and down I went. Sometimes slowly, sometimes quickly, and there was hardly any time to take in the view on the way as I spun around and bounced off the bright red tubes during my descent. I had hardly any strength left in my arms. I was struggling to catch my breath. Where had my strength gone? It was not until I was about a hundred feet from the ground that I looked down. I could see Ian taking photos.

"I finished the last twenty feet like a pro"

Then it became a lot easier and I finished the last twenty feet like a pro. When I landed, I must say I experienced the most amazing sense of pride and a genuine feeling of achievement. I had done it! No-one can take that away from me. Between the sixty of us that took part, we raised £30,000 for the children.

Job done, photos taken. Many thanks to Ian and his wife Michelle for supporting us on the day, for taking the photos of the abseil and for taking us home at nearly midnight. Thank you to everyone who donated on my Just Giving page and those people who put many pennies in my campaign bucket at work and outside Tesco's.

Reducing my hours

Friday 1st August   Blood Test

Today I signed a new contract with work. I was cutting down to four days per week and next year we hope to retire and move down to Dorset. Well, that's the plan. On Wednesday 20th August, it was my clinic day at Haematology. This time I saw a registrar, Doctor Jenny Bosworth. She was very friendly and happy to tell me that my bloods were good:

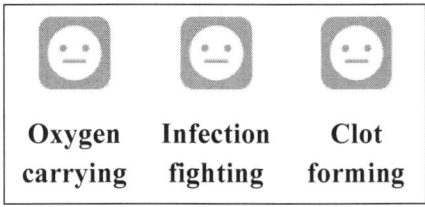

And as I had been in remission for nearly three years my next appointment would now be in six months' time. Whoopy! That gives us more time to think ahead and plan our lives without worrying about the next hospital appointment

On 23rd August, coming up to the Bank Holiday weekend, Chris and I went to the West End to see Les Miserables as a belated celebration of my 67th birthday. It was a fabulous show, emotionally draining and uplifting at the same time. I saw many a grown man cry during the performance. So, I thought it was all right to join in. Which I did unashamedly, while we were feeling sad. On the 24th August, yet another icon of mine, Sir Richard Attenborough, passed away aged 90.

October, November and December 2014   3 years cancer free

On the 17th October, I had been out of hospital for three years. There are just two more to go before I am considered *cured*. I am on the homeward stretch and although I can't quite see the finishing post, I know it's there and I can reach it. I have a new spring in my step and a more positive outlook now that I have got this far and to celebrate, we spent the weekend at Hayley and Joe's. Plus, we enjoyed a Sunday roast at the Weighbridge Brew House using some of the £2 coins that Chris has been saving up. We had our usual 10-night break in Tenerife in November, which was tiring getting there and back, but a welcome sunny winter break all the same.

When we returned home, I had a heart pacemaker appointment on Friday 21st November, but that was it for this year regarding hospital check-ups. Although I did pay a visit to the nurses and doctors on Onslow Ward to show my gratitude once again with a few Christmas goodies. Our Christmas holiday was a quiet affair at home and we invited my brother to stay for a few days over Christmas. Apart from that we just relaxed at home to the end of the year.

A New Year and my newfound strength

2015.

Welcome to 2015, the Chinese year of the Sheep. Quiet. Calm. Shy people by nature. I don't think I am a sheep person, do you, Mr Diary? There were to be occasions throughout this coming year that were life changing as far as my emotional health was concerned. They proved to be very difficult to deal with, but they gave me more confidence, inner strength and even a bit of extra courage that I thought I had lost since I was diagnosed with leukaemia.

The first involved a mate of mine, Barrie Gould. He had been diagnosed with prostate cancer sometime last year. I had been in touch with him from time to time and we used to meet on occasion for breakfast. I would keep our conversations brief when it came to mentioning how he was feeling or what treatment he was having at the time.

But this year was different. I spent more time phoning, texting and meeting up with him. I felt the need to spend time with him whenever I could or whenever he wanted to talk or meet up. I even encouraged him to talk more about how he was feeling, even though, as time went by, the more we talked the more I realised that his health was deteriorating.

It was strange. The more I reassured or empathised with him, the stronger I became mentally. I forgot my own vulnerability and concentrated on him whenever we made contact. I wanted him to get better as much as I wanted to get better myself. He used to say to me, *"You've done well." "You look good."* And I would reply, *"So, do you." "Just keep positive." "How are you feeling today?"* Stuff like that. I knew these were over-generalisations and it was easier said than done to be positive, but what can you do? I didn't want him to drop his head and give up. If he did, it would be difficult for me to be convincingly positive and to cheer him up because I was still vulnerable myself. I said to him during one conversation when he sounded very low, *"You are stronger than me mate, look at me now; if I can do it so can you."* I wanted to say anything that I thought could keep him in a positive frame of mind, just like anyone who knew him would do. I don't know whether my presence and encouragement helped him, I hope it did.

January, February, March, April and May 2015 Blood test

I am well and truly on the mend, mentally and physically. The first five months of the year just flew by without anything out of the ordinary happening, which is great news in its self. On February 25th, I attended my six-monthly leukaemia clinic. I was still a bit nervous while I was waiting in the anteroom listening to the doctor shuffling her notes or speaking to someone in her office. Yet again I needn't have worried. Everything was okay. My bloods were satisfactory. No, they were excellent! Wow!! Three blue smiley faces.

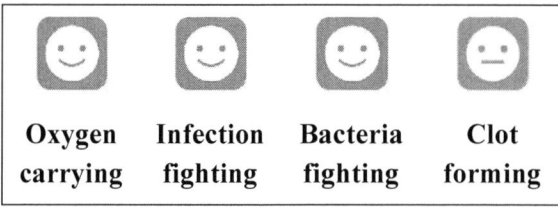

On the 7th March, Chris and I went to see The Phantom of the Opera in London. We always have a good time whenever we visit the city. The show was as good as ever, we'd seen it numerous times before. I did cry at the end, I always do. I felt sorry for the Phantom even though he was a murderer and kidnapper. Perhaps it was because he was alone, lonely and unhappy. Anyway, it's a fantastic bit of musical theatre that always manages to tug away at my heartstrings.

In May, we enjoyed ten days away in Tenerife and celebrated our wedding anniversary on our return. I am really enjoying life now. I feel happy, content and I am full of self-confidence. Almost superhuman. *Cancer? What cancer?!*

Finally retired

Friday 26th June

I have finally retired after fifty-three years of work. I don't know how long it will take before I get bored, because I have always worked, and worked hard.

I started my working life as a post boy in an office at Barry Staines Linoleum, 6 Old Bailey, London EC4. Nearly everyone that I knew managed to get a job in the city in the early sixties. White-collar jobs were plentiful. I think it was Alfred Marks employment bureau that helped me get the job. I remember my first day, Monday 3rd September 1962. It was exciting, yet daunting. I had only just turned fifteen. *Sherry* by the Four Seasons was top of the charts, and my favourites of the time, The Beatles, were about to release their first single, *Love Me Do*. America and Russia were on the brink of war. This was called the Cuban Missile Crisis. John F. Kennedy was also about to announce to the world that America would put a man on the moon before the end of the decade. Just a few weeks before this, in August, Nelson Mandela began a twenty-seven-year prison sentence, and a goddess of my time, Marilyn Monroe, died of an overdose. These were exciting times for an impressionable young boy like me, who was just about to join the world of the grown-ups.

Unbelievably, I remember clearly getting up very early that morning, to do my morning chores before going off to work. Every morning, I had to go to the local shops and buy the morning paper, then come home and make tea and toast for my parents, who were still upstairs in bed. I then had to clean out the ashes from the fire grate, leftover from the night before and prepare it for the coming day. Breakfast consisted of cornflakes or shredded wheat, accompanied by the cream from the top of the milk of at least three fresh bottles of gold top left by the milkman earlier. I used to take great care not to damage the bottle tops, as I removed the cream and replaced it with the ordinary milk.

It was always cold in our house early in the morning, regardless of the time of year, so I would light the gas oven, drop the oven door down and warm my feet while I ate. Then I remember getting changed into my newly acquired grey trousers with huge turn-ups, and a Prince of Wales check jacket, neither of which were chosen by me, and Hush Puppy shoes, which were. A white buttoned-down shirt and tie finished off my new attire. My parents paid for most of it with some help from money that I had earned on a milk round. When I was finally ready, I ran up the hill of Clock House Lane to catch the number 165 to Romford station, then the train to Liverpool Street and the underground to St Paul's. Once through the barriers, I remember stopping for a second to take in the awesome sight of St Paul's Cathedral to the right of me and staring at all the men in their bowler hats, while I munched on a Fry's Five Fruit Cream chocolate bar and a mouthful of Payne's Toffets that I had just purchased from the kiosk at the station entrance. I ran down Ludgate Hill, then right into Old Bailey (the street not the courts!) and into the offices of Barry Staines Linoleum to begin my adult working life.

Meeting Wally

I remember walking into the reception area where the receptionist smiled at me and asked, *"Can I help you?"*

I replied, *"I am Terry Barry."*

She looked shocked and then said, *"Are you the son?"*

I think I was temporarily lost for words. Was this my first working challenge to confirm that I was the son.

"I have come to start work. It's my first day. I have to report to Mr Wally Seaton."

With that, the still bemused receptionist directed me to the post room on the first floor where I met an elderly, regimental and rotund looking gentleman with a kind smiling face. He was frantically feeding envelopes of various sizes into a very noisy franking machine. I introduced myself.

"I am Terry Barry. I was told to report to you for work today. Alfred Marks recruitment sent me."

Wally stopped what he was doing for a moment and came over to me, shook my hand and put his arm around me in a reassuring way, which made me feel less nervous.

He said, *"I am Mr Wally Seaton. You can call me Wally."*

Almost immediately, Wally handed me a week's worth of luncheon vouchers. Then a lady came in with a trolley with a tea urn on it and handed me and Wally a welcome cuppa and some biscuits. I remember thinking to myself at the time, *"Blimey, if this is what working life is all about and they pay me for it as well, bring it on!"* And so, my working life began.

My first wage packet was five guineas per week, or five pounds fifty pence in new money. I had to hand five pounds of it to my parents, although they did let me keep the ten shillings a week or fifty pence in new money. I used to watch the comings and goings from the law courts at the top of the street. I remember seeing Christine Keeler and Mandy Rice Davis on many occasions during the Profumo Trial in 1963. I loved my first job. There is much more to tell about my teenage years, but it was a lifetime ago and a story for another book sometime. It will reveal what it was like for me growing up from the late 1940s to the young peoples' revolution of the 1960s.

But let's get back to the here and now and continue with the summer of 2015.

July, August and September 2015.

I spent some time in July talking to Sarah, the ward sister that looked after me when I was an inpatient. She, amongst others, was helping me edit and understand the medical side of my story which was partly their story as well. Sarah, Susan the dietitian, Jincy, Carol (another ward sister) and Doctor Louise were on hand to offer advice of how to translate the technical information into layman's terms so that we could all understand it. I also purchased my medical notes for £20.00; these covered all of my stay and outpatient notes for five years. I did attempt to acquire my notes from Frimley Park where I was a patient for a week but the process was more difficult and they wanted £50.00 for the privilege.

Breakfast with Barrie

Sunday 9th August
I hadn't heard from Barrie Gould for a while. I knew he was still having treatment and he had been in and out of hospital since last year.

I did visit him in hospital last December and we shared some caustic banter which always seemed to cheer him up no end. He used to cheer me up when I was in hospital and feeling low. I remember wheeling him around the hospital looking for a cafe, and wrecking the blinds opposite his bed when I was trying to cut out the sun, which was blinding him. It all helped him forget his illness for an hour or so before his wife Anne turned up. Then it was time to behave.

Anyway, I digress. I texted Barrie today just saying, *"How are you?"*

He replied after a while saying, *"Not good, I would like to be as fit as you."*

So, I rang him back and we had a brief chat. He sounded a bit down. I tried to cheer him up with some small talk but he just wasn't himself. Eventually, we arranged a breakfast date for Tuesday 18th August. I told him that I would pick him up at 9.30 am that day. I remember feeling somewhat troubled by Barrie's tone of voice during our conversation. He didn't sound himself, he sounded down. Who could blame him?

Tuesday 18th August
I drove to Barrie's home in Windsor to pick him up for our arranged breakfast date. He was waiting for me as I pulled up outside. We exchanged our usual good-humoured mutual abuse. Then off we went to one of his favourite greasy spoon cafes in

Cippenham, near Slough. He looked tired and unsteady on his legs. I offered him an arm for support which I thought he would not accept, but he did, gladly. We walked very slowly from my car to the cafe which was 200-300 yards away. This surprised me as Barrie was an independent sort of guy. A man's man, but there was no hesitation in accepting my arm that day.

During that slow walk, I realised how much Barrie's health had deteriorated. But once we sat down in the cafe he was his smiley self again. He said that he had never had such an appetite, as he munched his way through a massive fry up that included his favourite bubble and squeak. After our great value breakfast, I took him home. As I left him I could not help but think that his illness was beginning to get the better of him. There was nothing I could do about it except be there for him if ever he needed me. But he probably didn't, as he had fantastic support from his family and many friends. Barrie was a very popular, well-known and well-liked personality.

In a strange way, my friend's vulnerability and physical weakness somehow made me feel stronger and less vulnerable myself. Was this a selfish thought? Or was I truly and at last well again mentally?

Wednesday 26th August   Blood test

It was my six-monthly hospital visit again. Everything was fine. Blood results were:

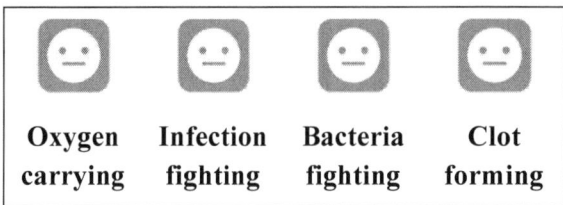

But I still get the jitters while I am waiting for my results.

Saying goodbye to my mate

Thursday 15th October
Today I phoned Barrie Gould's daughter, Denise. I had heard that Barrie had taken a turn for the worse and was now at home being surrounded by his family and being cared for by Macmillan nurses as it was only a matter of days. I telephoned Denise and asked her if I could go and see him and she kindly agreed. Chris came with me and sat in the car while I went inside after being greeted at the door by Denise.

I went into the lounge where Anne, Barrie's wife was sitting. She said that Barrie was just a few steps from the lounge in the dining room. I asked how he was.

Denise replied, *"They don't think he will last the weekend."*

I was shocked, sad, upset and sympathetic all at the same time. Denise walked with me part of the way to the dining room. Then stopped and let me make my way in to see him for one last time.

I was not prepared for what I saw. Barrie was asleep I think. He was in a hospital bed that had been provided for him. He looked peaceful, but his breathing was very shallow.

I leant over him and quietly said, *"Gouldy, it's me, TB."* I waited for a response, but there was none.

I tried again repeating the same words. Quietly. Sheepishly. I felt a bit self-conscious, I wondered whether Denise and Anne could hear me having this one-way conversation with Barrie. I felt a bit intrusive and secretive at the same time as I whispered stuff that Barrie and I used to laugh about when we were out together; it would probably mean nothing to his family, but I would usually get him to respond with a haughty laugh followed by a friendly retort. He lifted his arm up above his head at one point, but that was that. I started mumbling words. I can't remember what I said exactly. I didn't want anyone to hear me except him, I don't know why. I stayed for just a few minutes more before I thought it was time to leave him and his family in peace. I said *"Goodbye Gouldy"* under my breath, just in case he could hear me. I didn't want to upset him. It was very thoughtful and obliging of his family to let me see him just once more and I was so grateful. It was a heart-breaking thing to do and I will never forget it. I closed the door to the dining room and walked back into the lounge where Anne and Denise were standing looking at me pensively as I entered the room. They seemed apprehensive. They were standing side by side. They both seemed to be waiting for me to say something I thought. I don't know what I said exactly, except when I did try to speak as I walked towards them, I started to cry. I couldn't hold back. I apologised for my emotional outburst. Immediately they both took a step towards me and gave me a hug. Now we were all in tears. It was a welcome hug and I was grateful to receive it and I no longer felt intrusive. I sat beside them for a while. Then two Macmillan nurses knocked on the door and it was time for me to go. We said our goodbyes and I left. Chris was sitting in the car. She looked concerned. I got in and drove off. Neither of us exchanged words all the way home. She just glanced reassuringly my way a few times. It wasn't an uneasy silence. Just an accepted one.

Good news and sad news

Saturday 17th October   Four years cancer free
We were on our way to Bournemouth for the weekend. We were celebrating me being out of hospital for four years today; only

365 days to go before I was deemed cured. I received a text message as I was driving. I asked Chris to open it and read out the message. It was from Barrie's daughter Denise:

"Hi Terry. Just to let you know Dad passed away at 2.30 this morning. Will let you know arrangements, thanks Denise."

I felt emotional and numb receiving this sad news. I wasn't shocked, but it didn't take long before I felt grieved and somewhat angry that Barrie was no longer here. When we arrived at Bournemouth, I answered Denise's text message by just saying how sorry I was to hear the sad news. Chris didn't know what to say. I just said to her that we would celebrate and toast Barrie's 71 years of life that night as well as my four years of remission. But it was a bittersweet moment for me. More bitter than sweet.

Tribute to Gouldy

Monday 19th October

Barrie Gould
1944 - 2015

Just a little bit about Barrie's career as a footballer:

He started as a youngster at Arsenal and Chelsea and made his football league debut at Peterborough United in 1965. He made 15 league appearances for them over the next two seasons before going to Worcester, where he had four distinguished seasons, including a spell as captain. He went on to complete 188 first-team appearances and scored forty-four goals. He was given a free transfer in 1970 and joined Dover Athletic where he won a Kent Seniors Cup medal before going to

Guildford City and Cheltenham Town. He finally ended his playing career at Burnham, where he played and then managed. He will be remembered in footballing circles as a skilful midfielder and a great team leader on and off the park. I first met Barrie Gould some time back in the 1980s. It was a time when I was a member of a golf society called the Burnham Bandits. I knew of Barrie's reputation as a football player but I didn't really know him as a person.

The golf society was staying at a very basic hotel in Bournemouth. We had finished our day's play and met in the bar after dinner. Barrie was there in full voice and the centre of attention. He had a broom in his hand, which was his musical instrument and he sang Johnny Be Good about five hundred times. I remember him being quite noisy and my first impression of him was as a bit of an exhibitionist. He repeated his act throughout our weekend stay but by the end of it I finally twigged what Barrie was actually doing. He was attempting to bring everyone together as a unit, a team and guess what? He succeeded. Barrie was one of the most thoughtful people that I have ever met. He wasn't very good at golf but he loved being with the boys. He was a man's man with a heart of gold. He wouldn't stand for any nonsense either. If anyone in his company was out of order he would soon put them in their place. He was able to achieve this because he had the respect of everyone he came into contact with.

I phoned Julian Pugh today to give him the sad news regarding Barrie, but there was no reply. Julian is a club official of Worcester City FC. I had been in touch with him these past few months regarding Barrie and his illness. Barrie told me that Worcester was where he was happiest as a player. He was also the club captain and was featured in a book about the history of the club written by Julian, the club historian, and a colleague of his.

Julian did say earlier in the year that if Barrie wanted to be guest of honour at a game, he would make sure that the club made a fuss of him and would invite him to go onto the pitch in front of the players and fans as a form of a tribute for his services to the club. I thought Barrie would enjoy this and passed this kind gesture onto him but unfortunately and reluctantly he declined the offer as he was not well enough to travel that far.

When I finally got through to Julian and gave him the news that Barrie had passed away, he asked me to pass on his and the club's condolences to Barrie's family. He went on to say that the club would have a minute's silence in Barrie's memory and honour him at the next important home game.

I passed on these sentiments to Denise, Barrie's daughter and it turned out that Barrie's son Neil attended a match sometime later after his funeral and found it very emotional. Barrie would have liked that. R.I.P. mate, I will miss you.

As a post note to Barrie and what he meant to many people:

> I visited an old mate recently who I hadn't seen for some time. His name is Alan Brown and he is a lovely sentimental sort of guy and a member of the old Burnham golf society. Alan is not renowned for his golfing prowess but he is known for being great company; warm and genuine are just a few of his traits. We talked about various people that we knew and of course Barrie's name came up.
>
> After talking fondly about Barrie for a few minutes, Alan got up from his chair and said, *"I've got something*

to show you."

He opened a glass cabinet and produced a trophy and photo. He made sure that I couldn't see the writing on the trophy and he placed the photo face down on the table beside me.

He continued the conversation, saying *"You know I am not very good at golf and I have never won anything. Well we had a Burnham golf society Captain's Day after Barry passed away and when it came to the prize giving, of course I wasn't in the running to win anything. The prizes were handed out except for this one and the captain of the day, Keith Donavan, stood up and said we have one more trophy to present. It's not for the best golfer of the day but it is for one of our society's nicest members. He is warm, friendly and always has a welcoming cuddle for everyone. And it goes to Alan Brown."*

Then Alan turned the trophy around: THE BARRIE GOULD TROPHY and Brownie had won it. He then showed me the photo, which was of Barrie as we knew him.

I don't know anyone who wouldn't have given their right arm to win that trophy out of all the trophies that could have been won that day or any golf day whether they were good at golf or not. Alan stood up again at that point and looked out of the window with tears in his eyes. I felt his emotion too as we both silently remembered Barrie. After a while we began to talk about Barrie again.

I said, *"I miss Barrie too. I went to see him just a day or so before he died. His daughter Denise let me in and said* "We don't think he will last much longer. He is in a bed in the dining room" *and pointed to where he was. I opened the door."*

I hesitated in my conversation at that point. I looked at Alan and suddenly I began to get tearful and I couldn't stop. Alan said nothing at first and let me continue to be visibly upset in front of him. I apologised for my outburst.

He then said in a kind way *"I know mate, it's all right. Just let it out. Let it out."* And I did (I couldn't stop anyway).

Now you know what Barrie Gould meant to me and all that knew him. I am sure that most people who have lived a reasonably long life have a similar story to tell.

Friday 6th November

Today was Barrie Gould's funeral at St Edward's Church in Windsor. Chris and I attended. I said to Chris that I thought that it would be a big turnout and it was. Barrie would have been somewhat surprised and I know his family was. The church was completely full of people, some were even standing outside. There must have been four to five hundred people in attendance. It was a lovely service and very moving at times, especially when his young grandson Henry read out a brief reading in memory of his granddad as he stood by Barrie's coffin. Many a grown man shed a tear at that moment.

Death Sentence in a Public Hallway

**Thursday 12th November
to Tuesday 24th November**
We have had enough of bad news lately. Now we were off for a bit of winter sun in Tenerife, at our usual hotel in Playa das Americas. We had discovered a new place to visit, Les Galettes near Los Christianos, and a new cocktail called Mojito, made up from white rum, mint, soda water, lime juice and sugar. Well, it was new to us anyway.

As non-drinkers, we found Mojitos most refreshing. We did wonder why we were a bit wobbly after three or four of these as we strolled along the seafront with slightly spinney heads!

Everything was going great. The food, weather and atmosphere was fantastic. We always had our usual one-Euro ice-cold lager at Scratchy Balls Bar down on the seafront at Los Christianos. We were even recommended to a restaurant outside town where the locals go. We were taken there by the hotel reception guy as it was near his home. Chris had chicken and I had fillet steak but I had to send mine back because it was almost raw.

This was about three days before we were due to go home. The following day I started to feel unwell. I began to get the big D and although I was not physically sick, I couldn't eat much and started to develop a nasty headache. The following night, two days before we were due to go home, my headache became almost unbearable and I had a fever with a temperature of 39 degrees. We went to speak to the reception staff first thing the next morning.

They were quite helpful and suggested two hospitals. If we

wanted to be seen by the equivalent of the NHS, that hospital was quite a distance away and we would have to wait for hours before being seen and the language could be a problem. However, they suggested that we should go to a private hospital that was nearby. But they told us to be cautious: *"Don't have a drip. Don't have an X-ray."* Don't do this and that and most importantly, *"Don't part with any money!"*

To be quite honest, I felt so bad that I didn't care where I went. I just wanted a diagnosis and some treatment. So off we went over the road to the hospital. I showed the receptionist my expensive £145 for eleven nights' travel insurance, which she immediately dismissed by saying that her hospital didn't deal with this company. We left and went back to the hotel only to return for another try after a little while. This time they accepted my European Health Insurance card.

By now I was feeling pretty rough. I was ushered into a waiting area and after about half an hour a nurse took me to a very cramped cubicle with a bed. A doctor then came to see me. She asked a few questions about my medical history and current condition then left.

After about fifteen minutes a nurse came in. She took some blood, my temperature and put me on a drip. I lay there for about an hour. My headache was easing slightly. I was then sent for an x-ray. The hotel staff predicted these events. *"I hope I don't get the bill!"* I thought. After the x-ray, I went back to the cubicle where a young nurse came and took my temperature again. I asked him what the verdict was.

"Very hot," he said.

Another hour went by. I was then told to go back into the waiting area. Almost immediately a man dressed in white with ginger hair and South African accent came up to me and beckoned me away from the seating area into a public hallway.

He looked concerned and said, *"Here's the thing, the doctor is not happy. She said she would like to keep you in overnight for more tests."*

I replied, *"What tests? What for? I am going home tomorrow. What's the problem?"*

He then said, *"The thing is your looseemia might have come back."* He went on to say, *"It could be a gastro problem or it could be the looseemia. We must do more tests and it could be overnight."*

My blood ran cold. I didn't deserve this. I was petrified with what I thought he meant and what the outcome might be.

I said, *"Do you mean my leukaemia has come back?"*

"YES" he answered. *"What type of looseemia was it?"*

I could see that he was becoming unsure of himself.

"Acute Myeloid Leukaemia," I replied. *"It's not called Looseemia. It is highly unlikely that it has returned as I have been in remission for four years".*

"It can return at any time," he replied. *"It might be gastro or the looseemia."*

I was becoming increasingly agitated with the situation and him.

"Are you a doctor?" I asked.

"No, I am not."

This made me more uncertain about the situation and even more agitated.

"Let's get this straight. You are giving me a diagnosis which is probably a death sentence, whilst standing here in a public hallway and you are not even a doctor?"

He paused, then he asked me to wait for a minute so he could go and speak to the doctor. Why the doctor couldn't speak to me herself was beyond me.

He returned after a minute or two and said, *"The doctor isn't happy, but I recommend you go to see your GP when you get home."* He took me into an office to sign a few papers.

Before I signed I asked, *"Who is paying for the treatment I have had so far?"*

"The European Health Card agreement will sort it. They will sort it."

I signed and left with two prescriptions, one for antibiotics and one for paracetamol. How they determined what antibiotics were needed was beyond me because no stool sample had been taken to determine what type of gastro problem it was. We went straight to the pharmacy where we were told that the antibiotics would cost £52 and £6 for the paracetamol.

I paid for the paracetamol and thought I would wait until I got home the next day and book an emergency appointment with my GP for another blood test and find out what was required to get an accurate diagnosis of my illness if it was not leukaemia.

I couldn't wait for tomorrow. As soon as we got back to the hotel I phoned my hospital in the UK to speak to one of my haematologist doctors if they were available.

I spoke to a nurse on Onslow Ward who said, *"As soon as a doctor is free they will ring you back."*

After no more than 10 minutes, I received a call from a very senior doctor who had looked at my notes and listened to what I had to say about my symptoms.

He reassured me there and then by saying, *"It is very highly unlikely that the leukaemia has returned so don't worry. Enjoy the rest of your holiday and just to give yourself some piece of mind, arrange an appointment with your GP or come back to the hospital when you return from your holiday."*

Was I relieved? I certainly was, but I still had to get home tomorrow. My big D had not settled and I still had the journey home to get through. I managed to get a reasonable night sleep despite the day's events. Poor Chris! She couldn't even have a holiday without me being the cause of yet another medical crisis.

Tuesday 24th November
We couldn't wait to get home. However, our aircraft was kept for nearly two hours on the ground in sweltering heat in Tenerife because of some administration problem. We were sitting at the front of the aircraft and were told that the toilets there were for the crew only. We would have to use the ones at the back of the plane. As you can imagine, Mr Diary, that was most inconvenient and unwelcome.

Wednesday 25th November
I managed to get an appointment with my GP for early in the morning. I had a blood test and I supplied the required sample to determine what type of food poisoning I had. I made another appointment for the 27th for late afternoon when the results of my test would be back. I spent the rest of the day in bed.

Thursday 27th November
I visited my GP in the afternoon. The blood test turned out to be normal, bearing in mind what I have gone through over the past few days. The stool test confirmed that I had a severe dose of

food poisoning which had now been diagnosed and the correct antibiotics had been prescribed, which I began to take that day.

Sunday 6th December

This was the first of our 2015 Christmas events, Mad Trusts, A West End Christmas Show at the Actors' Church, Covent Garden in London.

"...the church was full of drag queens..."

It is a charity event where a host of West End stars of musical theatre come together to give a Christmas show. All the main musicals were represented. Les Mis, Phantom, Miss Saigon, Wicked and many others.

The show began with everyone joining in to *O Come All Ye Faithful*, followed by a singing and dancing procession of the West End Kids. Then the casts of War Horse, Miss Saigon and Matilda all sung songs in turn. Summer Strallen sang the *Christmas Song* and, ending the first act, The Commitments sang *The Fairytale of New York*.

My favourite entertainer was the lady who played the harp, Seana Davey, a young and very talented musician who accompanied a singer called Ross William Wild singing *Hallelujah*. It was fabulous. The second act was just as good. The team from Phantom sang *In Dulci Jubilo*, the Les Mis cast sang *Mary's Lullaby*, the Blues Brothers sang *Santa Claus is Coming to Town* and *White Christmas* followed by the company of Wicked who sang *Have Yourself a Merry Little Christmas*.

As a finale, the audience and cast members joined together and sang *Hark the Herald Angels Sing*. I didn't think Chris knew what to quite make of it and she was too self-conscious to sing aloud. Also, the church was full of drag queens dressed in outrageously over-the-top costumes, collecting money for a prize draw which took place at the end of the proceedings. We both enjoyed the show; it was certainly different from what we were used to.

The year was ending and so I made my usual pilgrimage to The Royal Surrey Hospital to distribute a few Christmas gifts before going on our Christmas Family Holiday in North Devon.

Tuesday 22nd December
This year's Christmas cottage turned out to be the best Christmas venue so far. It was called Bramley Meadow Farmhouse. It is three miles east of Coombe Martin. The farmhouse itself dates to the Magna Carta and is just a few minutes' drive from the village of Parracombe. It is set in 10 acres of farmland with sheep, horses, pigs and chickens. You can collect your eggs for breakfast. It also has two wood burners, one in the lounge and one in the kitchen. When lit, they make the whole place warm and cosy.

We were joined by nearly all the same people that came in 2011. Hayley came with her husband Joe, Oliver and Daisy and Granny Marion. Darren and his other half Jo and little Lucas were coming the following day.

We arrived at the cottage just after Hayley and her family. It took us ages to find it; our satellite navigation did not guide us to the exact spot, which was at the end of the world down a remote country lane.

We must have gone past the farmhouse a few times. It was pitch black and the rain was beating down hard on the windscreen and so it was almost impossible to see. We couldn't contact Hayley either, as there was signal on our mobile phones. Eventually, after both of us threatened each other with divorce a few times, we stumbled across the entrance to Bramley Cottage. The children greeted us at the door and we unloaded the car of food, luggage and presents. Our room was the oldest in the house. It used to be the pantry or bakery and the walls were about eighteen inches thick. The window had a view of fields that housed horses and sheep, although we couldn't see them that night. It reminded me of a poem by Bilbo Baggins to Frodo in The Lord of the Rings in which he warns Frodo of the dangers of travelling in wintertime:

> *When winter first begins to bite*
> *and stones crack in the frosty night,*
> *when pools are black and trees are bare,*
> *'tis evil in the Wild to fare.*

> *J.R.R. Tolkien*

After we unpacked, Chris and Granny Marion joined Hayley in the kitchen and put the rest of the food away and dressed the 10 foot Christmas tree that our landlords had kindly provided. More decorations were put up in the lounge and kitchen area.

It was about 7.00 pm. We had plenty of logs for the two burners, which Joe and I had lit and which were roaring away nicely.

After a light supper, the two children – already in their PJs - went to bed and we adults settled down in the lounge with a glass of prosecco each and a piece of pizza, plus a few of my homemade spicy hot pickled onions that I insisted everyone should try throughout our stay.

The flames grew higher and higher as the heat engulfed the logs that I had put on the fire just a short while ago. It had the usual hypnotic effect on me. The colours of orange and red soon gave way to yellow and white where the heat was at its greatest and the logs then slowly turned to a greyish white as the fire settled down with age. But still, the reflection from the flames made our faces glow in the dimly lit room. These are happy times. This is what life is all about for me now, happy family get-togethers.

13 Looking to the future

Sister Sarah's Farm

Wednesday 23rd December 2015
We were all up quite early and the children were ready to explore their surroundings. Darren, Lucas and Jo (Darren's new partner) arrived mid-morning. Lucas, Oliver and Daisy wasted no time in getting excited. They were always pleased to see each other and for a few minutes it was mayhem, but lovely to witness. I had arranged to go and see Sarah, my nursing Angel, who had looked after me when I was an inpatient. Sarah now lives not too far away from the cottage in Lynton. She and her husband Jason and children George and Charlie and the dog Albert have a smallholding where Jason farms pigs, sheep and chickens. Sarah has left the Onslow Ward and is now a specialist nurse in Taunton, about an hour's drive away.

Jason looks after the farm and even cooks the evening meal by all accounts while Sarah keeps the NHS going in North Devon. Chris and I made our way to Sarah's after breakfast. The farm was tucked away and difficult to find. As we were following a narrow lane close to our destination, we saw Sarah walking towards the farm entrance with her two boys and she directed us to the house. She invited us in to the kitchen / dining area through the oldest door I have ever seen and made us a cup of tea. It was a typical country farm kitchen; large and spacious with flagstone floors and low ceilings. We chatted for about an hour. As I have said previously, Sarah had been helping me with my book. We gave her a bottle of bubbly as a house-warming present and we exchanged Christmas cards. As we left, she gave us some freshly laid eggs which I must say were some of the best eggs I have ever tasted.

Sister Sarah

When we arrived back at the farmhouse, it was a hive of activity. The rest of the family had been out exploring the ten-acre grounds. They all had to wear their Wellington boots to go out due to the wet conditions. The three children were covered in mud and all had to have a hot bath, which they thoroughly enjoyed as they were bathed together to save time and hot water.

The bubbly continued to flow throughout the day. We must have got through between ten and twenty bottles of the stuff during our stay and I don't really drink. There was also plenty of food and, of course, my homemade pickled onions. The children played happily without bothering the adults and the adults chatted merrily without bothering the children.

Thursday 24th December   Christmas Eve

Organised chaos was yet again the order of the day. With breakfast over, the ladies - Chris, Hayley, Jo and Granny Marion - did some last-minute shopping. We then ventured down to the seaside at Lynmouth, where the children went exploring on the rocks for crabs, shells, seaweed and fossils.

When we returned to the farmhouse, we soon got back into the festivities of eating, drinking, laughing and joking. I kept up my duties of putting more logs for the fires in the lounge and dining room. Evening arrived before we knew it. It was not a very clear night, but clear enough to go outside and show the children the real Santa and his sleigh. He had just left the North Pole; the sleigh was laden with presents for all the children that had been good for most of the year. He was still thousands of miles away up in the sky but we did see him. We were not expecting him or his reindeer in Parracombe until all of the children in the world were fast asleep.

When we got back inside we heard a noise outside. A mini tractor was parked with its engine running outside the kitchen door. We all went out to investigate including the children who were there before us adults. There sat on the tractor was the smallest, youngest Father Christmas I had ever seen. In fact, he must have been the great-grandson of the festive icon. It was in fact the owner's son accompanied by the wife of the owner of the cottage and their pixie friend.

They stood outside in the rain looking very sheepish. The children beamed with excitement as we invited our new-found Christmas friends in for some festive beverage. I was unsure if the man in red with the white beard was quite old enough to drink. He then produced a sack of goodies for the children, giving them three nice presents each. What a lovely touch we all thought. The three of them were very friendly and wished us all a Merry Christmas before they left to enjoy their own Christmas. Of course, there was no stopping the three children from opening their unexpected gifts there and then. This was a great start to our forthcoming celebrations.

After a short while, it was bedtime for the children. They got into their PJs and their respective parents helped them put out mince pies, carrots and water for Father Christmas and his reindeer. They also sprinkled snow dust on the floor so they could see their welcome guest's footprints in the morning when they woke up. The children went to bed full of excitement, but soon settled down to sleep as they knew that it was not good luck to catch site of the real Father Christmas especially as he was delivering their presents.

We all settled down again in the lounge in this enchanting cottage and relaxed and chatted until bedtime.

Young Santa

Friday 25th December   Christmas Day

The plan was not to have our big Christmas dinner today, but on Boxing Day. Instead, we were having a buffet as most of the day was spent opening the presents and just chilling out.

We had our usual celebration breakfast of salmon and scrambled eggs with a drop of bubbly. Then it was into the lounge where the presents were piled high in the corner of the room.

Everything was ready for the distribution of gifts. We were all smartly dressed for the occasion and everyone had a drink. The fires in the lounge and the dining room were roaring away nicely. Joe, the allocated present distributor and assistant log stacker, was on his marks. The children looked like three little puppies waiting for a bone or two, huddled together just inches away from Joe. Then off we went. Black dustbin sacks waiting to be filled with discarded wrapping paper. Slowly but surely, we all received our presents in clockwork order. Obviously, we took our time and we had numerous drink and snack breaks in-between. We stopped for lunch, continued for a while in the afternoon, then stopped the distribution so that the remainder of presents could be opened on Boxing Day.

After a fantastic day, the children went to bed tired but happy and we grown-ups just relaxed and chatted for the rest of the evening.

Saturday 26th December   Boxing Day

The Christmas roast was in the oven. The table was laid out ready with crackers, poppers and festive confetti, and we placed a few of the remaining presents under the tree. Wellington boots were put into in the back of the cars. Granny was strapped in. Now we were off just down the road to the sea for an hour or so for some fresh air.

We were not out for long, just enough to get the cobwebs out of our heads. The children had collected a few pebbles and fossils to keep. This reminds me of my fascination with pebbles:

> Since I have left hospital, one of the things that I have become interested in is collecting interesting pebbles from the beach every time we visit the seaside. I know, it's boring, isn't it? And I am sure Chris gets fed up when I wander off onto any seaside beach that we are visiting, especially if there is a plentiful supply of these

ancient stones, but she always indulges me and sits on a bench or wall while I search for treasure. And as a token of my love and devotion, I always find and offer her one or two pebbles that are heart shaped for her to keep and she always accepts and keeps at least one.

They can be found all over our house. Some I put the date on if there is room and write on them where they were found. The smaller ones I leave blank. Some are almost perfect and some are less than perfect, but she keeps them just the same. I call them *Hearts of the Ocean*. I tell people, including my grandchildren, that they are hearts of souls lost at sea and they are returning to where they originally came from; whoever picks them up and gives them a home will have good luck in their lives. In fact, whoever is in possession of one of these stones will have good luck forever, providing it has been passed on to them with love or friendship and accepted in the same way. I hope people treasure them, but I suppose it depends on how they perceive the offering from me in the first place.

Now we were back to the cottage. The smell of our Christmas roast turkey cooking slowly in the oven greeted us as we walked through the door.

I put a few more logs onto the kitchen and lounge fires. Joe and Darren made sure everyone had a beverage of some sort and the children were being amused by Jo and Granny, while Chris and Hayley were sorting out the final preparations for the Christmas dinner.

After about an hour we were all called to the dining table to be seated. Poppers popped, crackers pulled, dinner in front of us.

Then we toasted the event, to each other and those who were no longer with us. I was sure that for that moment all the adults sitting around the table were thinking of someone that they missed. My first thoughts were to people recently departed: Barrie Gould, Peter Small and my sister-in-law Christine B. Although this year I felt stronger and less vulnerable myself and more able to cope with the emotion that any tragedy might bring, Barrie had only just passed away and I was thinking of how his family were coping at that moment.

The rest of the day went well. We all helped with the clearing up. The fires were blazing, everyone always had a drink of some sort in their hand and the rest of the presents were opened. The remainder of our day was just as enjoyable as the day before.

Monday 28th December
We left our holiday cottage for home mid-morning, everyone had a kiss and cuddle for each other as they said their goodbyes. A wonderful end to yet another memorable Christmas family gathering and a great way to end 2015.

This journey's end is in sight

2016
This year marks the final chapter of my leukaemia recovery. Everything seems to be under control and normal. The first two months of the year were uneventful although I did find myself reflecting on the past five years. On Wednesday 2nd March, I went to see Doctor Louise for my six-monthly blood test and clinic. Yet again everything was fine. Blood results were normal:

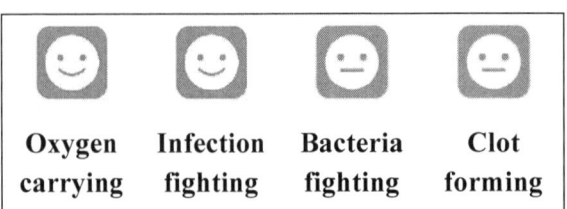

My final appointment should be on Wednesday 7th September 2016. That would be my five years of recovery process finally completed. I am looking forward to hearing my Consultant Doctor Louise utter the inevitable words, *"Everything is good"* followed by, *"Goodbye and good luck."* I will have to wait and see what happens between now and then. You never know what's just around the corner on any journey that has many twists and turns, do you? Oh look, two more smileys.

Meeting Emilie

Tuesday 15th March
I telephoned Emilie, Pete Smalls daughter. When she answered, I said,

"Hello Emilie, you don't really know me but I was in hospital with your dad nearly five years ago. You texted me about him passing away and his funeral arrangements."

She interrupted me and said, *"I know who you are, it's Terry, you have come up on my phone."*

This took me by surprise; I wasn't expecting her to keep my number. I told her that I was writing a book about my leukaemia experience and that her dad played a significant part in it. The reason for the call was to find out whether she and her family would be willing to speak to me about Pete and maybe share mutual experiences regarding what it was like for them during Pete's illness, as well as read what I had written so far just to get their approval.

She said, *"Of course, we would love to meet up. We speak openly about dad, I have kept all of his hospital notes and texts from his old mobile phone."* She invited me to her house on the 30th March.

When I arrived, Emilie introduced me to Pete's wife Pat and one of Emilie's sons and we sat around a table. I felt a bit apprehensive at first, but we soon broke the ice.

I began by saying, *"I am trying to put some dates together about certain events and I just need you to make sure the dates are correct."*

Emilie produced Pete's mobile and some diaries that she had kept from as far back as 2011 and said, *"Dad used to talk about you all the time. He used to say that you were in a bad place when you were in hospital with him."*

"Yes, we used to use each other as a crutch."

She produced all the information I needed to carry on with my writing and the family gave me their approval with what was written so far. My final question to Emilie was,

"How did you and the family cope with everything."

"Dad was my life. He was my hero. I think about him all the time."

After about an hour or so of friendly chat, we said our goodbyes. As I left, I couldn't help thinking that I had found some new friends. I was sure that we would keep in touch from time to time from that moment on.

I sat in the car for a while. I felt drained. The experience of meeting Pete's family was quite overwhelming, but I was glad that I had made the effort to meet with them, especially Emilie, who I felt somewhat drawn towards in a fatherly, protective way. I hope Pete would have approved. Emilie came across as a tower of strength but warm and vulnerable also, and a credit to Pete. But life without her dad was probably a void that she thought she could never fill. Pete's passing was still very raw to her. It can't be easy to move on when you lose a loved one, can it, Mr Diary?

Reunion with my cousins and the asthma run

Wednesday 16th April
Chris and I met up with my cousins in a pub near Romford in Essex where I grew up. They all looked the same to me as they did when we used to have our Boxing Day affairs at my Grandma Oakley's, just a bit older. We met for lunch and reminisced for a few hours; it was great to catch up.

When we left, I said to Chris it would be nice to go and see where I grew up and maybe revisit my asthma run. So, we drove to the old house. It hadn't changed much. It had a new front door and double glazing. Bygone memories began to stir. Especially of playing cricket with my mate in the narrow alleyway that separated the house next door.

> We used to use the dustbin between the two back doors as a wicket. We would play eleven-a-side county cricket matches during the summer season. I would be the

Essex team and my mate would be the eleven players from Kent. We used to share the game's commentary. I think we both tried to mimic the cricket commentator of the time, John Arlott. His voice was made even more famous years later in the Channel 4 film of P'tang, Yang, Kipperbang, one of my all-time favourite TV films. This was a simple coming-of-age film set in a grammar school in the London suburbs in 1948. It's a story of a young cricket-obsessed boy called Alan. He is also obsessed with a girl in his class who he hopes he will be able to kiss. He daydreams about his cricket and the girl and his thoughts are voiced by the very same BBC radio cricket commentator, John Arlott, in the style of a match commentary. The title phrase comes from a password used by members of Alan's gang. Anyway, you can only imagine the time it took for us to complete both innings and the racket we made in the process. I don't think such antics would be tolerated between neighbours these days but back then, no one seemed to complain. Ah, those were the days.

After drifting back in time for a while I eventually got back into the car and drove just up the road to the lane where I used to begin my asthma run over fifty-eight years ago. Chris stayed in the car as I began to retrace more of my childhood steps. To my right, there was now a scrapyard full of old smashed up cars piled high where there used to be a farmyard full of swallows, livestock and tractors.

As I continued walking up the now muddy lane I looked to my left where the cornfield used to be full of bright yellow corn. This was where my friends and I spent long summer days making camps out of the corn left behind by the farmers combine harvester. Alas, the cornfield was no longer there. Instead was an unkempt field full of lorry tyres and a few old retired horses grazing. I walked on and up the hill, I looked up into the sky where I used to see the skylarks hovering high above me. Their song always reminded me of the summer and warm sunshine. But not today. In fact, I haven't seen a skylark or heard the mysterious cuckoo call out somewhere in the distance since those summer days in the late fifties and early sixties. Maybe it's time I looked for them again now I am retired and reaching my twilight years.

> *Up with me! up with me into the clouds!*
> *For thy song, Lark, is strong;*
> *Up with me, up with me into the clouds!*
> *Singing, singing,*
> *With clouds and sky about thee ringing,*
> *Lift me, guide me till I find*
> *That spot which seems so to thy mind!*

The first stanza of "To a Skylark" by William Wordsworth

Eventually, I reached my destination at the top of the hill. To my delight the tree with the flat top was still there. But it no longer stood proud at the summit as I remembered it. It was almost unrecognisable. The top of the tree was not as flat as I remember. In fact, it was somewhat threadbare. Broken branches hung down looking lifeless, almost severed, but still managing to hang by a thread. Prickly, overgrown blackberry bushes and other thick undergrowth surrounded the trunk making access to it virtually impossible. But I made my way through the thorny obstacles in the hope that my name was still visible on the main trunk of the tree. But alas, there was no sign of the mark that I inscribed with the sharp stone all those years ago, bonding me and the tree together.

Reluctantly, I made my way out of the undergrowth and stood

there for a while looking all around me, feeling cheated and disappointed and desperately trying to remember what it was like for me finally reaching the top of the hill and breathing again all those years ago. But it wasn't the same. I didn't feel the same. Things change, places change, people change with time. But my memories of how things were will stay with me forever. They will never change, especially the happy ones. But on this occasion, all I felt was a sense of disappointment and confusion. Maybe I should have left the present reality of this memory alone.

Friday 27th May

Chris and I celebrated our 10th wedding anniversary. It is a shame that for half of our marriage, poor Chris has had to put up with me being ill or recovering from illness. She has more than shown her devotion towards me during that time. She has been my rock. Now we can toast our next 10 years together with renewed optimism. My struggle with cancer is almost over.

I no longer dread meeting my maker when the time comes, although I have no intention of meeting him for some considerable time. I have finally learned to accept my destiny. I only realised recently that I have always been able to accept whatever life throws at me. I am not brave; I am not clever; I have regrets; I have made, and still make, mistakes. I have even been guilty of pushing people away when they got too close. But not anymore. I used to think *why me* when it seemed that it was only me that was having all the bad luck, although I have always done my best to tackle life's problems head on. They won't go away on their own unless you are lucky and I don't have a lot of faith in luck. Luck is just a question of good timing.

Was it just good intuition that made me decide to go to the doctors that day back in June 2011, or was it fate? I will never know for sure. But I now know that I would have been dead in a matter of weeks if I hadn't been diagnosed. I didn't know that back then, nor did I ever think that I was not going to survive my ordeal. But I still feel upset when I think of what might have been. I have been asked whether I feel lucky to have pulled through my illness. My answer is no. I may have been lucky to have been diagnosed early. But I do feel fortunate. Mostly, I feel grateful to the people and science that have made my survival possible. In addition, I have discovered that I do have some sort of spiritual faith. I am not religious but I am sure many of us choose to believe in something that we don't fully understand, don't we? If we do, that is something to cling onto or look forward too. Maybe you must go through a near-death experience to understand fully these kinds of thoughts. Anyway, that is what I think.

I have mentioned earlier in my book that I am one of life's triers and rarely give up on anything. This is true. But having this sort of mentality has made it more difficult for me to consciously accept certain things, until recently that is. I am no longer consumed by that troubled restless spirit that had engulfed my very existence ever since I was a child. I have always felt that I have never been accepted or belonged anywhere in particular, especially in my childhood home.

> I did try to escape from my early home life on many occasions. I would walk miles to an auntie's or friend's house and knock on their door and wonder why, after a quick cuppa and a chat, I was never invited to stay for the night and so I felt that I had to leave. I don't know why, but I thought anyone who was related or kind to me would put me up! But I never plucked up the courage to ask if I could stay and when asked why I was visiting, I never gave the real reason (I didn't want to go home), so I left with nowhere to go. This could be the reason that to this day, I take a long time to take my coat

off when I am visiting or even when I return home. Or at least until I met Chris. Perhaps I had some of the mysterious cuckoo blood in me – I wanted to be in a nest that I had no right to be in! I even lived on an allotment for a few days once. But when Grandma Oakley got to hear about it, she took me in for a while. It didn't take me long to take my coat off when I was there. Perhaps Chris and Granny have something special in common!

I was a bit of a lost soul in many ways in those early days. I used to question everything including words and deeds of good intention. I rarely trusted anyone and was reluctant to receive praise even when I knew I deserved it. It was the world versus me. But not anymore. I now know for sure that you must fully accept the reality of any situation before you can move on from it. Maybe I had a problem understanding that in the past and that was why I struggled with some of life's realities.

I now also realise through recent experience that there is always someone somewhere out there worse off than myself and is suffering or has suffered far more than I ever could. My recent illness has taught me the reality of what suffering extreme trauma both mentally and physically really is. That is why I can now fully empathise with people who are or have truly suffered to the extreme.

Whether their suffering is more or less than my own, it makes no difference. I have entered into their world and experienced hell on earth. When did this realisation finally click? It was not until....

Friday 17th June

The sea was rough

We were on holiday in Cala San Vincente in Majorca, our regular mid-year holiday destination. I was sitting out on the balcony of our room looking out onto the small bay below. The sea was rough and so no one could go swimming. The weather was warm but overcast with a slight breeze. I had just come back from the hotel library where I found a Reader's Digest book of short stories that I thought would interest me.

What caught my eye was one of the titles *Anne Frank Remembered*, a condensed version of a book written by Miep Gies and co-written by Alison Leslie Gold. My interest was that Anne kept diaries just like me. They were true and honest accounts of the day-to-day existence of a young Jewish girl and her family who were caught up in and lived through Nazi-occupied Amsterdam. Eventually, most of them perished, including Anne, during one of the most horrendous of times in human history. I noticed a similarity between Anne's personality and my own as I became totally absorbed in her story, even though it was being told through Miep, the brave person who hid the Frank family from the dreaded Nazis.

As I read on, I began to feel as if I was in the room with her, as she and her family made the best out of the life they had been forced into through no fault of their own. Miep finally described returning home one day to the attic where the Franks were hiding only to find the place empty of people, just papers strewn all over the floor including Anne Frank's Diary. I imagined the horror that must have been on Miep's face as she entered the empty room with an intensity that I have never felt before. The fear, the panic, the betrayal they must have felt as Anne and her family were herded together and put into waiting trucks, like animals being taken to the slaughter. I could feel their fear. I felt sick, angry, guilty and upset as Anne's petrified big, brown, frightened, fifteen-year-old eyes looked up at me from the page. This was another new experience for me, a new kind of compassion and empathy that I didn't realise I had.

When I finished reading the book, it finally dawned on me that millions of people, old, young, past and present or in the future, have suffered, are suffering, or will suffer far more than I ever could. I felt almost ashamed that my own suffering was insignificant compared to what Anne Frank and her family and millions like her went through. That doesn't mean that I haven't suffered myself. I have and that is why I can empathise and sympathise with most people who have experienced trauma in the extreme, especially young people that have not lived a full life like I have. Outliving youth still makes me feel uneasy and guilty.

I have accepted my illness, treatment and recovery process. Until recently, I used to live in the hope that my cancer would not return. I now *believe* it will not return. So, hope, although an important emotion, no longer comes into it. I have now found the courage to live again with a different perception on life. In a way, my illness has taught me the true meaning of compassion and gratitude as well. At last I know for sure that, in comparison to many others, I have had a good life and if it was about to end now I wouldn't feel too sorry for myself. This young girl's brief existence and suffering has been my wake-up call to push aside any form of self-pity, continue to enjoy life to the full and accept my inevitable destiny.

My life has changed dramatically over the past five years but in the end, for me and one and a quarter million people like me in the UK today, *Life Goes On*. In a way, surviving cancer is like being reborn; it gives you the opportunity to reclaim your life, to be given another chance and to put right past mistakes if you get the opportunity to do so.

The more I struggled with my illness in the early years, the more hope had a major part to play in my day-to-day existence, probably because my future seemed more uncertain. I wanted to get better but I just didn't know if or when I would. I am sure that Anne Frank and her family felt this emotion and it probably got stronger with increasing adversity.

Enjoy life to the full. Take whatever life path decision is required and continue your journey and be happy until your journey inevitably ends. I no longer live in hope; I now live just for the day. I have gone through the tunnel and out into the light. I am cured in my mind's eye and I intend to be as happy as I can be for the rest of my life. I wish the same to everyone who has been in the same unfortunate position as me and my family. Something I read the other day sums up my last five years.

> *Grant me the serenity to accept the things I cannot change, the courage to change the things I can and the wisdom to know the difference.*
>
> *Reinhold Niebuhr*

It's a difficult task and easier said than done but it's better than standing still waiting to die, isn't it?

I would love to see one million cancer survivors and their families, get together with the loved ones who stood by them throughout their purgatory, including the nurses and doctors, and meet up just for one day and receive a badge or pin of courage, and embrace each other whilst being entertained by some grateful celebrities at various venues all over the UK. Just for one day. Organised collectively by the country's great charities. A massive task but it's a worthwhile dream that could become a reality. There is a worldwide cancer day, so why not a UK one? This gathering could also include the families of those lost to cancer and maybe together we could talk about the future and all the good things it has in store for us all. I believe passionately that our emotional and mental health is just as important as our physical wellbeing. It may not be easy for some people but believe me, it's good to talk face to face, especially if you have a shared experience.

My Dream

I have a dream that I hope will come true
That you will meet me and I will meet you.
I have a dream that throughout our great land
In country, in city, by coast and on sand
We could assemble, join hands and rejoice
United we stand, together, one voice
Embrace one another, enjoy a great day
Just for the day, maybe sometime in May.

Wednesday 7th September

I had my penultimate appointment with Doctor Louise. I thought this was going to be my last appointment before being discharged for good. But Doctor Louise decided to see me one last time in February 2017.

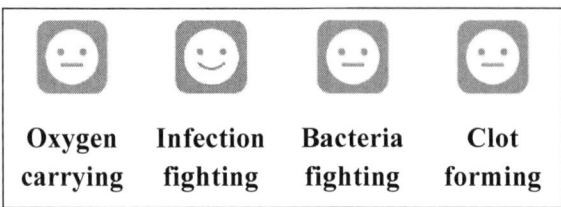

Monday 17th October   5 years cancer free!

We quietly celebrated me being out of hospital for five years today and even though I have one more appointment with Doctor Louise I am now cured as far as the NHS is concerned. Some of our friends didn't understand why we weren't having a big celebration. I know five years in remission is a recognised milestone but we have celebrated constantly almost every day since I was first in remission in 2011. Every time I had a positive blood test we celebrated. Every time I had a birthday we celebrated. Every day when I wake up and hear the birds singing for me it's a celebration of the coming day. We have enjoyed a lot of dinners, family barbeques, holidays, Christmases, bottles of wine and five birthdays of my own that I haven't taken for granted.

Another twist to my tale.

Tuesday 15th November
Chris received a phone call from our local GP surgery. She recently had a scan which showed some sort of abnormality. She was informed by the doctor that further investigations were needed, so a letter had been sent as a matter of urgency to a consultant to see whether she needed a biopsy. Chris took this news better than I did I think. But I did my best to play down the possibilities before we knew them. Now we had to wait for the appointment and possible biopsy to be performed. Chris was quite calm and took the news in her stride. What she didn't know couldn't hurt her. It was me that was thinking the worse even though I told her it would be fine.

She wanted to keep this news quiet until she had the biopsy and subsequent results.

Tuesday 22nd November
We both attended her appointment at Heatherwood Hospital in Ascot. I went into the consulting room with her. The doctor said that he wished to examine her and then perform the biopsy. This request took Chris by surprise as she was only expecting a

consultation. She disappeared into an adjoining room.

I heard her saying, *"Why is it hurting so much?"*

It turned out that the doctor needed to take two samples of tissue. I sat there wincing. The consultant came back into the room first and sat down opposite me. I took the opportunity to ask him what his thoughts were regarding Christine's examination while she was still in the examination room. He just said I can't discuss it with you until your wife is present. Chris came back into the room with the nurse and sat beside me, looking distressed. Then the consultant began talking into his Dictaphone. Normal this, normal that, unremarkable this and that. As you know, *unremarkable* is a medical term for normal.

When he had finished, Chris asked him, *"What happens next?"*

"You will receive a letter in the post. It usually takes two weeks."

"What do you think it is then doctor?" I asked.

He looked up at us both and said, *"We will know more once the biopsy results are in. But it's a 90% chance it's ok, 10% chance it's cancer."*

I turned and looked at Chris, she looked shocked. The word cancer had been directed at her personally. We thanked the doctor and left for home. Whilst walking to the car I could see that she was visibly upset. There were tears in her eyes.

I asked, *"Are you ok?"*

"I just hope everything is ok" she said.

Now it was my turn to support her in any way I could.

I said *"Don't worry, you are 90% ok. That's massive."*

It didn't help her much. The word cancer had terrified her, now we had to wait for the results.

This was something new again for both of us. However positive you are, you just can't help thinking the worse sometimes, can you? While we waited for the results, which were close to three weeks away, all sorts of things were going through my mind. What if she had to go through what I went through? What if the prognosis was not good? What would happen to us both? I didn't want to be alone and I didn't want her to suffer. I must be strong and positive for her sake. As it turned out all was well. Thank the Lord for that. No more scares please, Chris.

Christmas was a quiet affair at home. My final appointment with Doctor Louise was 22nd February 2017 and it went well. Bloods were normal:

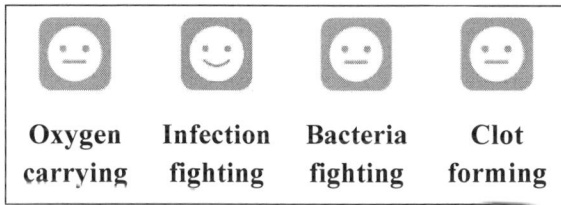

She told me that there was a slight risk of other cancers, especially skin cancers, following chemotherapy for leukaemia. But it was highly unlikely that I would relapse after five years. Well, that's all right then. I am unremarkable at last!

Half full or half empty?

I have been catapulted into a world that none of us expect to be in during our lifetime. But at time of writing, the reality is that

2.5 million of us in the UK have found ourselves in that world. One in two of the 2.5 million and their loved ones will struggle their way through it and rebuild our lives. Half of the 2.5 million will not make it and their loved ones will grieve to the end of their lives. Does that mean that the cup of life is half full? Or is it half empty?

> **Macmillan Cancer Support - Key Statistics**
>
> More than 2.5 million people are living with or beyond cancer in the UK, rising to 4 million by 2030.
>
> In 2012, almost 340,000 people were diagnosed with cancer in the UK and over 160,000 people died of cancer.
>
> By 2020, almost 1 in 2 people in the UK will develop some form of cancer during their lifetime.
>
> Over half of people living with or beyond cancer have had the diagnosis for over five years.
>
> UK cancer survival rates are worse than the European average rate. Cancer survival in the UK has doubled in the last 40 years:
>
> 40 years ago: overall median survival time was one year
>
> Now: half of the people diagnosed with cancer survive their disease for a decade or more
>
> For more details, see
> http://www.macmillan.org.uk/documents/aboutus/research/richpictures/update/rp-people-with-cancer.pdf

Life after cancer or any major trauma surely must take its toll. I know I didn't get off lightly. But half of us who have experienced it first-hand are still here to embrace our world. I believe that, given the opportunity, we could all rise and meet life's challenges head on with more courage and awareness than we had experienced before we were ill.

It just takes time and a positive frame of mind. I wish I had talked to someone in the early years of my recovery about my own fears. But I didn't have the courage to confront the werewolf. So, it took me longer to accept my situation and talk about it openly. I even avoided talking to anyone who may have been ill themselves or was currently having treatment. Maybe I should have found a solution to my fears sooner, instead of going into my shell and living the first two years in limbo and wasting valuable time.

I am not sure how the families of those who have not survived feel. But I, for one, would gladly offer my support to any one of them if I could. I feel guilty sometimes that I have pulled through my own ordeal and their own loved ones haven't. I may not know what to say to offer comfort, but I am a good listener and I think that at least we would share a common thread, a bond that unites us. The words would naturally come to me eventually if I was given the opportunity.

I also believe that communication through your peers can be beneficial. You don't have to talk about illness, it could be anything to do with everyday life. Maybe that's the best place to start (although I would probably begin with, *"How are you?"*). Even those loved ones that have been left behind would benefit from a genuine sympathetic ear occasionally. Do you believe in the old saying a problem shared is a problem halved? I know I do.

As my health has improved, so has my self-confidence and I have developed a new kind of strength and courage. When my friend Barrie Gould was suffering from cancer last year, I did my best to meet up with him whenever I could. It took me some considerable time to be able to get to the point where I had the courage to talk to him about his situation. I was a closed shop in many ways during the early years of my recovery. I also avoided talking to almost anyone who was suffering, even though I knew I had some empathy with them. It was like having an illness and not taking the medicine that you knew could make you better.

The drawbacks of my cancer experience are relatively few. The positives are many. I know more about myself, my capabilities, my faults. I have learned acceptance in its true form, of situations, others and myself. I wish I had done better in the past. That includes a healthier lifestyle, being a better person, taking education more seriously, being a better parent for example. There are many things about my past that I cannot change. Does that mean I am condemned? If we all thought that way, none of us would move on to the next positive step in our lives would we? We can create our own future by acting positively now.

I am coming up to my seventieth birthday. I have a few more aches and pains these days and a few more visits to my GP and I take a few more potions and pills. But, on the whole, I am okay. Increasingly, people of my age are getting illnesses such as cancer. There is no point in worrying about it. My generation are the baby boomers and we are living longer and I for one am grateful for it. I grew up in an age when it was cool to smoke, we ate suet puddings, bread and dripping. We even breathed in the foggy smog given off by fossil fuels because we didn't have any choice. But on the positive side, many of our parents and grandparents had allotments so we also had plenty of organic vegetables and fruit as well. But even with those few pluses, I don't think a lot of us led healthy lifestyles.

I don't think you have any choice as to the outcome of an illness such as cancer. You either survive or you don't. But maybe some of today's younger generation who think they are going to live forever, and quite rightly so, could take note of the latest cancer statistics that organisations such as Macmillan offer and look at prevention rather than cure. Maybe investigate what they can do to take better care of themselves, unlike me and some of my generation, and live healthy lives. If they have young children, make sure they do the same. Children will normally follow mum and dad's example anyway. That's all you can do. I know science is improving the chances of cancer survival as each day goes by, but if you take steps to avoid the risk of getting cancer in the first place you wouldn't have to put up with the after effects, would you? I don't mean to preach but I care about what happens to my children and grandchildren and I don't want them to suffer as I did (or worse).

I am the most contented I have been in years. I feel happy and safe with nothing much to worry about or prove to myself or others. I no longer have to compete with the world and my childhood perception of life has been reinstated once more.

Goodbye, Mr Diary

I woke up this morning at about 4.30 am and couldn't get back to sleep. Christine had been on at me to clear up my papers that were strewn about my makeshift office. Eventually, I got up and went downstairs and into the kitchen and made myself a cup of tea. It was getting light and the dawn chorus was starting. I then began to sift through the mountains of paperwork - drafts of my unfinished book and some old notes and letters, including doctors' letters, mixed up with the usual household paperwork that had been actioned but not filed away. I collected the few papers that I wanted to keep and opened what I thought was an empty sideboard drawer to put them away. Inside the drawer I found my old black 2011 diary. I took it out and sat down on the settee.

Just then, some movement in the garden caught my eye. I looked out of the window and there on the garden table was a robin. It seemed to be looking straight at me. I wondered if it was our resident robin who I hadn't seen for some time. I sat there for a while exchanging glances with my small feathered friend. Its liquid eyes looked very familiar. It reminded me of the same solitary robin that once perched itself on my shoe all those years ago, when I was a young boy sitting with my back against the flat-topped tree on top of the hill, feeling elated and hopeful.

I finished drinking my tea and looked out of the window once more. There was no sign of my friendly robin but I was sure that we would meet again soon.

I looked down at my diary. The contents of it no longer had any hold over me. There was no racing of my heart or a chill down my spine. It was just an old diary. I put it back with my papers in the bottom of the drawer.

I closed the drawer.

Goodbye, Mr Diary.

Acknowledgments

I would like to take this opportunity to thank the many people who have supported me and shown empathy and compassion throughout my past five years of uncertainty. I feel that it would have been more difficult for me to survive my emotional ordeal without them. Surviving a potentially deadly illness has allowed me to develop an enhanced gratitude towards people and life in general. To everyone that has been involved with my wellbeing and recovery process, no matter how small, I am and always will be eternally grateful. It is my wish to acknowledge everyone who helped but if I have inadvertently overlooked someone, I apologise in advance and my warmest thanks to you is no less valid.

Christine, my dear wife, who has spent at least half of our married life caring and supporting me through my unexpected illness and eventual recovery; my love and gratitude to you is infinite and goes beyond words.

Paul Watmore, editor. A friend who has helped and guided me through the conception of my book to its completion. Thanks for putting up with my constant pestering. *"It's 10.00 am Terry time"*. You must have the patience of a saint. Your help has been invaluable.

Doctor Louise. My Consultant and Guardian Angel who oversaw my medical care until my eventual cure. My family and I are eternally grateful.

Professor Smith and his team who first diagnosed me with my illness and gave me the inspiration and motivation to tackle my treatment head-on from the outset.

Doctor Marshall, the GP at my local surgery who sent me to Frimley Park Hospital for the investigation in the first place on the 14th June 2011, even though my symptoms were unrelated to my eventual diagnosis. Thankyou.

Dan Burge my director at work and the late **Chris Larkin** the Managing Director of the company Benchmarx of the Travis Perkins Group that employed me. For lifting any financial burden that I thought I might have while I was off work and for showing me genuine empathy and kindness throughout my months of convalescing. You have restored my faith in human nature.

The Onslow Angels who cared for me while I was an inpatient. Sisters Sarah, Jincy, Carol, Night Sister Afsa and Staff Nurses Toni and Betty. And the rest of the Onslow Ward team: Sue the Specialist nurse and Susan the Dietitian and not forgetting Atish the health care assistant. Also Costa Colin and receptionist Sylvia.

Barbara Binfield and her family who gave me permission to write and dedicate this book to the memory of Debbie, Barbara's daughter who succumbed to the same illness as I had many years ago. Debbie was constantly in my thoughts throughout my illness and still is today.

The late Pete Small. A fellow inpatient who showed me kindness and gave me optimism when I was an inpatient. The late **Pat Small** and **Emilie Shaw**, Pete's wife and daughter who gave me their permission to write about him in this book.

Anne and **Denise Gould**, wife and daughter of Barrie Gould, who gave their permission for me to write about my friend Barrie in this book.

My family and friends…Thank you for being there.

Norman Cottee. A friend from many years ago, who has also been invaluable in assisting Paul Watmore and me to review and help conclude my book in the most thorough and sympathetic way.

Other generous and kind advisors and reviewers who gave up their valuable time for me to complete this book are Val Coombes, Yvonne Smith, Sue Hawkins, Steph Richmond, Leesa from the charity Pride of the Isle and Shelley Rees.

List of characters

Alan Brown (Brownie)	An old golfing mate
Andy	Work colleague
Anne	Barry Gould's wife
Anthony	Work colleague
Atish	Onslow Ward Healthcare Assistant
Ava	Granddaughter
Afsa	Onslow Ward Night Sister
Barbara Binfield	Friend
Barry Gould (Gouldy)	My late friend
Beverley	My dentist
Brandon	Grandson (Jamie's son)
Beata	My son Nick's Polish girlfriend
Betty	Onslow Ward Staff Nurse
Carol	Onslow Ward Sister
Christine, Chris	My dear wife
Chris B	Cousin
Chris and Yvonne	Friend and old work mate and his wife

Chris Larkin	The late managing director of Benchmarx
Christine B	My brother Paul's late wife
Christine Earwaker	First girlfriend
Cloe	Registrar Frimley Park Hospital
Colin alias Costa Colin	Onslow Ward Housekeeper, tea man
Daisy	Granddaughter by marriage (Hayley and Joe)
Damian and Nicola	My middle son and his wife
Dan Burge	Director and work colleague
Darren and Angela	Stepson and his wife
Dave Gurling	Work colleague
Debbie	Barbara Binfield's late daughter, to whom this book is dedicated)
Denise	Barry Gould's daughter
Denise, Kerry and Kirsty	Barbara Binfield's daughters
Doctor Andre	Onslow Ward, Royal Surrey
Doctor Day	Microbiology, Royal Surrey
Doctor Louise	Haematologist
Doctor Marshall	Local surgery, Bracknell

Doctor McAllister	**Consultant Respiratory Physician, Royal Surrey**
Doctor Rayman	Consultant Haematologist, Royal Surrey
Doctor Gerry R	Consultant Haematologist, Royal Surrey
Doctor Tim	Consultant Cardiologist, Dorchester
Doctor Wong	Consultant Dermatologist, Royal Surrey
Eileen Sherman	District nurse
Elaine and Dave	Sister-in-law and husband
Emilie	Pete Small's daughter
Gary and Sue	Royal Yeoman B&B, Dorchester
Geoff	My sister Linda's husband
Graham	PICC technician, Frimley Park
Grandma Oakley	My granny from Romford
Harrison	My grandson by marriage (Matt)
Hayley and Joe	My stepdaughter and her husband

Ian and Michelle	Work colleague, photographer and abseiling friend and his wife
Immy	My granddaughter
James	Patient on Onslow ward
Jamie	My youngest son
Jincy	Onslow Ward Sister
Jo	Darren's partner
Joe	Hayley's father-in-law
Linda	My sister
Lola	My granddaughter (Sacha and Wayne)
Louis	My grandson by marriage (Matt)
Lucas	My grandson by marriage (Darren and Angela)
Marion	Mother-in-law
Matt and Gemma	My stepson and his partner
Maureen and Paul	Friends of Chris and I
Mr Diary	My imaginary companion
Narinder	Work colleague
Nick	My eldest son

Nicky	Onslow Ward Staff Nurse
Oliver	My grandson by marriage (Hayley and Joe)
Pat	Pete's late wife
Paul	Brother
Paul P	Work colleague at Benchmarx
Penny and Les	Friends from Sturminster Newton
Pete Small	Fellow inpatient on Onslow Ward and late friend
Professor Smith	My initial Consultant Haematologist at Frimley Park
Rafael	Reception manager, Hotel Molins
Sacha and Wayne	My daughter and her partner
Sarah (with Jason, Charlie, George and family and dog Albert)	Onslow Ward Sister
Scarlett	My granddaughter (Damian and Nicola)
Shelley Rees	Friend
Shay	Onslow Ward Staff Nurse

Sue Flaherty	Onslow Ward Specialist Nurse
Susan the diet	Onslow Ward Dietitian
Sylvia	Onslow Ward Receptionist
Toni	Onslow Ward Staff nurse
Uncle Les	My uncle
Wally Seaton	My first boss in 1962

List of Medical Terms

A

Acute Myeliod leukaemia, 24
Allopurinol, 23
AML, 24

B

blasts, 86
Bone Marrow test, 26, 97

C

cannula, 243
Clexane, 67
CRP, 61
Cytogenetics, 209

F

Forceval, 87, 91
Fountain Centre, 43, 77

L

Levomepromazine, 71

N

neutropenic, 49

P

Peripherally Inserted Central Catheter, 29
PICC, 29, 31
Piriton, 65

Pitting Oedema, 73
pulmonary embolism, 63

S

SATS, 99
Scandishake, 57
Sepsis, 58
stent, 66

Printed in Poland
by Amazon Fulfillment
Poland Sp. z o.o., Wrocław